Blood
In The
Parlor

Blood In The Parlor

Dorothy Dunbar

New York : A. S. Barnes and Company, Inc.
London : Thomas Yoseloff Ltd

A. S. Barnes and Company, Inc.

8 East 36th Street

New York 16, N. Y.

Thomas Yoseloff Ltd

18 Charing Cross Road

London W.C.2, England

9891

Printed in the United States of America

Contents

Contents

Background in Blood

REMINISCENCES OF A MURDER ADDICT

HOMICIDAL IMPULSE IS UNIVERSAL; fortunately giving into the impulse is less widespread. Everyone at some time in his life has, either in anger or in irritation, "felt like killing someone," but, happily for interglobal peace and population, it is a case of many are called but few are chosen. The number of potential murderers is large. The number of murders actually committed is much less, but perhaps it is this murder potential in all of us that accounts for the continuous popularity of "the fine art," as Thomas De Quincey has so succinctly named it. Since the antique day a disgruntled Cain decided that in life there must be death, the spectacle of one human depriving another human of his right to live has exercised a grisly fascination.

My interest in murder is personal, if not active. It started many years ago when my mother consigned me to the indulgent care of my grandmother and resumed her newspaper career. She worked for the Hearst paper in Seattle, and then, as now, murder consumed an impressive amount of the front page make-up. Every night I watched at the window for my mother to come home. When she appeared at the corner, I would run to meet her: "Tell me about the murderers you met today, mommy."

Being a conscientious parent, my mother tried in vain to arouse a healthy interest in Hans Christian Andersen, Mother Goose, or the Bobbsey Twins, but I was not amused. Perhaps the most trying phase of my mother's career was the time that orders came from San Simeon to do a fire-and-brimstone expose of vice. A

7

maliciously smiling city editor assigned mother to get herself put
in the local jail, make friends with some of the "girls," and report
her findings. I canvassed our neighborhood with devastating
thoroughness and great pride telling everybody that my mother
was in jail. Mother had a hard time reinstating herself with some
of our neighbors who didn't understand the finer points of
journalism.

Several years later, a bout with polio, involving innumerable
plaster casts and months in bed, coincided with the trial of the
"Tiger Woman," Winnie Ruth Judd, who had killed two women
friends, dismembered their bodies and packed them neatly in a
trunk. The crime might have gone undiscovered but for a blister-
ing Arizona heat wave. I had been following the case with
interest, and when my nurse brought my breakfast tray to me one
morning, I remarked with the precocity of the bedridden and
the callousness of an old murder addict, "This is a rather interesting case in Arizona." My nurse reported my reading material to
my mother in horrified disapproval. But mother had accepted my
preference for things homicidal, and I went on to the Lindbergh
kidnapping, the Black Dahlia, Madeline Webb and her Eli.

I can remember sitting in a hotel suite in a Tacoma hotel which
had been turned into a smoky, cigarette-littered press room after
the Weyerhauser kidnapping. An indulgent newspaper veteran
fed me ice cream with one hand, while the other hand was on the
extreme end of a bending elbow in the best fourth-estate tradition.
Strawberry ice cream has always been synonymous with kidnapping in my dictionary. As I was eating, my mother, who had
an open line on the telephone, called out that the little boy had
been returned safely. I tried *Nancy Drew—Girl Detective* and
Tom Swift, but they and the more adult refinements of Raymond
Chandler, Mickey Spillane et al., seemed anemic after my heady
environment of vice, murder, and kidnapping. I finally returned
to the raw material of true crimes and have spent many blood-
drenched, happy hours reading and writing about them.

Psychologists tell us that every act performed by man is done either directly or indirectly to satisfy the ego. Murder would seem to be the ultimate working of the ego to satisfy greed, love, or hate and sometimes—as in the murder for profit—the removal of an object for future gratification. To destroy one ego in order to build up another is the extreme expression of an overextended individuality. That is why murders are never alike. In a sense, a really interesting murder is a creative accomplishment. It is the plan of one man to match his own individual person against the sum total of custom and history, and the battle of wits between society and this rebellious sport is as fascinating as the crime itself.

Murderers fall into several categories. There are unartistic murders which De Quincey classified as "a knife, a purse and a dark lane." These are not creative murders and are usually committed by people who have no sense of symmetry or imagination in life, art, or crime. Gang killings of the Chicago variety, drug store robberies ending in wild shots from a shakily held pistol, and "thrill" crimes are wanton destruction, while juvenile delinquency is basically a problem of social adjustment. A first-class, bona fide murderer plans his murder with as much care and imagination as an artist blocking out a projected picture or a writer doing a first draft of his Great Novel. Of course, society doesn't ostensibly appreciate a Landru or an H. H. Holmes in the same way that it does a da Vinci or a Dickens, but there is an underlying feeling of admiration for the murderer. It is interesting to notice that during any well-publicized trial there is usually more interest and sympathy for the murderer than there is for his victim, whose life and character have become of secondary importance.

The "artistic murder" category eliminates such elements as habitual criminals, hired gunmen, maniacs, and perverts. The best ones usually occur in respectable settings and are perpetrated by people who have led hitherto blameless lives. Of course, there is always the question : "Aren't they maniacs or perverts, too?" It may be, but these murderers manage to hide their quirk, and, as to their sanity, it might be answered that they are crazy like the well-known fox.

The blood splashed on the walls and ceiling of the Borden home in Fall River suggests unrestrained violence and passion. The fact that the murderer was never caught would suggest a modicum of brain work behind the blood. Isaac Sawtelle of doggerel fame dissected his brother's body in a most violent way, but he was careful—or at least thought he was—to bury it on the side of the Maine-New Hampshire state line where life imprisonment was the highest penalty for murder. And Belle Gunness, with her ill-fated mail-order husbands, had a lime vat as well as a warm welcome waiting for her eager suitors when they arrived. She knew about habeas corpus and was an expert at butchering hogs.

In the nineteenth century, where the individual was making his last stand against mass production and the industrial age, murder as a fine art reached one of its highest peaks of artistry— a sort of homicidal renascence. Ladies whom their neighbors swore wouldn't hurt a fly were solicitously handing their husbands bowls of soup or gruel with a little deadly poison dashed in for seasoning. Dr. Bowers of San Francisco fed his wife phosphorus and inspired a song that was sung with gusto all along the Barbary Coast, "The Phosphorescent Bride of Dr. Bowers." Laura D. Fair, a lithe, accurate-aiming blonde, shot attorney Crittenden on an Oakland Ferry, but she presented such a picture of outraged, wronged womanhood as she sat in the courtroom in a rocking chair with a foot-warmer that the jury acquitted her. Adolph Leutgert of Chicago, a sausage manufacturer, mixed business with pleasure by annihilating his good wife and disposing of the corpus delecti in a sausage machine. Some people have even suggested that he realized some profit from the murder. Daniel MacFarland stalked Mr. Richardson, the journalist, and shot him for taking his wife's affections, while the lady in question occupied her time writing charming stories for children and giving recitations.

Florence Maybrick came to grief and within conversational range of the hangman, but her sentence was commuted because fair-minded people all over England couldn't decide whether she used arsenic on her complexion or her husband. Adelaide Bartlett walked out of the courtroom a free woman on the assumption that her husband drank a large glass of chloroform in a fit of pique after being denied his marital rights. And the anonymous-sounding G. J. Smith, creator of the perennial and euphonius "Brides in the Bathtub" case, found out too late that there was not safety in numbers. He extended into the twentieth century by fifteen years but had Victorian gusto.

THE AGE OF INNOCENCE

QUEEN VICTORIA HAD IMPLACABLE VIRTUE, nine children, and no sense of humor. She gave her country a good moral starching, which it needed after the risqué side effects of the French Revolution and the cavortings of four Georges. Trying to live up to her example of modesty and purity left several generations quite out of breath and produced an exclusively nineteenth-century disease—Victoriphobia.

Victoriphobia is the coexistence of fact and fiction, a running parallel of things as they are supposed to be and things as they are. Innocence was deified; sin was ignored. This dualism expressed itself politically in slogan-happy talk of peace and prosperity and lip service to the rights of man. Actually, it was an era of the self-appointed "white man's burden" and imperialistic bullying, and the soot-faced chimney sweeps of this age still evoke tattle-tale gray puddles of bathos. In religion, literal Christianity was a pillar of society, but biologists and geologists, including the colossus-type Darwin, were pointing out the fallacy of the Garden of Eden and calling unwelcome attention to the missing link. In art, literal flower studies, bucolic landscapes, and do-it-yourself china painting were the order of the day, while Corot, Manet, Renoir, and Whistler labored to infuse a little life into stage-prop decoration.

In literature, classicism, nature, and an over-the-tea-cup type of radicalism were metrically expressed by Byron, Wordsworth, Goethe, and Shelley, while Tennyson and Scott emasculated King Arthur and Richard the Lion Hearted, reduced the Knights of the Round Table to the level of drawing room gallants, and faded the raw splash of medieval splendor to an insipid pastel. And, to complete the parallelism, simultaneously, Flaubert, Thackeray and Stendhal were trying to point out that truth wasn't necessarily beauty, but their contemporary audience was small. And as a cultural culmination, there were the limp Pre-Raphaelites yearning for a return to preplumbing, premechanical days in the middle of a world-wide industrial revolution.

Victoriphobia is reflected in every phase of nineteenth-century life, and murder is no exception. Here is the fiction of gentility and the fact of violence. In most Victorian murders, murder is the act of removing an ugly fact to maintain a pleasant fiction, the grim reality of a dead body, or bodies, contradicting the fantasy of high-flown or obscure motives.

Madeleine Smith had to eliminate a persistent, socially impossible suitor to clear the way for a suitable marriage. The Duc de Praslin had to get rid of his nagging wife to avoid scandal and enjoy a blameless family life with his children—and their governess. Mrs. Wharton threw a house party that would have done credit to the old Romans, and she mixed antimony with hospitality to rid herself of a pressing debtor so she could continue to live graciously and respectably. And then, of course, there's always hatchet-happy Liz. No motive ever came out, but there must have been a whopper, because Miss Borden of Fall River was too strong-minded to do anything flighty like hacking her parents to bloody bits without a good reason.

All these crimes have the light and shade which De Quincey demands of a good murder, and they are the products of an age when the gold standard and the double standard flourished. It was an era when the libido was uncharted territory, when diagnoses as to the cause of death were hazy and "heart failure" could and did cover a multitude of sins, and when anybody who looked innocent was innocent until proven guilty.

Today artistry in murder, as it was practiced in the nineteenth century, is becoming a lost accomplishment; an ever-growing scientific and psychological knowledge has left the artistic murderer very little scope. The order of the day in most contemporary crimes is either a creditable pair of legs and the apologetically murmured, "And then everything went black," or, as in the case of Ruth Snyder and Judd Gray, a clumsy unimaginative job and bitter recriminations. By comparison with the past, murder in our own time has a flat, one-dimensional surface, and it is mainly on an economic level. The gang wars of prohibition, insurance hoaxes like those of Bluebeard Watson, petty pilferings practiced by Martha Beck and her south-of-the-border paramour through Lonely Hearts' clubs all have an aura of vulturing after the dollar. And the world-wide syndicate dealing in crime as a commodity has put murder in the distinguished company of big corporations and international warfare.

Even our "thrill killings" of the twentieth century lack color or contrast. The intellectual snivelings of Loeb and Leopold, William Heirens" psychiatric crutch, the fictional "George Murman," the "sick, sick, sick" refrain of the beatniks have too much monotony —not enough imagination. Only occasional touches, like the crab-apple-tree setting of the Hall-Mills Case or the "Walter Mitty Existence" of Edith Thompson revealed in her imaginative letters to Frederick Bywaters, shine as beacons in an otherwise dark world. But the nineteenth-century murders possess much imagination and can evoke as much nostalgia as a blurrily rendered version of "By the Light of the Silvery Moon."

In the following chapters, there is an abundance of Victoriphobia, and dualism rears its hydra head in each case. Robert Mathews dispensed sex under the guise of religion. He had to kill to prevent exposure and maintain the profitable myth. In the cases of Lydia Sherman and those suspicion-tainted tipplers, Mrs. Bravo and Mrs. Cox, they were pursuing the illusion of genteel, financially secure womanhood, although they had to indulge in a little realistic chicanery. Scott Jackson and George Hersey were both faced with keeping up the nineteenth-century fiction of premarital chastity, after some rather earthy interludes that literally bore bitter fruit. And Theo Durrant typifies the dualism of the age. A Sunday-school superintendent who assaulted women; a boy who was always good to his mother but had to have women— either dead or alive. It is this gaslight gentility contrasted with macabre darkness that gives Victorian murders a Dr. Jekyll-Mr. Hyde zip all their own. They belong to that happy era when crime, crinolines, and custom combined to produce murders that are a joy forever to the devotees of Mr. De Quincey's "fine art," and, from the safe, scientific vantage point of the twentieth-century arm chair, their specialized artistry can be fully appreciated.

Dr. Freud and his colleagues have given probers into the past a new tool : it is a second sight. That "things are not what they seem to be" is commonly accepted as axiomatic today, and with this second sight the dual psychology of the Victorian stands revealed. The repressions of the Victorians are very much like the corsets the ladies of the period wore. The figure of fashion with the hourglass waistline of sixteen inches tells the modern doctor the reasons for feminine vapors and internal injuries. The morality of the Victorians was corseted just as rigidly. It, too, repressed natural functions and caused warping. And when the moral drawstring snapped, it often resulted in—murder.

So, for murder *aficionados* who are weary of twentieth-century materialism, who are jaded from the negligee-ripping, I'll-blow-your-guts-out school of detective fiction, here are some gentle and gentlemanly fiends from a more gracious day.

I

The Girl Who Lost Her Head

IN 1896, THERE WAS NO SHORTAGE OF conversational topics; only the unimaginative or the uninformed resorted to the weather. William Jennings Bryan was defeated in his first presidential campaign, and John J. Sullivan fought his last fight. Utah, with its strange and bloody history, had been admitted to the Union, and Paderewski was making a triumphant tour of the United States. But on the morning of February first, a young Kentucky farm hand, John Hewling, discovered the headless body of a girl that became the main topic of conversation in Kentucky, Ohio, and Indiana for many months.

John Hewling worked on the Locke farm—a rich, rolling stretch of land in back of Fort Thomas, Kentucky, overlooking the Ohio River and the fast-growing city of Cincinnati. February first was a foggy, damp morning, and young Hewling walked briskly to work. As he reached a row of privet hedges that marked the boundary of the Locke farm, he saw a "heap of something" lying on the ground. He looked more closely and through the dim dawn made out the outlines of a bare, still hand.

Hewling ran the rest of the way to the farm house and told the startled Locke family that there was a body on their property. Farmer Locke cranked his shiny, new telephone, and, within an hour, police from Newport, Kentucky, were on the scene. The ground was torn up, and the privet hedge was trampled and bent. The body of a woman was lying face down, and a pale green dress with a small, black check was thrown over her shoulders and head. She had worn black cotton stockings, black kid shoes, and rubbers. A broken shoulder strap and a white corset cover lay a few feet from the body. At the woman's feet, soaking into her high button shoes, was a pool of black water. But as the watery sun broke through the fog, the black pool turned red, and, as if some alchemist were at work, the leaves of the privet hedge turned red, too.

Coroner W. Tingley had arrived with the Newport police, and he proceeded to do his job with efficiency if not sensitivity. He grasped the ankles of the woman's body to turn it over, and even the duty-hardened policemen gasped and refocused their eyes. The green dress had slipped down, but where the head by all biological laws should have been—there was nothing.

Something about the discovery of a headless body caught the public's imagination. Within a few hours after the discovery, surmises and conjectures were flooding the gaslit saloons, antimacassared parlors, and neat back fences of Covington, Newport, and Cincinnati. The Cincinnati *Post* added a finishing note of sex appeal by reporting to its readers: "The woman is young, and her form was that of a Venus."

Sheriff Jule Plummer of Newport quickly decided that this was no ordinary case and called his friend, Chief Philip Deitsch of the Cincinnati police, for help. Chief Deitsch sent two of his most experienced men over the river to lend moral and material help to the bewildered sheriff. These were Detectives Cal Crim and Jack McDermott. By Saturday afternoon, a neighbor of the Lockes had volunteered the information that she had heard a scream during the night. A passing hiker along the Alexandria Pike, which ran in front of the Locke farm, had found a woman's hat with torn red roses. Arthur Carter of Seymour, Indiana, was

brought to the scene of the crime with his three famous blood-
hounds, veteran criminal trackers in many Indiana cases. But the
situation was too nebulous for the three dogs. They sniffed, ran
around in half-hearted circles, and gave up. And to complicate
things still further, missing women were becoming epidemic.
Twenty-four women were reported missing in one day. Then the
great search for the head began. Ponds were drained. Culverts
and hollow trees were scrutinized hopefully. Even the Covington
reservoir was emptied. But the head was still missing, and the
body of the girl without a head and without a name lay in a
Newport undertaking parlor.

On Sunday, Sheriff Plummer and Detectives Crim and
McDermott got their first real break. In desperation, they again
went out to the Locke farm to see if they had missed any small
clue. Hundreds of people were milling around the spot. There
were people on foot. There were people on horseback. Matrons in
dignified carriages lifted their mitted hands in delicious horror,
and gamblers with their brightly dressed "female companions"
larked around the spot in dashing phaetons. Sheriff Plummer and
the detectives groaned at the sight. The blood-stained grass and
bushes had already been torn up or leveled by souvenir hunters,
and any faint possibility of clues vanished. L. D. Poock, a Newport shoe merchant, was in the curious crowd, however, and his
business instincts asserted themselves. Tapping Sheriff Plummer
on the shoulder, Poock imparted the pertinent information that
every shoe sold had a private number stamped on it by the manufacturer for their own records.

The sheriff and the two detectives jumped on this lead. A
horse-and-buggy dash back to Newport and a quick check revealed that the shoes found on the body had been made in Portsmouth, Ohio. A phone call to Portsmouth gave them the
additional information that the pair of shoes had been sent in a
big shipment to a Greencastle, Indiana, retail store.

On Monday there was an autopsy; the findings were varied.

The girl had died after 10:30 Friday night. There had been a heavy rain earlier in the evening, but the body had not been exposed to the downpour. There was evidence of cocaine in the intestinal tract, and pitifully slashed hands told the rest of the story. The decapitation was started while the girl was drugged but still alive. The sudden pain had revived her, and she had made a desperate attempt to fight off the knife with her hands. The amount of blood found by her body and splashed lavishly over the privet hedges, confirmed the doctors' belief that she had been beheaded while still alive—and at the spot where her body was found. But the autopsy finding that horrified a waiting and avaricious public was the fact that the nameless girl had not only lost her head; she had lost her virtue. The doctors, after sober conferences and endless tests and measurements, gave out the news that had the girl lived for another four months, she would have been a mother.

After the autopsy, Sheriff Plummer and Detectives Crim and McDermott left for Greencastle on the trail of their own clue. They had with them a small package containing a pair of high button shoes and the dead girl's clothes. As soon as they arrived in Greencastle, the men hurried to the Louis & Hayes Shoe Store. Luck was with them. The girl had worn such a small shoe that only two pairs of that particular style had been sold. One pair of the coquettish 3-B's had been purchased by a Greencastle matron who, a check by the detectives disclosed, was enjoying the best of health. That left one other name—Pearl Bryan.

Pearl Bryan, the man at the store told the detectives, was a local Greencastle girl. He reckoned her age at about twenty-two and suggested that her sister, Mabel Stanley, who owned a millinery shop in Greencastle, might be the person to see. The detectives found their way to the millinery shop, and Mabel Stanley answered their questions with increasing alarm. Yes, Pearl Bryan was her sister. Pearl had gone to Indianapolis the previous week to visit friends. Sheriff Plummer did not want to alarm the girl, but he made an appointment to go out to the Bryan farm later in the evening.

That evening Plummer, Crim, and McDermott hired a carriage and drove out to the Bryan farm. They found the family waiting for them in the large, immaculate kitchen of the farm house. There was Mr. and Mrs. Bryan, Mabel, and Pearl's brother, Fred. Their faces were puzzled and strained in the wavering light from the kerosene lamps.

Detective Crim asked a few questions about Pearl which Mrs. Bryan answered. Pearl was in Indianapolis visiting friends but would be home within the next few days. Pearl was an ideal daughter and never caused her parents any anxiety. "She is always happy as a lark and full of life." When Crim asked if Pearl knew anyone in Cincinnati, Mrs. Bryan admitted that Pearl had "an attachment" for Scott Jackson, a young dental student who was attending school in Cincinnati.

Detective Crim then opened the small brown paper package he had been carrying.

"Could you," he asked Mrs. Bryan softly, "identify the clothes your daughter wore when she left home?"

At the mother's affirmative nod, Crim showed her the contents of the package. At the sight of the green dress, Mrs. Bryan screamed with sudden, horrible knowledge. Pearl Bryan's murderer had taken her head but left the shoes. And now the headless body in the Newport undertaking parlor had a name.

Detective Crim went immediately to the Greencastle telegraph office to wire the girl's identity to Cincinnati. From the Greencastle telegrapher, the second vital clue in the case materialized.

"I think," said the telegraph operator, looking at the message, with small-town omniscience, "that Billy Woods is mixed up in this. He's been sending messages to Scott Jackson in Cincinnati about Pearl."

This was the second time the detectives had heard the name Scott Jackson in the last few hours, and a quick check with Pearl's family and friends disclosed some interesting facts about the man with the reoccuring name. He had been born in Jersey City, New Jersey. His father was a sea captain, and his mother was a militant nineteenth-century intellectual. Scott had worked for the Pennsylvania Railroad in Jersey City but had been fired after a disagreement with his employers, who used the word "embezzlement" with embarrassing frequency during the dismissal proceedings. At about this time, Mrs. Jackson, now a widow, moved to Greencastle. Her daughter had married Dr. Edwin Post, a professor of Latin at Depauw University, and she and her husband lived in Greencastle. Scott went to New York City where he sold advertising. In 1893, Scott Jackson came to Greencastle to live with his mother and sister. He was a dashing twenty-five, with blue eyes, a low, ingratiating voice, and a rakish blonde mustache. Because of his mother's background and his sister's marriage, the dapper, slightly effeminate Jackson was unquestionably accepted by the best families in Greencastle. He was unanimously described as a "fine young man" by eager mothers with daughters of marriagable age.

Jackson participated in the town's social life. He was popular with girls. He told stories of faraway places he had been and strange experiences he had had. Sometimes he made jokes in bad taste, and sometimes he drank a little too much. He was accepted, however, without reservations because of his mother's and sister's social position and his own marital eligibility.

It was not strange that Pearl Bryan and Scott Jackson should meet. They attended the same parties and graced the same impeccably correct parlors. Pearl was attracted to the "different" young man. And Jackson found it easy to respond to the flattering adoration of the young girl with blue eyes, strawberry-blonde pompadour, and hourglass figure. They made no attempt to conceal the fact that they were in love and boldly held hands in public. When Jackson left for Cincinnati in August, 1896, to study dentistry at the Ohio Dental College, people assumed he and Pearl would be married after he had finished school. He wrote to Pearl, with perhaps more truth than he intended, "I will always remember the summer of '95 as the happiest of my life."

Upon learning of Scott Jackson's relationship to Pearl, Crim sent a second wire to Cincinnati, asking for the arrest of Scott Jackson. Sheriff Plummer and the two detectives then left for South Bend where Billy Woods lived. Billy Woods was awakened by the detectives at 4:00 in the morning and given a hard choice for a sleepy man. He was told he could either go peaceably to Cincinnati as a material witness or he would be charged with murder. Woods agreed to go with the men and told them a frank story. All he had wanted to do was help Pearl. Woods claimed that he had acted from the best motives in a bad situation. He was horrified at the outcome and his part in it.

Pearl, Woods told the attentive detectives, had loved Scott Jackson with a reckless happiness. But happiness, Pearl found out, had its price. Several months after Jackson left Greencastle, she found out that—in the Victorian euphemism—"something was wrong." And as nature began to take its unmistakable course, she told her cousin, Billy Woods of her pregnancy. Woods had introduced Pearl to the young dental student and to some degree felt responsible for the situation. He immediately wrote to Jackson. At first the two young men had discussed the possibility of an illegal operation, but either Pearl or Woods, or both, objected. So, Jackson wired Woods to have Pearl come to Cincinnati. Tuesday night, January 28, 1896, Pearl Bryan boarded the train for Cincinnati after having told her family the little fib about going to Indianapolis. She believed that Scott Jackson, married life, and the end of her troubles waited for her at Cincinnati Depot. She was only partly right.

Meanwhile, in Cincinnati, upon the receipt of Crim's wire, Chief Deitsch had ordered the arrest of Scott Jackson.

"My God, what is this for?" Jackson asked the arresting officers.

He soon found out. It was a short walk from his rooming house to City Hall. He was taken to the office of Mayor John Caldwell for preliminary, tentative questioning. Jackson admitted he knew Pearl Bryan—had even taken her out once or twice— but he hadn't seen her since he was in Greencastle for the Christmas holidays.

"Didn't you read about the murder?" the Mayor asked.

"Yes," admitted Jackson with admirable delicacy, "but I couldn't talk about it. It made me sick at my stomach."

Jackson was charged with murder and searched. The police found three women's handkerchiefs in his pocket and two long scratches on his right arm. The handkerchiefs he had found on the street, Jackson said, and the scratches on his right arm were from vermin bites.

As Jackson was being led out of the Mayor's office, he suddenly asked, "Have they got Walling yet?"

And he refused to comment any further, but after Jackson's cryptic question Alonzo Walling, a stolid, black-haired dental student, was arrested on suspicion. Walling admitted having met Pearl Bryan in Cincinnati—invalidating Jackson's story—but denied any knowledge of the murder.

With the news of the arrests, witnesses, with suddenly refreshed memories, began to appear. Each one had a story to tell, and slowly the stories began to shape into one giant, accusing finger, pointing at the two young dental students. A cab driver said that at 7:30 the previous Tuesday night a pretty blonde girl had hired his cab at the Grand Central Station and asked to be taken to the Dental College. She had inquired at the door for Scott Jackson, but he was not there. She then asked the driver to take her to Indiana House, a rooming house in downtown Cincinnati. According to the records at Indiana House, a young blonde girl had engaged a room on that Tuesday evening and signed her name on the register "Mabel Stanley"—Pearl's sister's name.

William Wallingford, a saloonkeeper, heard of the arrests and told a strange story. Jackson and Walling were frequent visitors at his saloon. On the night of the murder, they had come in with a woman and sat in a private sitting room. The girl had ordered a sarsaparilla, and Wallingford was certain he had seen Jackson "slip something" into the girl's drink. At 10:30, Jackson had hired a carriage, and the girl and two men left the saloon together. Wallingford also volunteered the grisly information that on one of Jackson's rather frequent visits to his saloon, the dental student had expressed a desire for a human head to help him in his study of dentistry.

Several employees in a store located a few blocks from Jackson's rooming house came forward with information. They had been eating their lunch in the stock room, when an argument was heard out on the street. They looked out the window and saw two men and a girl. The girl was crying, and the two men were trying to pacify her. She said she was going home and tell her brother everything and he would "right the wrong." Jackson and Walling were identified as the two men.

Saloon keepers were very important witnesses. Jackson and Walling seem to have done everything but the actual murder in neighborhood saloons. Another saloonkeeper, John Legner, said that Jackson, late on the night of the murder, asked him to keep a valise. Legner agreed and put the valise under the bar. He noticed at the time it was oddly weighted and asked Jackson jokingly if he had a bowling ball in it. Jackson and Walling picked up the valise the next night. John Kugel, the third saloonkeeper, told the police that a man had left a valise with him two days after the murder. The valise was turned over to the police, and the bartender identified Jackson as the man who had left the valise with him.

The police examined the bag. It was empty, but detectives

found blood stains, privet leaves, and strands of long blonde hair clinging to the inside of the valise. It was identified as one of the two bags which Pearl Bryan had brought to Cincinnati. The second valise was left in the Lawrence Barbershop by two men identified positively as Jackson and Walling.

As the evidence piled up, Jackson and Walling began to trade stories. Walling accused Jackson of the murder. He said that Jackson had carried the head around with him, finally disposing of it. Walling concluded his version of the crime by saying: "I do not know who did it, but I think from what I've been told by Jackson that he did." Jackson believed in the old Roman law of an eye for an eye, and he applied it to both Walling and Woods. Jackson claimed he had spoken to Walling about "Pearl's trouble" and Walling had promised to help. It was Walling's suggestion that Pearl come to Cincinnati. Walling had thrown Pearl's head in the river. Mr. Jackson's final commentary was: "I did not do it. I think Walling did." William Woods was his nominee for the role of unmarried father of 1896. Jackson claimed that Woods had betrayed Pearl and he had merely been trying to help them out of a bad situation.

One of the grimmest scenes of the entire case took place in the funeral home in Newport. It was arranged by the police for its psychological effect on Jackson. Pearl's father, brother, and sister confronted Jackson and Walling over the casket which held the still headless body. Mabel Stanley, Pearl's sister, threw herself on her knees in front of Jackson and pleaded with him. "Tell me what you've done with poor baby's head. Think of her mother if nothing else. I am going to her tonight, and I want to tell her where baby's head is."

But Jackson refused to rise to the psychological bait. "I can't tell you anything about it," he said.

Walling, as usual, remained stolidly silent.

The investigation continued. A pair of Jackson's blood-stained trousers were found in Walling's locker at the dental college, and the search for the head continued. Sewers, ponds, even the river basin were searched. But still the head was missing. Nathoo, an alleged high-caste Brahmin from India, was followed by a faithful crowd of curious when he visited the spot where the body was found. He tried to locate the head by Yogi rites and incantations —without success. A mind reader named Thomas drove blindfolded in a carriage along the Alexandria Pike to the murder spot, trying to locate the head by means of vibrations. But his brain waves weren't strong enough that day. The head was still missing.

Cal Crim, in later years, said that to the men working on the case the whereabouts of the head was really no mystery. The dental school which Jackson attended was the proud possessor of a very modern, efficient incinerator.

In Cincinnati, an enterprising owner of a shooting gallery put up a huge sign, reading: "Put a bullet in Scott Jackson's heart and win a five cent cigar." Inside the effigy of a dental student did a "booming" business. And there was an ugly word whispered around in saloons and even church gatherings—"lynch."

Then, two weeks after the arrests, the final evidence arrived at Cincinnati Police Headquarters in the person of George Jackson, a very frightened young Negro. He had been too frightened to come sooner, but his evidence put the knot in the noose. George Jackson claimed that on the night of the murder he and some friends had been strolling along Plum Street, when a man came up to him and his friends and offered the enormous sum of five dollars to whichever one of them would drive another doctor and himself across the river to Newport with a patient. George accepted the job. The first stop was in front of Legner's saloon where they picked up another man who was supporting—or dragging—a young girl. George thought she was either very drunk or very sick. Just as the carriage reached Newport, one of the men came up front with the driver and told him, "If you get off this cab, I'll blow you to hell."

George had been thinking about doing just that. The woman

in the carriage had been groaning horribly. The night was dark, and the streets were deserted. They drove along Alexandria Pike until the man told him to stop. The two men dragged the woman out of the carriage and into the bushes. Then her groaning rose to a piercing scream, and George, by this time finding hell preferable, "never stopped running until I got back to Cincinnati."

George Jackson was then taken into a room where suspects, among them Jackson and Walling, were paraded before him. He unhesitatingly picked out the two dental students from the group and identified them as the two men he had driven along Alexandria Pike on the night of the murder.

Chester Mullin who owned a livery stable positively identified Scott Jackson as the man who rented a "rockaby" carriage from him on the night of the murder. The carriage was examined and the same pattern of privet leaves, strands of long blonde hair, and blood repeated itself on the back of the seat and on the floor of the carriage.

After endless legal counterpoint, Ohio handed over Jackson and Walling to the state of Kentucky for trial. On April twenty-first, Jackson's trial began in the Campbell County circuit court. As the witnesses trouped up to the stand and gave their evidence, it became increasingly difficult to believe Jackson's story of Woods as the betrayer and Walling as the murderer. Jackson was persistent in the face of overwhelming odds and pleaded "not guilty," but the jury disagreed with him unanimously. Scott Jackson was sentenced to hang.

On May twenty-sixth, Walling went on trial, pleading not guilty, and awarding the star role of betrayer and murderer to Jackson. Walling, who is described as slow, physically and mentally, and easily influenced went through his trial in a daze, refusing to look at his mother, who sat all through the testimony. But the jury decided that Mr. Walling had been too much in evidence during the time of the murder. He was sentenced to hang.

The two young men had friends and sympathizers, but the theory advanced by the prosecution was held by most people. Jackson had seduced Pearl Bryan. When Woods had broken the news to him, Jackson ordered Pearl to come to Cincinnati, but when she arrived his offer to her was not a trip to the altar but a quick visit to the nearest abortionist. Jackson probably weighed the impact of such a disgrace on his prominent mother and socially ambitious sister against his unwillingness to marry and had come up with the headless-body scheme. Possibly Pearl's overheard threat to return to Greencastle and have her brother "right the wrong" threw Jackson into a homicidal panic.

Walling's motive is not as clear. One detective at the time of the trial observed that Scott Jackson must have hypnotized Walling. Many old-timers speculate on the case, and while they remember with severe satisfaction that it took Jackson ten minutes to die, they don't discuss Walling's execution with the same relish. He was involved, but did he deserve to hang? Perhaps the answer lies in some of the adjectives found in the testimony and newspapers of the time. Jackson was "effeminate." Walling was "easily influenced." This combination is not unknown in either psychology books or the Bohemian set.

On the morning of March 20, 1897, a seething crowd of over 5,000 spectators gathered outside the jail. They were yelling, "Die game, Scott. Die game, Lonny." The Kentucky National Guard was called out. Even on the scaffold Walling looked at Jackson as if he expected him to say something, but Jackson, uncommunicative to the last said: "I have nothing to say." Walling knew it was all over, but in a low voice he maintained his innocence. "I am not guilty," were his last words. And so the two roommates who had lived together, died together.

Here again is the strain of dualism that distinguishes Victorian crime. In this case literally the facts of life or the fact of "what is" clashes head-on with the fiction of "what should be," and murder is the fusing agent that will bring the nineteenth-century pretty picture into focus again.

There are a lot of unanswered questions about the case, but there is one certainty. Pearl Bryan has become a Midwestern legend. Her headless body, dressed in her graduation dress, has been lying in the Forest Hill Cemetery in Greencastle for almost sixty-three years. But ask an older generation native of Ohio, Indiana, or Kentucky about Pearl Bryan, and their eyes light up with a reminiscent gleam, as if a dear departed friend had been mentioned. Men and women of middle age still recall playing a childhood game in which they took turns hanging each other from trees or staircases. The game was called "Jackson and Walling."

And the acid test of Pearl's perennial popularity is her frequent appearance in regional ballads. One of the dreariest and most enduring of these concludes:

> Pearl Bryan left her parents
> On a dark and gloomy day.
> She went to meet the villain
> In a spot not far away.
> She thought it was the lover's hand
> That she could trust each day.
> Alas! It was a lover's hand
> That took her life away.

II

Far from the Old Folks at Home

HISTORY IS NOT STATIC; it is quivering continuity. There is no such thing as a beginning or end, only illustrative peaks that punctuate the past, emphasize the present, and hint at the future. For example, the frozen body of Burgundy's Charles the Bold on the ice-swept battlefield of Nancy is an historical cliché that supposedly marks the end of feudalism and the emergence of Germany and France as national organisms. Actually, Charles's corpse is an illustrative peak in a trend that begins back in the time-shrouded days of Clovis, who divided the Frankish Empire between his four sons, and that can be traced through the shot-up Hapsburg at Sarajevo, into our own atom-ridden times. These illustrative peaks have their heroes, villains, slogans, and symbols —convenient subliminal pegs on which to hang historical hats : white-bearded Moses; Caesar and his to-hell-with-it-all attitude at the Rubicon; the bright flame of Joan of Arc's fire; the blood-stained prints in the snow leading to Valley Forge; Fort Sumter; "Remember the Maine;" V for Victory.

The history of crime has its own sanguinary thread of continuity, its own bloody peaks and gory symbols. Starting with the truculent Cain, murder has flourished as a national pastime through the ages. David's military tactics with Uriah the Hittite were definitely dirty pool. Nero was most unfilial when he poked holes in his mother's barge. Gilles de Rais (or Retz) had an inordinate amount of young children disappear within the melodramatic precincts of his medieval castle. The Marquise de Brinvilliers favored arsenic as a solution to family spats, and the examples are numerous in the nineteenth-century Renaissance of murder and the twentieth-century Restoration period of slaughter. As for symbols, there's Madeleine Smith's tasty cups of cocoa, Dr. Palmer's copious beakers of brandy, Neill Cream's "long pills," the Hauptmann ladder, and the Snyder-Gray sash weight.

For sheer Alpine altitude, however, in the illustrative peaks of crime, the blood-stained palm goes to Miss Lizzie Borden of Fall River, Massachusetts, and her inseparable symbol, the hatchet. Nineteenth-Century murder without Lizzie Borden is like Helöise sans Abélard, Dr. Johnson minus Boswell, or "Turkey in the Straw" without a fiddle. Lizzie isn't an example of nineteenth-century murder, she *is* nineteenth-century murder—a study in scarlet filtered to a pretty pastel pink by Victoriphobia.

In 1892, Fall River, Massachusetts, was an ugly but productive cotton-mill town of some 75,000 people. There was definitely a right and wrong side of the track, because a foreign-born element had moved in to labor on the business enterprises of the native born. It was one of those towns buttressed with community spirit that might be called nosiness by the uncharitable, and it had its own aristocracy of old Yankee families who defied the contamination of Boston or New York.

One of these families was that of Andrew J. Borden. He was one of Fall River's leading citizens. A home-town boy who made good, he started his business career as an undertaker, and, by a high death rate and caution with the dollar in 1892, Andrew Borden was worth over a quarter of a million dollars. He was president of a bank, an owner of profitable real estate holdings. This tall, slightly stooped, white-haired New England magnate was scrupulous and upright in his business dealings, but he was a fatally slow man with the buck. He was not above bringing a basket of eggs from one of his farms to sell in town. Although his one great love affair was with money, he married twice. His first wife obediently produced two daughters and died, and, at forty, Mr. Borden took a second wife—a palpitating, grateful spinster named Abby Gray.

For the past twenty years Andrew Borden had lived in a narrow frame house with the second Mrs. Borden and the two daughters of the former marriage. Ninety-two, Second Street was in a neighborhood that had seen better days, and Andrew Borden's house was situated on a narrow lot, hemmed in by other narrow houses and set almost flush with a busily trafficked street. Downstairs there was a sitting room, dining room, parlor, and kitchen, while upstairs there was the master bedroom, a dressing room for Mrs. Borden, separate bedrooms for each of the two daughters, and a guest room.

Andrew Borden was seventy with a lean, chipped-away, Grant Wood look. Abby Borden was sixty-four, short, and weighed a regrettable two hundred pounds. Miss Lizzie was thirty-two, a plump, unmarried lady with rimless eyeglasses who liked to try recipes, put bird houses in the garden, and read best sellers like *When Knighthood Was in Flower* and *Alice of Old Vincennes*. She was secretary to the Christian Endeavor Society, belonged to the Fruit and Flower Mission, and was active in the Women's Christian Temperance Union. She also taught a Sunday-school class and had made the grand tour of Europe in 1890. And Lizzie was a young lady with a mind of her own who took a very dim view of some of her father's convictions. She wanted to entertain lavishly, and she wanted a modern bathroom. To Andrew Borden the former was extravagant frivolity; the latter was downright decadent. Emma Borden, although nine years older than Lizzie, was like the negative to Lizzie's positive. She was much less active in church work, her tastes were much simpler, and she was caught up in the apathy of spinsterhood.

The fifth resident at 92 Second Street was Bridget Sullivan, the pert, Irish maid-of-all-work.

It was a portrait of New England home life in the nineties. Andrew Borden was one of those I'll-damn-well-have-the-final-word domestic patriarchs. Mrs. Borden, although a stepmother, seems to have gone about her household chores and domestic relations in an aura of unquestioning good will and easygoing plumpness. There was nothing of the "heavy" stepmother about her—except her weight. The two daughters of the house went their rounds of tranquil social life and light domestic duties. If it was a dour household, it was a righteous one, and what the Bordens lacked in humor or gaiety they made up for by relentless virtue and paying their bills on time. But, as in so many cases, this accepted picture of middle-class life had unexpected lights and shadows that blurred the focus, and the home that framed this portrait of domesticity was actually a house divided.

It is unhappy to relate that the two maiden ladies constantly squabbled with their father over property, money, and their standard of living. The girls, particularly Lizzie, wanted luxury—frosting on the cake. Andrew was content with life's necessities. And when Mr. Borden showed signs of helping his wife's step-sister financially, a restrained sort of hell broke loose. Lizzie expressed grim displeasure by ceasing to call her stepmother "mother" and, if forced to speak to her at all, called her "Mrs. Borden." The two sisters took their meals at pointedly different times than the old couple, and Lizzie even referred to the harmless Abby Borden as a "mean old thing" on several occasions, a statement that still stands unsupported as so many of Lizzie's pronouncements do.

The floor plan of the house further strained relations. The upstairs could be split into two separate parts by closing one communicating door, so that the master bedroom and dressing room could only be reached by the back stairs, the bedrooms of the two daughters and the guest room by the front stairs. The bad feeling seems to have been unanimous. The bolts were drawn on both sides of the crucial communicating door, permanently.

Late in July, 1892, Emma Borden went to visit friends in Fairhaven. Lizzie went to New Bedford for a visit but only remained a few days and returned home. On August third, Fall River was in the middle of a suffocating heat wave, but the sweltering monotony was broken by three interesting events. John Vinnicum Morse, a brother of the first Mrs. Borden, arrived at 92 Second Street for a short visit. He found Mr. and Mrs. Borden recovering from a sick spell the night before. They told him Lizzie had also been mildly affected. Miss Lizzie, in spite of the heat went out on an errand that afternoon. She went to a pharmacy and tried to purchase prussic acid to clean a sealskin cape. The druggist refused to sell her such a potent dry cleaner, but Lizzie was never one to be easily discouraged. Eli Bence and two other drug clerks later identified Lizzie as the would-be purchaser, but she flatly said she wasn't. Then, Lizzie visited a neighbor and family friend, Miss Alice Russell, and carried on like the voice of doom. She told Miss Russell of the daylight robbery that had taken place last year, of the Bordens' illness of the previous evening. She was afraid the milk might be intentionally poisoned.

She feared her father had enemies, the barn had been broken into twice. She was afraid an anonymous *they* "would burn the house down over us," and her last word on the subject was "I feel something hanging over me, and I can't throw it off." Miss Russell suggested the barn might have been broken into by boys chasing pigeons. As for the other gloomy forebodings, she had no answer. It was probably too hot to cope with such things. Most of this sounds like conversational heat lightening, but one statement was based on fact, not humidity. There had been a daylight burglary at the Borden home in June, 1891. Mr. Borden's desk had been broken open, and he was relieved of eighty dollars in bank notes, twenty-five to thirty dollars in gold, some streetcar tickets, a watch and chain, and some small trinkets. His thrifty

soul outraged, Mr. Borden called in the police, who looked help-
lessly at the ravished desk and nodded sagely when Miss Lizzie
said the cellar door was open and *they* might have come in that
way. However, a few days later Andrew Borden told City
Marshal Hilliard: "I am afraid the police will not be able to
find the real thief." Whether it was some inflection of voice, the
curious choice of the word "real," or his uncharacteristic readiness
to abandon the inquiry, there was a definite feeling at the local
precinct that Mr. Borden was not entirely in doubt as to the
robber's identity.

At the trial, Lizzie's lawyer blamed the curious conversation
with Alice Russell on her monthly female condition. In the neo-
Lydia Pinkham era this was a shrewd gambit, and Lizzie, at the
inquest, used her condition as a neat bit of insurance just in case
any blood was found on her clothes. The assertions about poison
were probably wishful thinking after her disappointment at the
drug store. The milk and the stomachs of Mr. and Mrs. Borden
all registered negative on poison tests made after the tragedy.

On August fourth, life at 92 Second Street started out in a
routine swelter. Mr. and Mrs. Borden and Mr. Morse ate a truly
terrifying breakfast at seven, prepared and served by Bridget.
There are many elements of horror in the Borden case, but one
of the worst was the August fourth breakfast—mutton, sugar
cakes, coffee, and mutton broth. Bridget was later ill in the back-
yard, and if she ate that breakfast she deserved it.

By 9:15, Mr. Morse had left the house to visit relatives. Mr.
Borden set out to make a few business calls, defying the heat in an
inferno-like, black broadcloth suit. Miss Lizzie had come downstairs and was in the kitchen, sensibly sipping a frugal cup of
coffee, while Bridget washed the breakfast dishes. Mrs. Borden
asked Bridget to wash the first-floor windows inside and out and
said she was going to put fresh pillowcases on the pillows in the
guest room. Bridget got her pail, brushes, and clothes and went
out through the side door, leaving it unlocked. She talked over

the fence to Mrs. Kelly's girl for a few minutes and then started sudsing her way methodically around the house. It took an hour, and, as she washed, she looked in each ground floor room and never saw anyone. Mrs. Borden and Lizzie were inside, and it is evident from later medical testimony that Mrs. Borden experienced the abomination of forseeing her own death and knowing her executioner before blood and blackness engulfed her life and her world.

Bridget came in the house, locked the side door, and started washing the windows inside. At about 10:45, Mr. Borden pounded on the front door. He had forgotten his key, and that was no light matter if you lived at the Borden house. It was a veritable Bastille. The side and back doors were wooden and locked and they both had screen doors with hooks on them, the front door had three fastenings—a spring latch, a bolt, and a lock which operated by key—and Bridget had to let Mr. Borden in. As she fumbled at the three locks, there was a laugh, which has been described in terms running the gamut from "low and amused" to "high and maniacal." Whatever it sounded like, there was no doubt where it came from. Bridget turned around and saw Miss Lizzie standing at the head of the staircase a few feet from the open door of the guest room. Lizzie came down the stairs and told her father : "Mrs. Borden has gone out. She had a note from someone who is sick." Mr. Borden took the key to his bedroom from a shelf, went up the back stairs to his bedroom and a few minutes later came downstairs and went in the sitting room to rest. He took off his coat and, as further proof that New Englanders are impervious to the weather, put on a cardigan jacket before he stretched out on the couch to rest. He lay on his right side with his congress shoes hanging over the side on the floor. He was in the same position less than an hour later, but he wasn't in such good condition.

In the meantime, Bridget was washing the windows in the dining room and Lizzie joined her there to start ironing handkerchiefs. Bridget went into the kitchen to wash out her cloths, and Miss Lizzie followed her : "There's a cheap sale of dress goods on downtown. They are selling some kind of cloth at 8¢ a yard."

But Bridget was not to be tempted by the vanities of the world. She had been up since six, she had been sick, and the heat was shimmering in a haze off the street. Bridget decided to go up and rest for a few minutes before lunch. Lunch was to be cold mutton and mutton soup, which makes death lose some of its sting.

Bridget lay down in her attic room and heard the clock strike eleven. Fifteen or twenty minutes later Lizzie called up to her, "Come down quick. Father's dead. Somebody came in and killed him."

Bridget was sent for the doctor. Dr. Bowen, an old friend of the Borden family, found Andrew Borden lying on his side on the couch, his head thoroughly bashed in, blood all over his face. The wounds, it was later proved, were caused by a sharp instrument dealt by a person of ordinary strength and inflicted from behind. But at the moment, the chief fact that struck Dr. Bowen was that the face of his old friend was "hardly to be recognized by one who knew him."

The neighbors, including Mrs. Addie Churchill from next door and Alice Russell, the police, and a curious crowd had gathered with disaster-inspired speed, and Dr. Bowen left to send Miss Emma a wire in Fairhaven. By the time Dr. Bowen returned to the house, Bridget and Mrs. Churchill had found Mrs. Borden, adrift in her own blood on the floor of the guest room. And it was written literally in blood that Miss Emma and Miss Lizzie were inheritors of $175,000 each. Coagulation, and lack of it, showed that Abby Borden went to her reward a good ninety minutes before her husband.

In a montage of curiosity, heated discussion, and growing suspicion on the part of the police, the funeral and the inquest took place. Miss Lizzie, so clearheaded and composed during the nerve-wracking morning hours of August fourth, a pillar of

strength to those who had come to comfort her, at the inquest,
under the questioning of District Attorney Hosea Knowlton,
became confused and snappish by turn, and she literally just
didn't know where she was on the crucial morning. Seven days
after the murders, Lizzie Borden was arrested for the murders of
her stepmother and father. And the world became "Lizzie
conscious." Coffee and conversation percolated with equal heat
at the nation's breakfast tables, and the question was hotly asked
and hotly answered, "How could a woman do such a thing?"
Some people thought it impossible, but some nasty-minded
skeptics thought it was not only possible, it was highly probable.
But Lizzie had moral support from Lucy Stone and her following
of suffragettes. Mrs. Susan Fessenden and the W.C.T.U. got
behind Lizzie, and she had physical as well as moral support from
her pastors, Reverend Buck and Reverend Jubb. She usually
made her appearances leaning on the arm of one or the other.
"Unfortunate girl . . . innocent . . . persecuted . . . harshly treated"
were adjectives and phrases that were loosely bandied about, until
it seemed as if the Commonwealth of Massachusetts should be
indicted and tried for their treatment of Lizzie Borden.

Children in the street chanted, "Mr. Borden he is dead, . . .
Lizzie hit him on the head." And one of the barbershop witticisms
of the time was: "What did Lizzie Borden say when someone
asked her what time it was? 'I don't know, but I'll go axe father'."

So Lizzie added variety to an already spicy situation by the
quantity of answers she gave to the increasingly pertinent
question: "Where were you when it happened, Miss Lizzie?"
She always had a ready answer, each one different. She told Dr.
Bowen she was out in the yard when she heard a groan. Mrs.
Churchill was informed, "I went to the barn to get a piece of
iron. I heard a distressing noise and came back and found the
screen door open." She told Patrolman Harrington she was in the
loft of the barn and heard nothing. The loft was examined and
found to contain a pristine layer of dust untouched by human

hand or foot. It was so hot in the loft the patrolman had to leave gasping for air after a few minutes. But "Asbestos Liz" swore she had been there about twenty minutes. To Miss Russell she again gave the "looking for a piece of iron to mend a screen door" version. Now, these variations could be excused on the grounds of excitement and confusion, but at the inquest, Miss Lizzie claimed she strolled in from the barn, casually took off her hat, and accidentally discovered her father's body. There's just too much variation between hearing a noise and running in to find your father hacked to bits and hearing nothing and coming upon the disaster accidentally. Also the point was brought up that if Lizzie thought someone had come in and killed her father as she said to Bridget, it was either extremely foolhardy or extremely courageous to stand in the hall, just a few feet from where fresh blood spilled and reeked, and call up to Bridget. Rushing out on the street, away from the carnage, would have seemed more likely. Her account at inquest of her activities during the time between Mr. and Mrs. Borden's deaths was just as erratic. She gave lie to the axiom a person can't be in two places at the same time. She was reading an old Harper's magazine in the kitchen, and she was upstairs in her room sewing a piece of tape on a dress.

Then there was the curious question of Miss Lizzie's elastic wardrobe. At the inquest, she testified that she wore a blue-and-white-stripe dress the morning of the murders but changed to a pink wrapper after somebody told her to. (The case crawls with anonymous collective nouns.) Nobody admitted giving this bit of advice. Both Bridget and Emma Borden said Lizzie was in the habit of wearing a cotton dress of light blue with darker-blue figure in the mornings. At the trial, Dr. Bowen confusedly described Lizzie as wearing a drab colored calico-type dress. Mrs. Churchill said Lizzie was wearing a light-blue cotton with a darker-blue shape. However, when Lizzie was asked by the police to turn over to them the dress she wore on the morning of the murder, she handed them a dark-blue silk dress which she had been wearing during the morning since the murder. Shown the dress at the trial Dr. Bowen had no resort to the indecisive word "drab." "I should call it a dark blue." Mrs. Churchill when confronted with the dark-blue silk reluctantly admitted that "I did not see her with that on that morning."

Then Alice Russell, torn between friendship and conscience, finally told the following story. After a visit Saturday night following the murders from the mayor, who warned Miss Lizzie she was under suspicion, Miss Russell found Lizzie in the kitchen on Sunday morning, burning a light-blue, cotton-cord dress with a dark figure. Emma Borden at the trial said there was paint on it, and she had urged Lizzie to burn the dress. However, police officers who had searched the house said they never saw a dress smeared with paint, and Miss Russell saw no paint on the portion of the dress Lizzie was burning. Lizzie's militant advocates were delighted when the news came out that Lizzie seemed to be the one Borden in the house without blood on her the morning of August fourth. It was proof of her pure innocence. However, the story of the dress could knock the props out of this. Miss Lizzie had some sort of a blue-and-white cotton dress that she was in the habit of wearing in the morning. She was wearing it the morning of the murder, according to witnesses. However, after the murders she changes into a pink wrapper, and for the next few mornings wears a dark-blue silk dress, which she turns over to the police when they request the dress she wore on the morning of the murder. She is found burning a dress that resembles the one she wore on August fourth—after she is told that she is under suspicion. She says she wore the blue-silk dress, which is produced in court. Witnesses say it is not the dress she wore. Emma says the burned dress had paint on it, Lizzie said it had paint on it. Police say there was no paint-stained dress present when they examined the clothes.

The problem of blood could have been easily taken care of after the first murder. There was ample tidying up time, since

Bridget was outside washing windows for about an hour. As to the second murder, where time was more tricky, one look at an extant photograph of Mr. Borden's body as it was found gives a pretty adequate idea of what could have happened. The couch on which he was lying was directly to the side of the sitting-room door, against the wall. With Mr. Borden lying on his side, the back of his head would have been to the door and the murderer could merely have reached an arm and an aiming eye around the door and started banging away. If a few spots of blood were later discovered on the sleeve of the dress, they wouldn't have been obvious to excited eyes, but might have been apparent if tested, so the dress was disposed of just in case. The other theories of Lizzie stripped to the buff or Lizzie in some sort of all-enveloping waterproof garment gave color to the conjectures of the time, but they don't hold water. Even if Lizzie had betrayed her Puritan upbringing by hacking her father to death without any clothes on, she wouldn't have had time to get dressed again, considering what the ladies of the 1890's considered "dressed." Nothing resembling a waterproof garment was ever found.

But whatever theory was believed, there was one certainty in the whole mixed-up matter of Lizzie's dress : Alice Russell was crossed off the Borden Christmas-card list. There was nebulous gossip, too, about Lizzie's lover. The leading candidates were a nonmaterializing young man she was supposed to have met during her European trip and a shadowy clergyman. But there was never any tangible proof of a romance in Lizzie's life. Like her spiritual ancestress, Elizabeth I of England, she died wearing the righteous if unwelcome crown of virginity, and any tangible lover remained conspicuous by his absence.

There was also the matter of the note Mrs. Borden received. Protestors of Lizzie's innocence were faced with the uncomfortable fact that not only did the sick person never come forward, but the messenger also disappeared from the face of the earth. Lizzie's lawyers never made too much of that. The law takes little notice of anything other than the first, second, and third dimensions, and with the eyes of the town, the country, and the world turned on Lizzie, the sick friend and the messenger boy must have indeed been fourth dimensional characters not to come forth.

On a warm June day in 1893, the thirteen-day wonder, noted in legal documents and court transcripts as the Trial of Lizzie Borden, opened in New Bedford. It was held in a bare, white-walled room with chairs, desks, and settees. The three superior court judges required by law wore regular business suits and fanned themselves with palm-leaf fans. Thirty or forty members of the press, including representatives from the New York Sun and the Boston Globe, were poised to rush news to a breathless, waiting world, and finally Lizzie Borden made her entrance in the grand manner. Walking sedately, flanked by Reverends Buck and Jubb, she wore a new, stylish black mohair dress with leg-of-mutton sleeves and a black lace hat with rosettes of blue velvet and a blue feather for properly subdued dash.

Mr. Hosea Knowlton and Mr. William Moody conducted a fair, accurate case for the commonwealth. Under more ordinary, less-emotional circumstances they had a case as strong as that which has sent many protesting innocents to their final reckoning with state executioners and the Almighty. The trial revealed little news, although Mrs. Hannah Reagan, the matron of the Fall River Police Station, heard the following conversation between Emma and Lizzie Borden: "Emma," said Lizzie "You have given me away."

"No, Lizzie I have not," was the reply.

But Lizzie insisted "You have; and I will let you see I won't give an inch."

It's cryptic conversation to put it mildly, and, as it stands so starkly without any context, it is open to all sorts of interpretations. However, Reverend Buck made it seem more important than it actually was, when he visited Mrs. Reagan and tried to get her to sign a statement retracting her story of the conversation. It is gratifying to learn that Mrs. Reagan refused to sign the retraction, and Reverend Jubb, a vehement and vocal champion of Lizzie's innocence, was told by the Fall River officials in no uncertain terms to mind his own business.

A gruesome touch was added when a plaster cast of Mr. Borden's head with appropriate blue marks to indicate the wounds was introduced as part of the medical testimony, and Miss Emma Borden snatched the headlines from Lizzie for one golden moment. Miss Lizzie entrenched herself on her constitutional rights as firmly and eagerly as any object of a twentieth-century Senate investigation, and her sole statement has a familiar ring. "I am innocent. I leave my counsel to speak for me."

The only time Lizzie had really run into trouble was during District Attorney Knowlton's merciless barrage of questions at the inquest. She had withdrawn from this encounter bruised and punchy. She wasn't about to get back in the ring for another sparring session with the question-happy District Attorney, and Emma Borden was an ideal substitute. She could testify on everything that happened before and after the murder, but she could not be cross-examined about the morning of August fourth. Emma came out strongly on her sister's side and said it was she who had urged Lizzie to burn the controversial dress.

The commonwealth based its case not only on the fact that Lizzie had the opportunity and motive but the question, "Was there an opportunity for anyone else?" There was no sign of housebreaking, no struggle, nothing taken. They were hampered by the exclusion of both the pharmacists' testimony on Lizzie's abortive attempt to obtain prussic acid and Lizzie's suspect inquest testimony. The other weaknesses of the Commonwealth's case were the inability to prove that the ax found in the Borden home was the murder weapon, even though it showed signs of recent washings and scrubbings with ashes and fitted the length of the wounds by an exact three-and-one-half inches; and not being able to come up with conclusive evidence that the blue dress Lizzie wore was the same one that met a fiery end in the Borden's kitchen stove. Otherwise, the prosecution anticipated Dragnet by fifty years and presented the facts, clearly and damningly. It was an appeal to the intellect.

As for the defense, it was more colorful, if less creditable, and Lizzie had an ideal legal figure in her lawyer. Ex-Governor of Massachusetts, George Robinson was a shrewd Yankee who knew the value of the cracker-barrel approach on a New England jury. Lizzie was her own worst enemy geographically. She was flitting all over the house that morning—upstairs, downstairs, in my lady's chamber—and yet in this narrow house with its communicating doors and thin partitions, the defense maintained, there was a very tangible messenger of death, slaughtering Mrs. Borden in her own guest bedroom, waiting in a small closet yet leaving no traces of blood or physical presence for an hour and a half until Andrew Borden decided to come home and lie down and take a nap. This hypothetical killer then struck again, took the hatchet down to the basement and got out of the house without being seen by Bridget or Lizzie, then walked down Second Street invisible to all the neighbors and off into some fiendish limbo.

Lizzie's guilt might have violated every Victorian precept of gently nurtured female, but the story of her defense violated every known limitation of time and space. Ex-Governor Robinson's closing speech for the defense typifies his whole argument : "To find her guilty, you must believe she is a fiend. Gentlemen, does she look it?"

The jury looked at her, the tasteful clothes, the rimless spectacles, the air of gentility, backed by her pastors and her family, and they brought in a verdict of not guilty.

After the jury congratulated the vindicated darling of the Women's Christian Temperance League, to a man they headed for the nearest hotel bar to celebrate a job well done.

Lizzie may not have been the most beautiful or the sexiest lady ever to flutter a courtroom, but she was the luckiest : She got acquitted. Today a great gulf yawns deep and wide between the jury that acquitted Lizzie Borden and the lawyers, writers, and crime fanciers who study the case today. Faced with the fiction of a church-working spinster who couldn't even have such a thing as murder enter her pure thoughts and the fact that no one else could have done it, the Borden jury bought the whole fiction package. It was dogma in 1892 that a woman couldn't do such a thing, but twentieth-century courts are more skeptical and have been known to hand dcwn verdicts where looks gave way to facts and have indicated that moral turpitude does not guarantee the difference between guilt and innocence on a capital charge.

Anna Marie Hahn looked like a comfortable "Cincinnati Dutch" housewife, but the mortality rate of old men she loved and left landed her in the electric chair. Mr. Chine, the ex-choir singer, appeared like a harmless little man addicted to buttermilk, until he started cremating his wives with undue haste. Major Armstrong was the spit-and-polish image of military propriety, but he bought too much arsenic to take care of his dandelion problems. James P. Watson, alias "Bluebeard"—and that was no courtesy title with sixteen wives unaccounted for—was a mild-spoken, highly successful business man who was tenderhearted and easily moved to tears. Louise Peete was the epitome of refine-ment, but corpses kept turning up with embarassing regularity wherever she lived. And Dr. Alice Wynekoop, well-known doctor, club woman, and social worker just couldn't account for her daughter-in-law's body in her examining room. None of these ladylike or gentlemanly paragons were acquitted.

There has been no change or developments in the Borden case since the warm June day when the daughter of the house was acquitted to wild cheers and hosannas. There were, indeed, dark hints about a jet-propelled Emma Borden quickly sneaking into her home and then flashing back to Fairhaven. John Vinnicum Morse came in for his share of dark mutterings, but both his alibi and that of Miss Emma were checked and not found wanting. Bridget has been mentioned as a suspect. But she had a good character, was contented with her job, and it was unlikely that she would put such a strain on employer-employee relationships. Also Miss Lizzie was Bridget's alibi, as she could never be Miss Lizzie's. There was, of course, the usual rash of wild-eyed men, maniacs waving hatchets that dripped with blood in broad daylight, and deathbed confessions—all adding up to a big fat zero.

Miss Lizzie and Miss Emma moved to a larger, more-spacious home about a mile and a half from Second Street, and it is to be hoped that it had a modern bathroom after all the sisters had been through. In February, 1897, Lizzie hit the front pages again. "Lizzie Borden again. A warrant for her Arrest has been issued. Two Paintings missed from Tilden-Thurber Company's store. Said to have been traced to Miss Borden's Home in Fall River." No more is heard of this matter except that an "adjustment was made out of court." It brings to mind the burglary of 1891.

Lizzie lived on in Fall River in her fine new home. She preferred Washington and Boston where she was an inveterate theatregoer. She seldom patronized Fall River stores and was not seen on the streets of the town except for brief glimpses of her in her carriage and later her motor car. At any rate, guilty or innocent, it seems that Lizzie, who changed her name to Lizabeth A. Borden, didn't win any popularity polls in her home town. She loved the theatre and seemed to have a school-girl crush on a favorite Boston tragedienne, Nance O'Neil. She shocked Fall River by throwing a big party for Miss O'Neil after a local performance, and there is an even more amazing record that she rented a house at Tyngsboro and entertained Miss O'Neil and her company for an entire week, an almost Roman entertainment for a gentle New England spinster. Evidently, all this was too much for Emma. She left Fall River shortly after this saturnalia and was heard of no more until she and Lizzie got into a legal hassle over the sale of a building from the estate in 1923.

And that's the story of Lizabeth A. Borden, who lived happily until her death in 1927. On June 1, 1927, Lizzie died at her home in Fall River, and on June 10 of the same year, Emma died at Newmarket, New Hampshire. Lizzie left an estate of $265,000 to friends, relatives, and the Animal Rescue League.

Lizzie was not only lucky to get acquitted. She did herself comfortable—to use a local expression—with her home, cars, trips, and theatre jaunts, but it all has that "company look" of dutiful smiles and empty conversation. Did the blood-stained images of Second Street ever gibber idiotically at her memory? Did the wet footprints of the past walk through her mind? There's no way of knowing. Her life after the double murder appeared as placid, although more independent and luxurious, as it had been before the one violent eruption in continuity, and the dark truth lies under a tombstone at the foot of Andrew Borden's grave, marked simply Lizabeth A. Borden.

But she belongs to the world, and it has given her an epitaph in poetry, not in stone :

> Lizzie Borden took an ax,
> Gave her mother forty whacks.
> When she saw what she had done,
> She gave her father forty-one.

Lizzie is a legend. The ax is immortal, and for those interested in the influence of heredity, Lizzie inherited the right to use the Borden coat of arms from her ancestors, Joan and Richard Borden, who pioneered in the locale of Portsmouth, Rhode Island, around 1638. The coat of arms is a "Lion Rampant, holding a Battle-Axe, proper."

III

Portrait of the Monster as a Young Man

MONSTERS, SPRINKLED LIBERALLY through history and literature, have exercised an eternally lurid fascination. The ogre of the fairy tale, the cyclops of mythology, and the medieval conception of the devil have all enjoyed a macabre vogue. And murder is no exception. Here, too, the monster holds a secure place in the popular affection of the public, unrivaled by the more rational perpetrators of the gentle art of elimination. Murder for profit, murder for necessity, or murder for any number of pressing and diverse reasons is always interesting, but it is the monster's murderous escapades that are immortalized in song and legend.

Criminologically speaking, there are two types of monsters. There is the slinking, anonymous monster who creeps around dark alleys and gloomy boardinghouse hallways waiting for a victim. The graphically named Jack the Ripper; Earl Nelson, who enjoyed a brief glory in the headlines as "The Dark Strangler" of the West Coast; and Dr. Neill Cream of the bland name and not so bland prescriptions fall into this category. But the psychological monster, when driven to murder, is the most beloved of them all.

The psychological monster offers contrast. It can be an upright member of a community, a successful business man, a loyal,

48

devoted wife or a spinster of impeccable reputation. Some of the finest monsters come from peerless families and blameless backgrounds, and, when murder breaks out against such a background, it has many of the characteristics and all of the fascination of *Dr. Jekyll and Mr. Hyde.* The idea of a bloodthirsty "Mr. Coffee Nerves" lurking ectoplasmically behind a respectable façade is intriguing, and when it breaks out, the press and the public literally give the devil his due of undivided attention, front-page space, and sometimes even thinly disguised admiration.

When Robert Louis Stevenson visited San Francisco in 1879 to carry off the palpitating Miss Osbourne, he did not possess the gift of foresight and had no way of knowing that in sixteen years the higher moments of his brain child would be acted out in life against the clanging, rugged setting of the last frontier. On the other hand, there is no evidence that a young student attending San Francisco's Cooper Medical College in 1895 had ever read a book by a Samoan recluse called *Dr. Jekyll and Mr. Hyde.* But the resemblance is there, and so are the basic ingredients for every bona fide psychological monster—the struggle of good and evil in one man. In most murderers, the presence of glaring megalomania is present and evident. But the monster is the unhappiest of all criminals, because his ego isn't pitched up to that hysterical conviction of "I can do no wrong." The monster's ego is split. One part of him yearns for normalcy and respectability and fights with the antisocial nemesis of his other personality.

Born in Toronto, Canada, in 1871, Theodore Durrant had all the prerequisites of monsterdom. He and his family moved to San Francisco, where his father had an executive position in a shoe factory, and the Durrants moved in the higher circles of church and social activities. Young Theo graduated from Cogswell's Polytechnic and entered Cooper Medical College. In 1895, the year that was to be so fatal for him and several other people, he was a senior at the medical college.

Theo was a member of the Emmanuel Baptist Church where

he was the assistant superintendent of the Sunday school and church librarian. He was also secretary of the Young People's Society of the church and a member of the Second Brigade Signal Corps. He was popular, bright in his studies. His closest friends found him interesting and amiable, and the young ladies of San Francisco considered the tall, slim young man with high cheek bones, blue eyes, and an interesting pallor handsome. His mother constantly regaled her friends with conversation about Theo and what a fine boy he was. All things considered Theodore Durrant was an exemplary young man of the turn-of-the-century school. But Theo not only had the personal requirements. He had the stage props, too. There were two beautiful girls and a "hoodoo" church.

The Emmanuel Baptist Church was almost as old as San Francisco. It was a large, red wooden building on Bartlett Street between Twenty-second and Twenty-third Streets. It had been standing when the great bay city had been a drowsy Mexican settlement. The mission beside the Laguna de los Dolores and the Presidio Barracks with Bay Shore houses dotting the sand dunes were the extent of the architecture, and soldiers, mission fathers, and Indians were the main inhabitants. The red wooden church had witnessed the gold rush, when money and murder were unrestrained. It had seen the Committee of Vigilance take the law into its hands in 1851. It was still standing in 1870, when Laura D. Fair proved the accuracy of her marksmanship and the inadvisability of Attorney Crittenden's making promises of marriage he had no intention of keeping and in 1885, when the body of Dr. J. Milton Bower's wife was said to gleam and glow in the gloom of the city morgue and the worthy doctor sat in a cell contemplating the susceptibility of his three wives to the grim reaper. The church, like San Francisco, had a history. By 1895, San Francisco was a city of law and order, clanging cable cars, and water-front melee, but the Emmanuel Baptist Church had acquired a reputation. It was called the "hoodoo" church.

It had been struck by lightning. Some of its trustees had defaulted with church funds, and one of its pastors had committed suicide after killing the proprietor of a newspaper. Some citizens had advocated burning the church down. The idea was a good one, because the church made a valiant effort to live up to its name.

Blanche Lamont was a member of the red wooden church. She was eighteen. She was pretty, and she was romantic. After her father's death in Dillon, Montana, Blanche and her sister, Maude, had come to San Francisco and lived at the home of their aunt and uncle, Charles and Tryphena Noble, at 209 West 21 Street. She was active in the church society and attended a city normal school. Her tall figure, incredible eyelashes, and soft brown eyes guaranteed her an enviable popularity with the the opposite gender, and unfortunately it attracted the attention of Theodore Durrant.

At the church where she met the young Sunday-school teacher, Blanche also made the acquaintance of Minnie Williams. Although some accounts picture the two girls as friends of the bosom, Mrs. Noble and Maude Lamont both denied that the girls had been anything but casual acquaintances, with their church work in common. But they were wrong. The two girls did have something else in common—Theo.

Minnie Williams was small and frail with black curly hair and a gamin's face. Blanche was a pretty school girl and the possessor of a conservative upbringing and conservative ideas, but Minnie is almost as interesting as the monster. She was not a "lady," since she worked for a living, and she was of secondary social rank in the hierarchy of the church. Minnie, like Theo, was born in Canada and had moved to San Francisco with her family. When she was fourteen, Minnie somehow discovered that her father was involved in an extramarital escapade. She made her plans well. She forced her smaller sister to make friends with the daughter of her father's "friend," and through this junior Gestapo, Minnie learned that her father and the woman had an appointment to meet at the Emmanuel Baptist Church. Like an avenging fury, Minnie dragged her mother to the church, and there found Mr. Williams and the lady in the middle of what is politely termed an assignation. It would seem that churches in the days of the Barbary Coast were used to assuage the needs of the flesh as well as those of the spirit. It is interesting that in the days when a young lady's sex education was based on the axioms that "nice girls didn't talk about such things" and that babies were the exclusive handiwork of the Almighty, Minnie didn't indulge in hysteria or seem shocked at the discovery. She made her plans cooly and carried them out with a malignant calculation.

Unfortunately, Mr. Williams's mistress had gained control of the Williams property and negotiable assets, so when Minnie took her mother to the church she was responsible for breaking up her family financially as well as emotionally. The church took up a collection and sent Mrs. Williams and the younger children back to her parents in Canada, but Minnie decided to stay in San Francisco. The church promised to watch out for her, and in a sense she became a ward of the "hoodoo" church; and, as if to add the finishing touches to an artistic masterpiece, Minnie found employment in Alameda, in a casket factory.

Clark H. Morgan was head of the factory and soon began to notice the small girl with a suggestive sparkle in her eyes and a naughty innuendo in her speech. Mr. Morgan adopted her into his home as a combination companion and maid to Mrs. Morgan. Minnie was sedate and shy with her women employers and with people whom she considered her superiors. Reverend Cressy described her as "quiet and retiring." Dora Fales, a friend of Minnie's, described her rather guardedly as "an exceedingly discreet girl." And Jennie Williams, another friend, said "Minnie was smart in concocting plans." But with the sedate, bearded Mr. Morgan, Minnie was far from reticent. They discussed life and men and things even more specific. She told Mr. Morgan that

Theo Durrant had taken her to Fruitvale one Sunday and propositioned her in a lonely spot. Of course, she had refused. She also told her elderly confidant that the relation of Blanche and Theo was "of a nature to startle anyone." Theo might have boasted to Minnie, or Minnie may have been jealous of Blanche's social position and assurance. But it was a vicious thing to say about a girl who had always been pleasant and kind to her, even trying to get Minnie work in her aunt's house. But while Minnie had the appearance of an engaging little minx of the nineteenth century, she had the mind of a procuress and a prying preoccupation with sex that suggests the voyeur. She liked to talk to Mr. Morgan. She told the ever-attentive Jennie that she had been deceived by an "older man with elegant rooms in San Francisco." Her interest in Theo and the nebulous gentleman with the "elegant rooms" are the only tangible evidence of men in her life, but the San Francisco police files were full of her unhealthy monologues and observations. Talking about the ever-interesting subject seemed to give Minnie a perverse satisfaction.

Theo, too, was interested in the subject treated by such divergent talents as those of Ovid and Havelock Ellis. As early as 1893, Theo confided to a fellow medical student that he had "no knowledge of women." For the sake of at least three people it might have been preferable if the young man had remained in his primeval state. In the later part of the same year Miss Annie Welming told a friend, Miss Clayton, that Theodore Durrant had conducted her to the Emmanuel Baptist Church, had seated her in the church library, and asked her to wait there for a minute. She claimed the young Sunday-school superintendent left the room and when he returned it was not with the apparent purpose of teaching Sunday school. He was in that condition which has not been considered proper since the original sin or, as Miss Welming delicately phrased it, "in his birthday suit." The young lady departed with alacrity, eyes averted, and confided the happening to Miss Clayton, who in turn passed it on to a reporter from the *Examiner*. Miss Welming repudiated the story with maidenly indignation, and peace and sanctity were restored. It was treated as one of those titillating but not too reliable vignettes that young ladies spending the night in each other's company often exchange. But whether Theo actually stripped or whether Miss Welming enlarged upon a furtive attempt to snatch a kiss, it is an indication that the young man was beginning to acquire a curiosity about the more earthy phases of life. And it is also an indication that he was conducting his investigations in a place that had been used before for similar purposes—the Emmanuel Baptist Church.

It is interesting to notice that Eullah Durrant, Theodore's sister, had gone to Germany to study music. Later she changed her name to Aude Allan and was a sensation on the continent with a terpsichorean striptease called "The Vision of Salome." Theodore didn't dance, but there is a family resemblance.

In December, 1894, Blanche and Theo went for a stroll through Golden Gate Park. It was very late when he brought her home and apologized to Mrs. Noble for keeping her niece out so late. Mrs. Noble didn't seem to mind, but Blanche did not allow Theodore to call upon her for several months. Theo was evidently still at work enlarging his "knowledge of women," for when a young lady stays out with a young man until a late hour and then refuses to see him again, it is a sure sign that maidenly honor has been under siege but has not surrendered.

Blanche left her aunt's house on the morning of April 3, 1895. She told her aunt she was going to a Young People's Society meeting that night and hummed a song as she closed the door and walked out onto the street. She was wearing a dark full skirt, a nipped-in basque jacket, and a big floppy hat with ribbons and flowers. The tall girl must have made a pretty picture, and, unfortunately for Durrant, the bright hat, the pretty face, and the admirable figure made people notice Blanche Lamont wherever she happened to be on that last day.

Blanche met Theo on Mission Street at 8:15. They must have decided on the meeting at church. It was the first time Blanche had consented to see Theo privately since the late homecoming in the previous December. Blanche had evidently come to some conclusion about the stroll through Golden Gate Park. Together, they boarded an electric car, and Henry Shellmont, the conductor, noticed that Theo seemed "to be talking sweetly to her." They separated for college and school, and Theo swore he never saw her alive again.

Blanche dutifully attended some cooking classes, and, although several of her classmates said that she was dreamy and pre-occupied, it is understandable. She was young and romantic, and a young man had been speaking "sweetly to her" on the electric car that morning. At 2:55, Minnie Edwards, Alice Pleasant, Mary Lanegan, and Blanche Lamont left school together. It is hard to think that Theo had murder on his mind that April day. He was an intelligent young man, and yet he left a trail of his activities across the city of San Francisco. A string of witnesses saw them from the time they met until they entered the church together.

Theo was waiting for Blanche when she came out of school. "He ran like a boy" and jumped on a waiting cable car where Blanche joined him. Miss Edwards also boarded the car, but the other two girls continued walking down the street and had just reached the corner of Powell and California when the car appeared. Blanche and Theo were sitting on the "dummy" deep in conversation. Miss Edwards had entered the car proper. All three girls were positive in their identification of Theo. He too was very stylishly and noticably attired that day in a blue coat, cheviot vest, and knobby hat, and one of the girls remembered that he wore his hair "exceedingly long for a gentleman." Being curious about Blanche's beau, it is reasonably certain that in the universal way of school girls they gave Theo more than a passing glance.

Mrs. Vogel, who lived opposite Blanche's school, was worried about recent burglaries in the neighborhood and had been watching the young, well-dressed young man loitering on the corner. He waited for about an hour before Blanche arrived and they boarded the car. Mrs. Elizabeth Crosset, who had known Theo for four years, passed him on a car going in the opposite direction and wondered who the pretty girl with him was. She saw the couple transfer to the Valencia car, and Blanche must have made a pretty picture, laughing up at Theo and clutching the floppy hat, which the notorious San Francisco wind was threatening. Mrs. Crosset added with delicacy and some confusion "her clothes blew considerably around her limbs—her form—her dress, that is." Martin Quinlan, an attorney, saw Blanche and Theo a few minutes later, and they were walking in the direction of the church. Mrs. Teake, who lived opposite the church and had known Theo for several years, saw Blanche and her young man enter the church by the side gate on Twenty-third Street at about 4:20 in the afternoon.

All of Blanche's actions on the last day of her life were those of a girl who is thinking about a pleasant future with a young man in it—the coquettish hat, the meeting with Theo and the dreamy manner. The witnesses who saw Theo and Blanche together that afternoon all agreed that she was accompanying Theo happily and that, even as they entered the church, the young man opened the door for her and she entered first, smiling at him over her shoulder, which speaks for Blanche's unawareness of her peril as well as Theo's gallantry.

After Theo closed the side door of the church, no one can say with any certainty what happened, except that the young Sunday-school superintendant by some obscure alchemy of personality turned into a perverse Quasimodo. Blanche, as a member of the church, must have been cognizant of its reputation in respect to mundane activities. She had evidently made up her mind about Theo, or she would not have accompanied him there in the middle of the afternoon without the intention of indulging in a little "spooning." But something pushed the monster across the line of safety. Perhaps Blanche coquetted too much and too long. Perhaps Theo became too imperative in his demands or actions. There was a struggle. As she fought, Blanche must have seen something in Theo's face that made her realize she was fighting for her life as well as her virtue. She was a large, strong girl, but according to the medical testimony she lost both. But whether Theo killed her by accident or in what the tabloid called a "fit of passion" is a question of endless surmise.

Whatever his reactions were, Theo worked quickly. He dragged the body by the hair to the alcove in the church library, through the door to a staircase, upwards into the Sunday-school room, up to the gallery floor, through the door to the belfry staircase and tower. He dropped her body on the bare boards of the belfry room. He crossed her hands on her chest, after stripping off all her clothing, and put several small pieces of wood under her head to hold it in position. Medical students call this "blocking," and Theo's training was telling in a moment of stress. He stuffed Blanche's school books and clothes between beams and rafters. What happened then, is, according to the coroner's report, exclusive subject matter for Kraft-Ebbing. When Theo left the belfry tower, the bright hat that had started out so gaily in the morning was wadded under a rafter, and its owner rested on the floor below.

At five o'clock, George King, the church organist and a friend of Durrant's, entered the church. He wanted to practice the music he was going to play for the Easter service. The notes of the organ in the empty church echoing up to the belfry where Theo was finishing his self-imposed labor must have added the last touch of horror to the tower-room scene. A few minutes later King heard a noise that startled him, and then a trembling, perspiring, and very white Theodore Durrant appeared in the doorway of the chapel. He told King he had been repairing some wires around the church and that a gas jet had leaked. He was feeling quite ill from the fumes and would George please go to the corner drugstore and get him a Bromo-Seltzer. King was concerned about his friend, but when he came back with the medicine, Theo seemed to be feeling better, and they left the church together.

Mrs. Noble in the meantime had become uneasy because Blanche hadn't returned home for dinner. She knew her niece had been planning to attend a prayer meeting that evening, and, thinking she might be there, Mrs. Noble went to the meeting. Durrant sat directly in back of her and asked Mrs. Noble: "Is Blanche here tonight?"

Mrs. Noble said, no, that she hadn't seen her and was worried.

"Well," answered Theo, "I regret that she is not with us tonight as I have a book called *The Newcomes* for her, but I will send it to the house."

At this point, the prayer meeting was called to order, and Theo joined in the prayers with fervor and piety.

Although Mrs. Noble stoutly and firmly maintained that there was no lover or elopement, the good Tryphena waited several days before she notified the police. A search was made in San Francisco and Oakland for the missing girl, but nothing was found. The newspapers ran brief items on the disappearance, but disappearing girls weren't extremely newsworthy in a water-front town. Durrant, who was known to be acquainted with Blanche, said he knew nothing about her absence and helpfully hinted that she had "gone astray." Theo insisted he had attended medical school that afternoon, but later investigations brought out the facts that no one could swear that he was in class as the attendance was large, that a friend answered his name at roll call, and that Theo had asked a fellow student, Glover, for the loan of his notes for the lecture given on the afternoon of Blanche's disappearance. Later investigations also showed, with a parade of witnesses, that Theo was every place else that afternoon but Cooper Medical College.

The next week was a busy one for the incipient monster. Part of the time he was acting as Theodore Durrant, model student and Sunday-school teacher, and part of the time he was behaving in the irrational, meaningless way of the monster. Theo and George King paid Mrs. Noble a visit. The two young men chivalrously offered the worried aunt any assistance they could give in finding Blanche, but Durrant, forgetting his chivalry for a moment, again intimated that Blanche had met "a fate worse than death." Oppenheimer's Pawnshop on Dupont Street was honored by a visit from Theo. He was trying to pawn several women's rings, but the canny Mr. Oppenheimer didn't think they were worth his investment. Later in the week Mrs. Noble received three rings of Blanche's wrapped in an old copy of the *Examiner* on which were scrawled the names of George King and Professor Schonstein, Blanche's music teacher. The handwriting was identified in court by experts as Durrant's.

Minnie Williams was getting her share of Theo's fatal attention, and within twenty-four hours after Blanche's disappearance Minnie was telling Frank Young, who ran a bakery shop in Alameda, "I know too much about the disappearance of Blanche." And she told her friend Jennie that Blanche had "met with foul play." Whether Theo had actually hinted these things to Minnie or whether she was employing her usual sensation-seeking tactics is debatable. The fact that she voluntarily made an appointment with Theo for the following Friday indicates that she was not frightened of the young man personally.

The last day of Minnie's life was a busy one. On Friday, April twelfth, Minnie left the Morgan's to go into the service of Mrs. Voy in San Francisco. From vague hints, it has been suggested that Mrs. Morgan was becoming a little uncharitable about the serious talks that Minnie and her husband were having about men and life. So, Minnie Williams moved her personal belongings from Alameda to San Francisco, kept an appointment with the hair dresser in Alameda, and took a ferry to San Francisco at

four o'clock in the afternoon. The hairdresser's appointment is
another indication that Minnie thought her appointment with
Theo was a standard "date" rather than a rendezvous with
a murderer.

Unfortunately for Theo, he was once again the victim of a
series of witnesses. Three fellow medical students saw him at the
ferry depot, wearing a long coat. He told them he was going
across to Mount Diablo for military exercises with the Signal
Corps and asked one of them to answer for him the next day at
roll call. Frank Sademan, the janitor of the church, was in the
neighborhood on some obscure errand and saw Theo who told
him that he was tracking down a clue to Blanche's disappearance.
He volunteered the information that a strange man had stopped
him on the street and asked him if he were Theodore Durrant.
When Theo replied that he was, the stranger hissed, "If you
want to find out about Blanche Lamont, watch the ferries." Frank
Sademan didn't question the story, but the prosecuting attorney
and the jury did when Theo told it in court. Adolph Hobe, an
Oakland commuter, saw Theo talking with a small, slight woman
in a cape at about five o'clock.

Between six and seven, Minnie settled herself and her things at
Mrs. Voy's. Minnie told Mrs. Voy that she was going to a
Christian Endeavor meeting at Dr. Vogel's house. Mrs. Voy gave
Minnie a latch key, warned her not to stay out too late, and that
ended one of the shortest employer-employee relationships on
record.

At eight o'clock, Ann McKay, a Scotch laundress, passed the
Emmanuel Baptist Church on her way home and saw a tall man
in a long coat (she later identified Theo) and a small girl in a cape.
The cape Minnie wore seems to have attracted as much attention
as Blanche's hat. The man was pleading, and the girl was protesting. At 8:10, J. P. Hodgkins, a freight claim adjuster, was coming
home from the drugstore and saw Minnie and Theo in front of
the church. Durrant was acting, said Mr. Hodgkins, in a "manner

unbecoming to a gentleman." Hodgkins went to the rescue. Peace was restored, and Minnie took Theo's arm. They were about three hundred feet from the church when Hodgkins went on his way, puffing his cigar, and feeling a kinship with St. George. At 8:15, C. Y. Hilly, a boy from the neighborhood, saw Theo entering the back door of the church, and Alexander Zengler, a member of the church who lived just across the street, saw Minnie and Theo enter the church and decided to time them. The church had long been suspected in the eyes of the older members. There were rumors that the young people were practicing more than brotherly love within its precincts on week nights. Mr. Zengler did not like these stories about "gay times," so he waited to see how long Theo and Minnie would remain inside. Some time later, Theo walked out of the church alone. According to the medical testimony, Mr. Zengler's fears were well founded, but the doctor also added a verdict of asphyxiation and hemorrhage which would explain why Theo came out alone.

Again there were witnesses to all of the acts leading up to the crime, but again the church was the only witness, and a mute one, to the actual murder. Who killed Minnie Williams is obvious. Why she was killed remains a mystery. Both Minnie Williams and Theodore Durrant are enigmas. Did Minnie try to blackmail Theo into marrying her with some half-knowledge that she had ferreted out? Perhaps she began exercising her unhealthy curiosity and hit accidentally upon the truth. Perhaps the influence of the church itself was active, and a similar situation produced similar results. But Minnie Williams, who had been a secretive girl in life, had no secrets from the medical examiner in death. She did not fight off Theo's advances as Blanche had done. She surrendered gracefully, but still he killed her. A knowledge of things past rather than sex appeal is probably the reason for Minnie's death, but paradoxically enough if Durrant had not killed the second girl Blanche's body might not have been discovered for

months or even years. The belfry was never used, and the tower
room was well ventilated.

At 9:30, Theo arrived at Dr. Vogel's house for the Christian
Endeavor meeting. His hair was disarranged. His face was paler
than usual, and he was covered with perspiration. He begged his
host's permission to wash his hands before joining the meeting.
For the rest of the evening, it was remembered, he was good-
natured and active, joining in the talk and refreshments. Afterwards, many people who were there refused to believe that Theo
Durrant was guilty. No one, they argued, could have acted as he
did that night if they had just committed murder. But then Harry
Hayward attended the theatre after sending Kitty Ging on her
last buggy ride, and Edward Small had for himself what men like
to refer to with a cocked eyebrow and a leer as a "hell of a time"
in Boston while awaiting to receive word that his cleverly wrought,
mechanical deathtrap had worked and that his wife was dead.

The meeting adjourned at 11:25, and the young people went
home—with one exception. Theo said he was going back to the
church. At midnight, he let himself into the church with his latch-
key and prowled around the scenes of his earlier activities. There
are certain scenes from certain murders that stand out with horror
and clarity: Marie De Brinvilliers sitting on one side of her
husband at the dinner table feeding him arsenic, while her
cowardly lover sat across from her and fed the unsuspecting
husband antidotes for the wife-administered poison; Burke, of
Burke and Hare notoriety, breaking the back of the small boy
who sat trustingly on his knee; Belle Gunness with her sleeves
rolled up efficiently butchering "hogs" in her well-equipped basement. And Theodore Durrant prowling around the gloomy, gaslit
church is entitled to the same remembrance.

On the next morning, the Emmanuel Baptist Church was the
scene of great activity. The Ladies' Society of the church was
decorating the chapel for Easter services the following day. A
group of ladies decided to indulge in a little rest and a little

gossip and went into the library. There was a small room opening off the library which the pastor used as a study. One of the ladies opened the door for some reason, which was quickly forgotten, and discovered the mutilated and bloody body of Minnie Williams. There is an old sketch of the scene. Three or four shirtwaisted, pompadoured ladies are looking into the small room with varying expressions of polite interest on their faces while the upper part of Minnie's remains emerge. Minnie also wears an expression of polite interest, and to the left of the door is a sampler bearing the legend, "In God We Trust."

The police were notified, and within a few moments the police and a large crowd of curiosity seekers had stormed the church. The coroner looked at the body. Minnie had been choked by forcing parts of her underclothes down her throat with a stick, stabbed in each breast with an ordinary table knife used at church refreshments, and the arteries in her wrists were severed. Even the coroner looked as if he might be sick.

While the frenzy of discovery was going on at the church, a reporter from the San Francisco *Chronicle* paid a visit to the Durrant home. Theodore was out. He had been up with the birds and on his way to Mount Diablo to join in the Signal Corps trips. He should have stayed home. The reporter talked to Mrs. Durrant, who was horrified at the news of the murder and even more horrified at the reporter's polite hint that her son might know something about the crime. Mrs. Durrant immediately launched into her favorite subject about what a good boy her son was. She told the newspaperman that Theo always kissed her whenever he left the house or came home. A statement which the reporter thought seemed strangely empty in view of his suspicions and the scene he had just left at the church.

Mrs. Durrant was cooperative. She allowed the *Chronicle* man to examine the clothes Theo had worn the previous evening. He found no bloodstains, and that was the beginning of the resurrection of the Borden theory. The Borden theory, so popular when the absence of blood on the Fall River spinster's clothes puzzled the nation, is that the criminal either wore a melodramatic, all-enveloping cape or nothing at all. And in the context of the Durrant case the revived theory had psychological as well as practical implications. While the reporter found no bloodstains or missing buttons, he did find a woman's purse in the suit-coat pocket. He quietly slipped the purse in his own pocket and took it back to the *Chronicle* office. When the purse was opened, it contained a small amount of change, a few trinkets, and ferry tickets for boats between Alameda and San Francisco. Mr. Williams, Minnie's straying father, received an urgent message to come to the newspaper office, and when he arrived identified the purse as his daughter's.

Easter Sunday, the *Chronicle* ran the story of the purse and accused Durrant of the murder of Minnie Williams. The civic-minded paper also suggested that if the police would take the trouble to search the rest of the "hoodoo" church, they would find Blanche's body. The police took the suggestion and returned to the church. They searched the lower part of the building with negative results, but the door to the steeple which had no bell and was never used showed signs of having been forced open. The officers broke down the door, followed some footprints on the dusty floor and found Blanche Lamont. The body was nude with blue marks on the throat. The police began searching for the clothing and gathered it piece by piece from rafters, beams, and every conceivable cranny. The coroner contributed the information that the girl had not "parted with life and honor without a struggle" and that the "outrage had probably occurred after death."

The signs pointed to Durrant. Minnie's purse, the "blocking" of Blanche's head, the fact that Blanche had been strangled by a left handed person and that Theo was known to be ambidextrous. The police sent out a call across the bay to pick up Durrant while, as one contemporary writer exquisitely phrases it : "The

auditorium below was decked with a profusion of flowers in com-
memoration of the Risen Lord. Above, in the dark church tower,
lay the disfigured and dishonored body of one of the fairest of
the flock of believers."

Detective Anthony of the San Francisco Detective Bureau was
sent out to bring Durrant back. He caught up with Durrant at
Walnut Creek on the way to Mount Diablo, and told Theo that
he must return to San Francisco for questioning. Word had
traveled faster than the detective and his charge. An immense
crowd waited at the Oakland Ferry landing to see the subject of
future headlines. It was a threatening crowd, and it required an
ample supply of police protection and patrol wagons to get
Durrant to the city jail unharmed and in one piece. San Francisco, in spite of its cosmopolitan veneer, was still a Western town,
and the Vigilance Committees were personal recollections rather
than abstract history to many of its citizens. Both Theo and his
escort heard the word lynch more than once as they moved from
the ferry landing to the jail. Theo spent the night in the protective
shelter of the jail, and on Monday morning Detective Anthony
arrived at the jail with a warrant for the arrest of Theodore
Durrant, charging him with the murder of Minnie Williams. Mr.
Durrant, Sr., arrived on Anthony's heels with a lawyer. Theo was
sullen and Mr. Durrant was terse at their first meeting. The
lawyer looked harassed and worried.

Within twenty-four hours after the arrest, Police Captain I. W.
Lees, the white-haired, plump, goateed impresario of the case,
was the recipient of an avalanche of information. Within the
same space of time, Theodore Durrant had changed from the
pleasant, popular young medical student and Sunday-school
teacher into a full-fledged monster. Information poured in. Theo
was depraved, vicious, and perverted, and everyone had evidence
to prove it. A parade of necessarily nameless young ladies had
stories of propositions from Theo, all received indignantly, of
course. The descriptions of the propositions were so graphic that

if the accounts were fictitious it is hard to tell how the girls acquired their material in an age when *Beverly of Graustark* and *When Knighthood Was in Flower* were the accepted standard for what every young lady should read. But if the stories were true and Theo was really refused by this legion of young ladies, we need look no further for his motive. He murdered out of sheer exasperation over his unpopularity. The debauching life of medical students was given attention and criticism, and, in an age when the mention of limbs was considered indelicate, it is easy to see how young men who practiced dissection were irreparably damned. Hints of necrophilia gave the whole case a purple tinge. Thomas S. Duke in his *Criminal History* says that he was the possessor of a photograph of Theo taken at a school picnic. The picture is not obtainable, but Mr. Duke assures us that the boy's position "proves degeneracy even as a child." And a German professor whose writings had charted the unknown region of the libido and an English poet whose writings had glorified paganism received their share of public condemnation as accessories to the fact by proxy and incitement.

Monday afternoon, Theo was taken to the office of Chief Crawley, and Blanche's three girl friends identified him as the young man who had met Blanche after school on the day of disappearance. Durrant still claimed that he had never seen Blanche that afternoon, that he had never seen these girls before, and that at the time they claim to have seen him he was in class listening to Dr. Cheyney give a lecture on milk sterilization.

But in spite of Theo's often repeated protests that he was innocent, on April nineteenth the Coroner's Jury found that Blanche Lamont had come to her death at the hands of Theodore Durrant. Theo had been arrested for the murder of Minnie Williams, but the state had decided to try him for Blanche's murder. One reason was that the witnesses who identified him on the day of Blanche's murder were people who knew him. Several of the witnesses who identified him the day of Minnie's disappearance had not known

Theo personally and could be made suspect in the eyes of the jury by skillful cross-examination.

Theo was returned to the jail to await trial, still sullenly but not very convincingly proclaiming his innocence. Hooting crowds still loitered outside the jail, and young women with flowers and oranges began to make their appearance, a sure sign that Theo had reached a mature monsterhood in the eyes of the public. Sergeant Whitman found a cardboard box in the jail hallway addressed to Chief Crawley. It contained a lady's glove dipped in red ink and a few strands of hair with a note: "You are on the wrong trail. Got the wrong bird. My Handiwork. Find me if you can. (signed) Harry the Hacker." Chief Crawley, like Queen Victoria, was "not amused," but his vocabulary was more colorful than the good queen's.

The public and some sections of the press will never believe that the person arrested for murder is the real murderer. They think that the police picked someone at random and arrested him. The facts of evidence and investigation and that the prisoner is usually in jail for a very valid reason are ignored. If the whole world loves a lover, it is also true that a great portion of it sympathizes with a murderer. To prove that the martyred hero is innocent, public suspicion and innuendo will focus on another suspect—the somebody else who could have done it. Of course, should the police take the suspicions seriously and jail the favorite suspect, he would, by the same metamorphosis, become wronged innocence, and the same loiterers would stand outside the jail, and the same women would bring him flowers. Although public opinion had been violently anti-Durrant at the time of Theo's arrest, the moment he entered the city jail surrounded by forces of law and order, he became "that poor boy" and another suspect became imperative.

The suspect was George Gibson, pastor of the Emmanuel Baptist Church. The main grounds for suspicion seem to be that Mr. Gibson did not visit Theo after he was in jail. The public was ecstatic when Mr. Gibson was summoned to the police station, but it turned out to be a routine questioning. He was, however, given police protection, confirming the rumor that some of Durrant's friends had threatened to assassinate him. There is a curious letter which the pastor wrote to a friend in which he refers to Mr. Duprey, Theo's lawyer. "What do I know? Mr. D. has not the genius to find out. Had he made a friend of me instead of an enemy he would have succeeded better. If he had only taken me into his confidence, as he did the other witnesses of the mission how different his case would have been." But in view of the evidence against Durrant and the bad taste of Durrant's lawyer reviving the suspicion against Gibson at the trial, injured feelings rather than sinister knowledge might account for the letter. After the hysteria subsided, Mr. Gibson continued for many years in his capacity as the church's pastor.

The trial began on July 22, 1895. Judge Murphy presided. One month was spent in selecting a jury, and more than one thousand prospective jurors were questioned before the panel was approved by the State and the Defense. Definite opinions had evidently been formed by the citizens of San Francisco on the pros and cons of Theo's guilt.

When the actual testimony began on September first, the courtroom was crowded, and Judge Murphy used his gavel more than once to restore legal calm. "The Sweet Pea Girl" contributed a note of color to the rather dry legal proceedings. She was a regular courtroom habitue during the trial, and, every morning as Theo was escorted in to face his "jury of peers," the young lady would attempt to pass him a fragrant, colorful cluster of sweet peas. She sent him gifts to the jailhouse, and Theo thanked her kindly for a copy of *Beside the Bonnie Briar Bush* which he had enjoyed reading. Her name was Rosa Holland, and she claimed that she had known Theo through church activities. In view of the facts of the case, this is a somewhat elastic phrase. One group of reporters claimed she was Rosa Holland from Oakland. Another school of thought and journalism claimed she was the wife of an unknown Mr. J. C. Bowers. Amid protestations of belief in Theo's innocence, she finally admitted to the reporters that she was both Rosa Holland and Mrs. J. C. Bowers. Theo backed up her story about their acquaintance, but nothing else did. Her sole contribution to the story of Theo is a bunch of sweet peas and one deathless line, irrefutable in its logic. When asked about herself, she declined to reply and profoundly observed : "I guess everyone has troubles of their own."

Fifty witnesses testified for the prosecution, including the incredible string of people who had seen Theo on the day of Blanche's death. The evidence was circumstantial, but it was strong. He was found guilty in spite of his repeated plea of not guilty, and a sweeping denial of all state testimony. Theo was sentenced to hang on February 7, 1896. The jury was out for five minutes.

Legal appeals occupied two years, and Durrant waited in San Quentin while his lawyers, family, and friends pleaded for his life. Many people believed that he was innocent, but on April 3, 1897, the Supreme Court affirmed the decision of the lower court, and Governor James Budd refused to intervene. And for the fourth consecutive time, Theo was sentenced to hang.

In the meantime, Durrant had become a personality. At his trial his sulkily handsome face had been fine grist for the mills of professional sketch artists, but he had made poor copy for the journalists. In jail, Theo became publicity conscious, and so did his parents. He played the part of injured innocence with almost professional timing. He had high moments of exhalted martyrdom, especially when the press was present, but at night the guards would hear screams coming from his cell and see him groveling on the floor. Perhaps Blanche and Minnie were indulging in a belated revenge. He spoke of his hopes for a pardon and of his plans for practicing herb medicine in Central America. "I believe I would like a tropical climate," he said. And there were many people who believed that the legal processes of the State of California had every intention of accommodating him. Day after day, Theo wrote busily and mysteriously in his cell, and his father ostentatiously carried away the manuscript, page by page. It was never seen again in spite of Durrant *pére's* dark hints of things to come.

Theo had what he called "prophetic" dreams. While in a state that was between waking and sleeping, he saw Reverend Gibson appear to him in his cell and display a scroll upon which pictures moved. The pictures showed a shipwreck, and Theo's dream was prophetic in two ways. There was a ship disaster three days later, the Coléma, and he described the motion picture which was an unknown art in 1895. He also saw words on a scroll which told him about the perpetration of the murders with which he was charged, but Theo did not give such a detailed account of this vision. One famous writer on things criminal has compared writers who figuratively dig up dead men and attempt to analyze them in an amateur way to manufacturers of quack medicine who diagnose through the mails. If the people who knew a man admit that they did not understand him, how can someone fifty or a hundred years later hope to understand the same man? The answer is obvious. Contemporaries of Theodore Durrant, Lizzie Borden, or Jesse Pomeroy, "the white-eyed boy," didn't know about the trinity of the twentieth century : the id, the ego, and the super-ego. A specific example of this is found in the case of Theo. In any modern book on psychology, there are descriptions of visions and half-waking, half-sleeping hallucinations of great distinctness. They are under the bold-type heading of *schizoid,* and almost any doctor or student of the subconscious, if he possessed a drop of gambling blood, would be willing to give good odds on the possibility of Theo's hearing prophetic voices if suffering the extreme penalty hadn't ended his career prematurely. Theo himself was conscious of the lurking monster. "It seems," he mused to a newspaperman, "that I were two persons, so distinct are my physical and spiritual nature."

Theo was conscious of three things. His innocence, a sudden

pride in the Durrant blood, and his dual personality. He announced repeatedly that he was "going to die like a Durrant" and that he was innocent. He obviously had no intention of making a last-minute confession to satisfy the consciences of those who were responsible for his death, and, as his pride in his family name grew, the chances for a scaffold declaration decreased even more. But his many references to his dual nature show that at least Theo was conscious of the duality and perhaps by indirection he was justifying his acts of violence. Theo, the innocent, was putting the blame where it belonged—on the monster. And in this way, he could justly claim that Theodore Durrant as a person was innocent.

The day before the execution, reporters were admitted to the jail to offer sympathy and publicity to the Durrant *famille*. But Warden Hale was in a testy mood: "Don't talk to me of sympathy for those people," he roared. "Mr. Durrant now says he will break any camera in the execution room and pummel every artist. What rot! Why he has been to me with a kinetoscope man and has gone down on his knees to me to allow Theodore to go out of his cell, pick a few flowers, scatter them on the walk and go back to his cell while the kinetoscope man takes snapshots. They have been trying to run the execution. They behave to me as if they were proud of all this."

A kinetoscope is a device which these days deals almost exclusively with hula dancers and strip teasers. Pictures are taken, clipped together, and as the spectator riffles through them they appear to move. Mr. Durrant had decided, with a touching paternal sentiment, that a kinetoscope treatment of Theo would be a fine tribute to his boy and incidentally have some merit and attraction as salable souvenirs.

When the reporters were admitted to Theo's cell, they found him in one of his exalted moods. "It is not awful to go to such a death. Such a death as mine may be the means of abolishing capital punishment in this state."

His mother, hovering around like a harpyish caricature of motherhood, bolstered his morale. "It will be a grand death, Theo. Think of how Jesus died."

But the effect of all this piety and martyrdom was slightly marred when Theo added, "I have been accustomed to remuneration when talking for publication." And when the hint was not immediately adopted by the fourth estate, Mrs. Durrant told her son snappishly, "Theo, you have said enough." Even exaltation has its price.

On the evening before the execution, Theo sent for Father Logan. In the early days of his imprisonment, the Rev. William Roder had been Theo's spiritual adviser, but the Durrants had told him that his services were no longer required when Theo became a Catholic convert. The Reverend Roder said that he was afraid he had not been "successful in concealing his conviction of Durrant's guilt." And although the minister said that Theo had made no formal confession, when asked what his opinion of Durrant was, Reverend Roder replied that he was a "psychological monster." Theo must have said more than he realized about his dual personality.

Father Logan answered the summons and spent several hours with Theo. A guard in the hallway heard Theo declaim in carrying tones to the priest, "No, I will not confess the murders because I am not guilty."

On the morning of the execution, Theo was calm enjoying the usual "hearty meal," and Dr. Lawley, the prison doctor, felt professional admiration for a man who with such a short time to live had a pulse beat of seventy-four. Mrs. Durrant was waiting in a room adjoining the execution chamber. Mr. Durrant was being escorted into the execution chamber, having insisted on seeing his son's last moments. Amos Lunt, the hangman, confined himself to a liquid diet, and the witnesses, who were sheriffs from all the counties of California, arrived at San Quentin and were led into the death room. Some of the officials from the more rugged sections of the country had to be asked rather emphatically to park their shooting irons outside.

Theo entered the white-washed execution chamber with Father Logan. He mounted the scaffold without looking at his father and informed the nervous hangman, "Don't put that rope on, my boy, until after I talk."

The newspapers marveled at the brave way in which Theo died, but from many accounts of executions, the murderer who displays cowardice or has to be carried to his execution is the exception rather than the rule. Dr. Pritchard, who disposed of his wife and mother-in-law, went to the gallows "as if marching to the strains of martial music." Guiteau, President Garfield's assassin, stood on the scaffold and recited endless verses of his postimpressionistic poetry, and Carlyle Harris, a young medical student in New York around 1893, met his death very much like Durrant, with protests of innocence and a reverent little speech. The activities of these two young men were similar in many ways, but there was a difference. Harris had a motive in his madness.

Theo delivered a convincing scaffold address. A reporter who was present in the execution chamber says that his references to the Almighty were made with pious intonations, that he showed just the right amount of Christian forbearance and forgiveness toward the San Francisco press, and that his rhetoric was flawless. But it failed to convince the reporter of Theo's innocence.

"To those who wish me to say something," Theo began, "I wish to say this : that I have no animosity against anyone but those who have persecuted me and hounded me to my grave, innocent as I am. I forgive them all. They will receive their justice from the Holy God above, to whom I now go to receive my justice, which will be the justice given to an innocent boy who has not stained his hands with the crimes that have been put upon him by the press of San Francisco. I forgive them all, for I do not hold anything against them for it.

"I do not look upon people now as enemies. I forgive them as

I expect to be forgiven for anything I have done, but the fair fame of California will forever be blackened with the crime of taking innocent blood, and whether or no they ever discover the committors of these crimes matters little to me now, for I appear before the whole world innocent, to proclaim my innocence for the last time, and to those who have insinuated that I was going to spring a sensation of any kind, I can say that there is no sensation other than that of which I have spoken.

"They must consider for themselves who wished to start up a sensation. That I am innocent I say now, this day before God, to whom I now go to meet my dues.

"I am innocent. . . ."

He had not finished, but Amos's nerves were quivering, and on the last "I am innocent" Theo was dropped into eternity.

Mr. Durrant and some of their friends joined Mrs. Durrant in the next room. In a few minutes Theo's body was brought in, in a black coffin, and the parents kissed Theo's mortal remains and wept together. Williams, a convict of English extraction, asked Mrs. Durrant if he could bring her some tea. She thanked him and said she would like some. Williams, upholding English tradition and custom, returned with his version of tea, a tray loaded with every sort of food, and served it on a table not more than three feet from the coffin.

Friends and witnesses, thinking that the couple would like some privacy, busily gathered in little groups or looked out of the windows, and, for those who believe that monsterhood can be inherited, here is confirmation. As the people in the room continued to speak softly or studiously study the scenery, the voice of the bereaved mother was heard. "Papa," she said plaintively, "Give me a little more of the roast."

The body was taken by an impressive carriage procession to the Durrant home on Fair Oaks Street. No crematorium or cemetery would accept the body. Mr. Durrant spent his days looking for a last resting place for his son, and Mrs. Durrant employed her time in sitting by the coffin in the front parlor where she talked to Theo for hours every day. The Pasadena cemetery agreed to accept the body on the thirteenth of January, and how Mrs. Durrant passed her days after that is not known.

An anonymous reporter who wrote a contemporary account of the Durrant case summed it up more accurately than he knew by his choice of an adjective. He said: "It was a most monstrous murder."

IV

The Flowering of George Hersey

GEORGE HERSEY WAS A YOUNG MAN who lived and worked in South Weymouth, Massachusetts, in 1860, and Fate, with an unfortunate emphasis on coincidence, was hard on him.

He seemed like the average gentleman of his day. He was personable, neat, always asked permission to smoke in the presence of ladies, and he is interesting for several reasons. He was the possessor of a pioneer spirit, and, although his field of activity was a strange one, he explored it with the fortitude and thoroughness of a trail blazer. By his pioneering, he drastically weakened the time-honored institution of the shot gun for redress of certain grievances and gave a new pattern of procedure to that most unfortunate class of men—unmarried fathers. He set an example that was followed by such fateful fiends as Herbert Hiram Haydn and the Reverend Richeson, when the problem of unwelcome paternity was forcibly brought to their attention. Their respective victims, Mary Stannard in her red calico dress crumpled on the garden path and Avis Linnell, the school girl, collapsing in agony over a porcelain bathtub, owe much to Mr. George Hersey of South Weymouth, Massachusetts.

The Tirrell Family from which Hersey drew material and inspiration for his pioneering venture was one of those New England families that rival the Indians in totemic clannishness.

76

In 1860, South Weymouth was its stronghold, and the small town was glutted with Tirrells. There was Wilson Tirrell, the owner of a prosperous leather business and a man of competent social standing, his wife, and three daughters. Wilson's brother, Kingman, had sired two sons and two daughters. Wilson Tirrell, Jr., and his wife, Nancy, had already begun perpetuating the family line with hereditary fecundity. Susan, Wilson Tirrell's oldest daughter, married William Hersey of Hingham, and Mr. Tirrell's two sisters had settled down with two worthy citizens of the town, Jairus Vining and Randall Richards. And to complete the solid family front, at the time of the murder, none of the Tirrells lived more than a quarter of a mile distant from each other.

In the case of the Tirrells, it would seem that the unkind fate which hounded Mr. Hersey's well-polished, gentlemanly boots was accompanied by an implacable, avenging fury. In 1845, a Mr. Albert Tirrell of South Weymouth was charged with the murder of Mrs. Maria Bickford, a woman whose name was not mentioned in front of wives and daughters. He was acquitted on the interesting assumption that Mrs. Bickford, with feminine ingenuity, had set fire to herself and then almost cut off her head. Fifteen years later, two Tirrells lost their lives by violence.

In the fall of 1859, George Hersey was a widower. His brother had found him employment in South Weymouth at the shoe manufacturing company of Nathaniel Shaw, and George moved from his parents' home in Hingham to South Weymouth, where he boarded with Jairus and Mary Vining, the aunt of William Hersey's wife. George roomed with Gus, the Vining's son, and Gus formed a great admiration for his man-of-the-world roommate. One night, Hersey pulled a small vial from his bureau drawer and gave Gus a knowing wink. "There," he told the impressed Gus, "is something to kill young ones."

The relations between the Herseys and the Tirrells were intimate, and it was no surprise when Wilson Tirrell's daughter, Mary, announced her engagement to George Hersey. But before the congratulations had subsided, Mary became violently ill, and on January 2, 1860, she was dead. Hersey was at her bedside constantly during Mary's illness, and everyone who saw the young man thought that fate was dealing most harshly with him in the matter of wedded bliss. Later, it was thought, both officially and unofficially, that perhaps George had helped fate along. Mr. and Mrs. Tirrell were so touched by the young man's grief that they invited him to live with them for a while. The inference was that it would be one continuous wake, with the lover and family of the dead girl keeping her memory alive with a barbaric intensity. It was board and room in exchange for companionable grief, and, before the funeral was over, the ill-omened housing arrangement was in effect.

The gloomy household consisted of Mr. and Mrs. Tirrell, Betsy Frances, a daughter by a former marriage, and twelve-year-old Louisa, a daughter of the present marriage. In contrast to her sister Mary who was a carefree, golden-curled belle of South Weymouth, Betsy Frances was sallow, thin, and "given to melancholy." She was twenty-five years old, and in those days a woman who remained unmarried at that age had already begun to assume the autumnal crispness and dryness of spinsterhood. Betsy Frances, with her prim body encased in the cumbersome costume of the day and her prim soul encased in the equally cumbersome morals of the period, emerges from the cold intricacies of the trial testimony as a pathetic figure. Hers was a rigid Victorian personality with a stiff backbone of grim New England Puritanism and a hint of insanity, and when her crinoline, literally as well as figuratively, fell before attack, both she and her attacker violated the stern ethics of their society, and somebody had to pay the ever-demanding piper. Betsy Frances dared to emerge from her shell of layers of petticoats and morality for a brief moment and found beauty and color in a life of bleak monotones. But Victorian society, which refused to recognize the existence of legs as well as basic functions in man, demanded a high price for this deviation. It was paid in full. George Hersey had more of a choice. He could have settled on just being a cad and taken the advice of Horace Greeley, but his pioneer instincts were too strong.

Hersey, after his entrance into the Tirrell home, and Betsy Frances were constantly in each other's company, and the family regarded it as a rather touching brother and sister relationship. The girl had been almost abnormally attached to her sister, and the presence of her sister's ex-future husband must have been food for her libido. They were both in mourning and shunned society, walking, riding, and attending church together and unchaperoned. They spent many evenings together in the Tirrell front parlor after the rest of the family had retired. Hersey showed an interest in Frances' clothes and personal purchases, and Frances, by way of reciprocation took charge of his clothing and lovingly stitched cambric shirts for him. They were allowed a staggering amount of freedom, in the days when a man and a maid were meticulously protected against their own baser natures. But Mr. and Mrs. Tirrell were immersed in their grief and never considered that two very much alive young people of the opposite gender might have more than a morbid interest in common.

After Hersey had been living with the Tirrells for about a month, the family and friends noticed a decline in Frances' health, and Hersey remarked to several of her relatives that he wouldn't be "surprised if Frances made away with herself." Her melancholy was attributed to Mary's death and was left to the minstrations of time. "Melancholy" is the word that is again and again appearing as a qualifying adjective next to Frances' name in the trial testimony, and the terminology is insidious. In 1860, it could mean anything from a sensitive temperament to raving mania, and Dr. Appleton Howe, the family physician, uneasily admitted under oath that the first Mrs. Tirrell, Betsy Frances' mother, had died in 1845 from a general breaking up of the system and complete debility. The year of her death, Dr. Howe had been called in to dress a wound in Mrs. Tirrell's throat made with a sharp cutting instrument. He didn't ask how it happened or who did it, and Mrs. Tirrell, during the time he was treating the wound, remained in a completely passive state. Melancholy was part of Betsy Frances' heritage.

For the first month after Mary's death, Hersey did not go to work. He gave ill health as an excuse, and Mrs. Tirrell noticed that he "read considerable." Mrs. Tirrell made several visits to a sick sister in February and the first part of March, and Mr. Tirrell was away on short business trips. Betsy Frances and Hersey took care of the house, and twelve-year-old Louisa was the only chaperone they had.

The last part of February, Hersey returned to work, and when he took his place at one of Mr. Shaw's stitching machines, it was evident that he had found several things to take his mind off his loss. He was studying chemistry and talked very lucidly and expertly to the men at the shop about poisons and their various effects. He told Wilson Tirrell, Jr., that he was going to California to do some kind of chemical research and with a laugh and an unintentional bit of prophecy repeated the current "Pike's Peak or Bust" slogan.

At the same time Hersey returned to his job, he began spending his evenings away from his adopted home. Mr. Hersey was evidently a great believer in love on the rebound, and he had an almost elastic quality of being able to bounce from one woman to the next. His newest petticoated consolation was Loretta Loud, a popular young girl in South Weymouth. In March they became engaged, but at George's request it was kept a secret to spare the Tirrell family. Loretta had a healthy feminine curiosity, and tried to make Hersey admit that he had been interested in Betsy Frances, but his answer was an emphatic denial that he had ever been in love with her and an emphatic assurance that he never would be. George also told Loretta that if Frances "did not get better soon she would not live long." Loretta, fortunately for her

future health and happiness, broke her engagement with Hersey
when she found that he wanted a more tangible sort of consolation
than she was prepared to give him.

In the meantime, Frances was becoming more and more
depressed. Hersey's sister, Caroline Cushing, came to visit the
Tirrells, and Frances told her hysterically that she wished that it
had been she that had died rather than Mary. Caroline suggested
to Betsy Frances that a change of scenery would be a good tonic
and invited her to come to Hingham. Frances accepted the invitation and went to Weymouth Landing to buy material for a new
dress, but Mr. Hersey remarked gloomily to several assorted
Tirrells that he didn't think Frances would live to wear the dress.
It looked as if he knew what he was talking about because at
approximately the same time, George Hersey went to Boston and
had an interesting conversation with Alfred Coburn, who was
employed by the Ellis F. Miller Pharmacy on Hanover and Union
Streets. It seemed that Mr. Hersey was troubled with a vicious
dog. Could Mr. Coburn give him a little strychnine to remedy the
situation? Mr. Coburn was obliging, but he warned Hersey that
it was against the law, and he hoped there wouldn't be any
trouble. The prospective canine killer assured Coburn that he
"would never hear from that." He also bought some Lubin perfume wrapped in a bluish-purple paper, a hair brush, and a comb.
Hersey walked out of the pharmacy, and the next time he saw
Coburn it was under less commercial circumstances in the Dedham County Jail. Mr. Coburn may not have been an ethical
druggist, but he had a good memory for a face.

Mrs. Tirrell was having a trying time. Nobody would talk
to her, and George was "acting different toward Frances than
what he did before." Alma Tirrell doesn't sound like a garrulous
woman, but the house was beginning to pluck at her nerves. She
said to Frances, "I wonder what George is put out with me about.
He don't talk with me and don't stay in the house when I am
here." But Frances had problems of her own and replied absently

that Hersey "talks as much with you as he does with me." The noncommunication was contagious. Frances, too, became more silent than usual, and Mrs.   Tirrell's later testimony presents a rather cheerless picture of their home life. She said that sometimes she and Frances "would sit for hours and nothing would be said if I didn't speak." Frances said she "just didn't feel like talking." And Mrs. Tirrell noticed other things. At first, George had responded to Frances' attentions; now he avoided or rebuffed them. He made excuses to go to bed early on his infrequent evenings at home. Frances still sewed buttons on his shirts and brushed his great coat, but George remained aloof. In fact, Mrs. Tirrell was afraid that "something was not quite right."

On the afternoon of May Third, Frances' sister, Susan Hersey, left her little girl with Frances while she went shopping, an indication that perhaps Frances had already fallen into the mold of the maiden aunt. When Susan called for her daughter, Frances asked her to stay for tea, and Susan noticed that her younger sister seemed happier than she had for many months. She seemed almost gay as she sat sewing on a shirt for George and humming a rather lilting popular song. Frances told Susan that she was feeling much better and added, with a knowing, very unspinsterish smile, that George wouldn't be going to California. George came in the room and smiled affectionately at Frances. Mr. Tirrell came in from his garden where he had been puttering away the bright May afternoon, and Frances served tea. Susan left soon after the meal, and that was the last time she ever saw her sister.

As Frances was putting away the tea things, Hersey said he was supposed to take the horses and carriage and pick up Mrs. Tirrell who had been spending the day with her brother and his family. He asked Frances and Louisa if they would like to come along for the ride. The girls agreed and settled their mountainous crinolines in the carriage, and when they arrived at the Blanchard house, Mrs. Tirrell asked Hersey if he would take Louisa to the barber's for a haircut. He agreed, and Mrs. Tirrell and Frances waited at the Blanchards. Frances showed her aunt and cousin a brooch she had made from a lock of Mary's hair and joined quite vivaciously in the conversation. Her relatives were delighted to see the girl feeling so much better. Hersey returned with the newly shorn Louisa, and while the women made their prolonged birdlike farewells, he and Mr. Blanchard "passed the time of day."

The ride home found George in his usual silent mood. At the trial the district attorney asked: "Was he then revolving in his mind this dreadful deed?" At eight o'clock the carriage pulled up in front of the Tirrell house. Mr. Tirrell was waiting for them on the porch. The family adjourned to the front parlor, and Hersey, after unceremoniously taking off his shoes, said that he had a bad headache and was going to bed.

Betsy Frances brought in the evening paper and read aloud the items of interest to her parents. The Seccession Meeting in Charlestown was erupting in hot issues and hot debates. Miss Florence Nightingale was writing a handbook for nurses which would sell for twenty-five cents. The D. Appleton Publishing Company announced the advent of a new book by the author of *Adam Bede,* and a ridiculously angular man with a ridiculously euphonious name was being mentioned as a dark horse in the presidential race. Frances finished reading the paper and answered a knock on the door. The boys of the neighborhood, in accordance with local custom, had left several May baskets hanging on the door knob. She brought them into the parlor and said that she would take them up to show Louisa. Mr. Tirrell, in a benevolent mood, offered to take the family to the circus in Fall River the next day, and Frances told her mother that she would get breakfast in the morning. She walked out of the brightly lit parlor, up the stairs, down the dim, gaslit hall, swinging the gay May baskets on her arm, and walked right out of life.

Frances went into the room where she and Louisa slept, woke

Louisa and showed her the May baskets. Louisa was drowsy and didn't notice what her sister was doing. She heard Frances leave the room for a few minutes, probably to put her clothes in the closet at the end of the hall. Frances returned, moved around the room for a few minutes and crawled into bed. A half hour later, Louisa was wide awake. The bed was rocking, and Frances was twitching and trembling violently.

"Mother! Mother!" called the frightened Louisa. "Frances is in a fit."

Mr. and Mrs. Tirrell and Hersey rushed into the room. Frances was screaming, "I shall die. I shall die." She was suffering the usual symptoms of strychnine poisoning, and her pain was a horrible thing to see. Hersey was sent for Dr. Howe. Mrs. Tirrell tried to massage Frances' legs and arms and apply hot poultices. Mr. Tirrell, feeling the need for his family at such a time, went out and roused the clan like a latter-day Paul Revere. Within a half hour, Albert and Austin Tirrell were at the house. Mrs. Vining and her husband were trying to straighten out Betsy Frances whose back had arched from the muscular convulsions. Mrs. Richards was wiping away the blood that trickled from the girl's badly bitten lips. By the time Dr. Howe arrived, Betsy Frances had fulfilled her own prophecy. She was dead.

After Frances' death, the family became practical. They were all afraid of being poisoned and even boiled the water they drank. Albert Tirrell suggested an autopsy, remarking with real New England thriftiness of phrase that he didn't think the death was a "natural stoppage" and that "here are two droppings away so suddenly and they should be examined." The rest of the family agreed with the young man. All except Hersey who denounced the practice of post-mortems and called it "butchery" and "shocking mutilation," saying that he would never allow a friend of his to be opened. But the family, sitting in the parlor while Frances' still warm body was in the room above, overruled Hersey's objections and asked Dr. Howe to make the necessary arrangements. Hersey became very quiet and was evidently so upset at the thought of the autopsy that he forgot to advance his pet theory about Frances' suicidal tendencies. That night Louisa slept with Hersey in his room. The Tirrells seemed to tempt fate when they were grief stricken.

On Friday, the day after the death and the day before the autopsy, Hersey went into his shop and visited the various Tirrell domiciles. And he talked too much. He stopped at the house of Wilson Tirrell, Jr. Nancy Tirrell said it was strange that Frances should die so suddenly, and Hersey's reply is one of the few true statements he made. He said that he thought Frances had died of a broken heart, and, in a more literal sense than Nancy Tirrell realized, added that she seemed as near like his wife as anyone could.

He visited the home of Kingman Tirrell and talked to the two girls, Charlotte and Ann. Charlotte observed that it was strange to have two such sudden deaths in the family, and Hersey countered by asking, "Can it be that Mary and Frances have met in Heaven?" If they did they must have had a great deal in common, even for sisters.

Hersey told the girls that on her way to the clothes press, Frances had stopped at his door and asked about his headache. He said he was just about asleep when he heard his name called and rushed into Frances' room where he found her sick—"Just like my wife; although Hannah suffered longer," he added reminiscently. Charlotte asked if Frances could have taken poison, and Hersey, in spite of his gloomy prophecies on the subject, replied "No. I do not think so."

He told Jairus Vining the same story, and the versions he repeated to Dr. Howe and Spencer Gurney and Edward Lewis, who worked in the shoe shop, didn't vary from the original. But Louisa firmly denied that either she or Frances had called Hersey's name that night and that the first time he came into the room was with her parents. When the prosecution pointed out that Betsy Frances would naturally call to the person she knew to be the source of her sickness, Hersey and his defense quickly jumped on the bandwagon, backed up Louisa's version, and denied that he had ever said anything else.

The autopsy was set for Saturday morning, May Fifth. The Tirrells were almost as upset as Hersey at the prospect of desecrating their dead, but they had concluded that some of the niceties could very well be overlooked in view of the high mortality rate of the daughters of the house. Late in the morning, Dr. Howe, Dr. Fifield, and Dr. Towers arrived on their grisly errand, and Hersey, in spite of his avowed horror at the proceedings, asked if he might be allowed in the autopsy room. The doctors didn't object, and he entered the room with them. Frances' body was placed on a wooden board which rested on the sitting room table. The doctors opened their bags, gathered around the table, and the grim business began. Dr. Howe must have been expecting an unusual disclosure, because he had found "unusual indications" that did not jibe with Frances' marital status, when he made the examination the night of her death. The autopsy confirmed his worst fears. Betsy Frances was in a state—some three months advanced—in which no nice young lady finds herself without benefit of clergy, plus at least nine months of married life.

Hersey was asked to leave the room, and the doctors, after a brief consultation decided to call in the coroner and gave Dr. Howe the thankless duty of telling the family of their findings. While Dr. Howe was saddling his horse to go for the coroner, Hersey approached him.

"Have you found the cause of death?"

"No. What did you expect we would find?" The doctor answered with a certain amount of testiness born of suspicion. "But I suspect she has been poisoned."

"Heavens and earth," was Mr. Hersey's shocked comment, and he threw his hands over his face.

The coroner arrived at sunset, and the autopsy proceeded. The organs were found to be in a healthy condition and were placed in earthen jars, sealed and delivered the next day to Prof. A. A. Hayes of Boston. He and Prof. E. N. Horsford of Cambridge were directed by the government to make separate investigations for poison. They obligingly and scientifically extracted from the parts given them a large portion of strychnine—it totalled about $2^7/10$ grains. George Hersey took no chances; half grain is a dangerous dose.

Following the autopsy, the Tirrells, en masse, indicated very clearly to Hersey that while they believed babies were the result of divine will, a little human intervention was necessary. And since George had been the only young man with whom Frances had any contact during the "critical" months, it was evident that he had exceeded the fraternal bonds. Mr. Tirrell with a very real sense of melodrama and a very real sense of grief ordered Hersey out of his house in sonorous, meaty phrases.

Mrs. Vining had been the first to tell Hersey that Frances was "in the family way," and Hersey reached heights of hypocrisy or biological ignorance when he exclaimed piously, "It cannot be that Frances was such a girl as that. I would as soon think (it) of my mother." But the uncomfortable fact remained that Frances had been in an embarrassing condition, and Hersey was the most likely person to have put her in it. His only comment after the autopsy was that the weather was "very warm."

After being ordered out of his "second home," George went to his brother's house. Mrs. Hersey was torn between being a good wife and offering shelter to her husband's brother and being a good Tirrell and ordering him out. She finally compromised by admitting Hersey to her parlor but subjecting him to a grueling, feminine cross-examination. He was crying and wailing, "It will be laid to me." Susan told him it was impossible for anyone else to be guilty. His only reply was that he "couldn't bear the disgrace of this." Mrs. Vining was present and aided and abetted

Susan. She fixed Hersey with an unfriendly and imposing look and asked him if he could swear he was innocent. He said he could. But then George Hersey wasn't a follower of the sweepingly romantic English poet who thought that beauty and truth were synonymous.

It was evident to Hersey that South Weymouth was not going to be a congenial place to live, so Sunday morning he asked his brother to arrange for transportation to Hingham. William asked Mr. Cyrus Sherman, a local business man, if he would drive George to Hingham. Mr. Sherman agreed, and by ten o'clock Sunday morning George Hersey rumbled out of South Weymouth in Mr. Sherman's cart, and Mr. Sherman probably told the story around many warm New England firesides on many cold New England nights of how he had driven the "South Weymouth Poisoner" home on that bright spring day.

At the time that irresistible George was being conveyed from the scene of his activities, Ann Tirrell and Mrs. Tirrell were searching Hersey's room. Mrs. Tirrell found some colored paper that might have been the Lubin perfume wrapper, but she burned it as "trash." In Frances' room, Ann discovered a silver spoon in the fireplace behind the fireboard. There were small dabs of fruit preserve clinging to it, and the women gave it to Dr. Howe. Upon examination the spoon was also found to have small dabs of strychnine clinging to it.

During the trial, the defense returned to two points with regularity. Why was the spoon thrown behind the fireboard? And why hadn't Betsy Frances accused George Hersey in her last painful moments? The defense was making a valiant effort to prove suicide and also maintained that she had been so cheerful on the day of her death because she knew that "on the morrow she would be with her Heavenly Father."

Most girls admittedly are not as cheerful as Betsy Frances when their "young man" is rendering such a service. But Hersey was not a stupid man. He ended his days in the Dedham County

Jail because he lacked variety, not intellect. He probably told Frances that it would never do for them to marry and produce a six-months' baby. The thing to do was take the medicine he would give her, clear up the situation, and then they would be married with impeccable righteousness. That would account for her willingness to take the medicine and her good humor the day of her death. When Frances stopped at his door to ask about his headache, Hersey made provisions in case the medicine took time to be effective. He told Frances that she might be sick for a little while and to throw the spoon behind the fireboard so that no one could find what she had taken.

Frances' cries that she was "going to die" were probably those of a frightened girl, but she had expected to be sick, and she certainly wasn't going to say to a roomful of aunts and cousins that George had given her medicine for an unmentionable purpose and ruin their bright future. She was sure the pain would pass, and she and George could go ahead with their plans. Why should she spoil everything because she was frightened and the medicine was making her sick? And for the last ten minutes before she died, Frances was unable to speak. George Hersey was capable of gaining limitless trust from the women who loved him.

The following week, George Hersey was arrested at the home of his parents. He submitted gracefully with the fatalistic phrase, "I am ready."

On April 4, 1861, the Grand Jury of Norfolk County returned an indictment which found that "the said George C. Hersey, had willfully feloniously and with malice aforethought had administered strychnine to the said Betsy Frances Tirrell. . . ." The indictment contained four separate counts which were wrangling material for tortuous legal skirmishes, but all four points, regardless of wording, had the same thought; that George Canning Hersey "did deprive of life the said Betsy Frances Tirrell. . . ."

On May twenty-eighth of the same year the trial began. It had attracted wide interest not only because of the *modus operandi* but also because Hersey was the first American disciple of one of the major Wicked Men of all time, William Palmer, the jovial English rural physician and horse player who murdered with strychnine and joked with his victims while they died. Pages of the trial testimony concern the medical and chemical tests used in detecting strychnine, and contemporary medical and legal men read it with professional interest.

The Hon. George T. Bigelow was chief justice with Associate Justices Harles A. Dewey, Pliny Merrick, and Reuben Chapman. Counsel for the commonwealth was headed by the Hon. Dwight Foster, attorney general, and the Hon. Benjamin Harris, district attorney. Hersey had requested for his defense George S. Sullivan, Esq., and the Hon. Elihu C. Baker. The jury was empaneled with Jeremiah Allen as foreman. The indictment was read, and Hersey again pleaded not guilty.

Mr. Harris opened for the prosecution. He pointed out to the jury that American law operated on the innocent-until-proven-guilty theory and told the twelve men what the state must do to prove guilt. It must prove that Betsy Frances Tirrell had died a violent death, that she died from strychnine which had been administered by the prisoner. The district attorney indulged in very little embellished oratory, although a phrase did slip into his speech about the "life and fair fame of a young and beloved daughter being cruelly destroyed."

Mr. Baker made the opening speech for the defense. He pointed proudly to the fact that his client's position in the community was a good one and rather unwisely called attention to Hersey's triple bereavements—the loss of a wife, a fiancée, and pseudo stepsister. It started the jury thinking about the mathematical possibility of three coincidental deaths in three years. Baker tried to shift the blame to an anonymous "destroying angel who spreads his dark wings over that stricken family."

He adopted the attitude of an indulgent but slightly disapproving father toward Betsy Frances and in trembling tones said that she had "yielded what a woman prizes above her life—her virtue. . . . She had loved not wisely but too well. . . ." He then explored his client's sterling character and ended up with a flourish. "Poison under the guise of love . . . this needs the heart not of a man but of a fiend incarnate . . . a heart whose every muscle and sinew has been tempered and steeled in the very fires of hell. . . ." The suicide theory was advanced, Mr. Baker claiming that Betsy Frances had a motive, since she had "lost that bright precious jewel of her queenly crown" and calling attention to her "melancholy."

The Tirrell family streamed steadily into the courtroom and with eyes averted from George Hersey, offered their scraps of information which accumulated into a pattern of damning guilt. Apothecaries from Derby and Weymouth Landing testified that neither Hersey nor any member of the Tirrell family had purchased poison from them. The careless Mr. Coburn had identified Hersey and repeated his identification of Hersey and their conversation to the twelve men in the jury box.

The medical testimony for the state was brilliant. Dr. Hayes gave a scholarly dissertation on Frances' intestine which was stimulating to chemists if not to the palpitating spectators who had come to hear about sex, not strychnine. He eagerly offered to make some of his color tests in court, but the judge wearily sustained the objection of the defense. Dr. J. B. S. Jackson, Professor of Morbid Anatomy at Harvard, and Professor Horsford confirmed Dr. Hayes's testimony. The defense failed to shake any of the witnesses in cross-examination, but a persistent effort was made to prove that at some time during the months before Betsy Frances' death a small brown dog had been found poisoned on the Tirrell property. The small terrier continued to pop up in incongruous places throughout the trial as the sole recipient of Mr. Hersey's Boston-imported strychnine.

The sensation of the trial, both from a journalistic and a medical viewpoint, was Frederick Morrill, a Boston physician, who practiced at 9 Howard Street. He had made a commercial success of "induced miscarriages" and was in a rather delicate position as a state's witness. In the last part of 1857, he testified, Hersey had seen his advertisement for medicines for females. Hersey told him he needed advice for females in the family way. Morrill told the worried young man that he had medicines but did not sell them for that purpose. Hersey had then asked about an operation, and the "doctor" told him that it was safe in the hands of one who understood it but not in the hands of those who did not. Morrill was evidently testifying with an uneasy eye on the state. He said that Hersey left and did not return to his offices until early in 1860. If Hersey was the victim of coincidence in the other two deaths, his visit to Morrill in 1857, the year his wife died, was another unfortunate marker.

On Hersey's second visit he told Morrill that he had come for a friend who was about three months advanced in pregnancy and about twenty-five years old. He finally admitted that the case was his own and priced "suppression" medicines and operations which ranged from two to five hundred dollars. Hersey protested that he was "only a mechanic" and couldn't afford it, adding the interesting information that he could get something "to get rid of it for fifty cents." He also confided to Morrill that he was unfortunate in getting into such scrapes. Women were pretty much alike, he said, and he could generally do anything he wanted with them—except control their fertility.

"That rather touched me. . . ." Morrill righteously told an attentive courtroom. "I told him I would rather not talk with such a man."

Hersey tried to pacify the "doctor" by saying that he could send him a great many cases, but Morrill testified, piously, that he refused the offer and the chance to sell some of his medicine.

Hersey also wanted a little strychnine to kill a dog. Morrill again refused.

The defense treated the Boston practitioner rather roughly, forcing him to admit that he was not a "regular physician." Morrill studied his fingernails assiduously and declined to answer "whether I keep medicines for sale to procure abortions." When questioned about his advertisements, which suspiciously stated that "persons wishing them may have rooms," Morrill volunteered the information that "I have had Females come to the city to be treated for lameness." He studied his hands again when he "declined to state whether I have ever procured an abortion."

The state rested its case with a short summation. Mr. Foster said that George Hersey had had his choice of marriage, exposure, or murder, and that the prosecution had certainly proved the latter. He asked for a verdict of first-degree murder.

The defense based its case on Hersey's good character, the fact that no actions had ever been witnessed between Hersey and Betsy Frances, and the rather ex post facto question concerning Betsy Frances: "Was she up to the standard of our New England girls?"

Hersey's lawyers, while they used the letter of the law skillfully, are a good example to any law student of what to do if you want to see your client hung. Baker, particularly, had no understanding of the jury or the small New England community, and he antagonized where he should have appeased, ranted and raved when he should have retrenched. He made remarks about the personal appearance and habits of people who were considered leading citizens of the small, compact town. He accused the state and the Tirrells of collusion. He said that Dr. Howe, whom he called "old Weathercock" because of a slip of two weeks on the age of the foetus, had shown an indecent interest in the conviction. He hinted that Frances had not been a virgin when she met Hersey. He implied that Albert or Austin Tirrell were as likely candidates for the unwelcome paternity as George Hersey. He called Mrs. Tirrell "a hard, thin, sharp-featured woman" and claimed that Betsy Frances had committed suicide.

The jury was out five hours and came back with a verdict of guilty of murder in the first degree. In February, 1862, Hersey was given a lecture and the death sentence by Judge Bigelow. He was executed on August 8, 1862, and his brother requested the body.

Just before his death, George Hersey handed the following statement to the warden:

I, George Canning Hersey, being now about to appear in the immediate presence of the all-seeing God and Judge, hereby declare in what respect I am guilty, in the matters which have been charged against me.

As to any act or even thought of procuring the death either of my wife or of Mary Tirrell, of both of which I have been suspected, I am wholly innocent. So Help me God! Nor did I ever use means with either of them for any purpose resulting in their death. So help me God!

I hereby acknowledge in the sight of God I am guilty of the death of Betsy Frances Tirrell, for which I was indicted and for which I am now to suffer.

I hereby warn all young people by my experience and fate against the indulgence of lustful passions. These have brought me to my untimely end. GEORGE C. HERSEY.

Whether George Hersey was responsible for the first two deaths or whether they were coincidences is a matter of opinion, but Hersey, who was unwilling to forego the comfortable respectability of South Weymouth, had the singleness of purpose that belongs to the pioneer, the scientist, and the murderer. And perhaps the personality of the gentlemen from Massachusetts contained a little of each.

V

And to Hell with Burgundy

SOME WOMEN ATTRACT MEN; some women attract trouble.
Florence Bravo was a double-barreled magnet; she attracted
both. Her small voluptuous figure, which no corset or bustle
could distort, her coquettish chestnut hair, which no curling iron
or crimpers could restrain, and an irresistible siren song of help-
lessness made up a small but potent package of sex appeal. It
was just her luck to fatally fascinate an alcoholic, a married
man, and a spoiled boy.

As for trouble, Florence was a feather, caught in every
emotional downdraft that came along, and she got trapped in
some cross-ventilation when she overstepped the unalterable code
of Victorian womanhood. In an age when the sanctity of woman
was as jealously institutionalized as chivalry had been in the days
when knighthood was in flower, the pattern of Victorian dualism
fell into inflexible categories. A woman was either "pure" or
"fallen." She had to be one or the other, and there was no room
for a twilight zone, such as our current popular myth of the
"prostitute with the heart of gold." A pure woman was a virgin
with chaste thoughts and sexual *rigor mortis,* a woman who
granted her husband bleak conjugal submission and periodic
heirs, or a spinster who lightened the heavy load of her days with

the subliminal sop of John Ruskin's Italian-art criticism or pure-thinking literature like *Sesame and Lilies*.

A fallen woman encompassed everything from the dashing, feather-boa-ed belles, who toyed with champagne and men in private dining rooms, to gin-logged slatterns. But Florence Bravo didn't realize that never the twain shall meet. If she had followed the rigidly mapped course of either a good or bad woman, there would have been no nineteenth-century shocker known as the "Balham Mystery," but because she wanted to have her cake and eat it, too—Florence Bravo was just plain murder!

Florence Campbell was the daughter of Robert Campbell, a wealthy London merchant. Everything points to a spoiled, petted childhood and to a familiar twentieth-century spectacle—well-meaning parents who are unable to cope with the teenaged Frankensteins they have created.

In 1863, when she was eighteen, Florence visited Montreal, and, to her, one of the greatest attractions of the brave new world was Captain Ricardo of Her Majesty's Army. Captain Ricardo listed as assets a dashing uniform reminiscent of a Strauss operetta, a name with an evocative Latin ending, and a comfortable fortune. In 1864, two doom-ridden events took place: Maximilian, that harassed Hapsburg, became Emperor of Mexico; and Florence Campbell married her colorful captain. Some men accept marriage with stoicism, while others luxuriate in the matrimonial state. There are men who fight it—wifebeaters, etc., and there are men who avoid it, e.g., bachelors. Captain Ricardo by nature and inclination, belonged to the latter group. He had an inordinate liking for women, and he was an avid companion of the grape. Florence, at a dewy, well-developed eighteen certainly must have appealed to him, but marriage was the price for capitulation. So Captain Ricardo bartered bachelorhood for maidenhood.

Like most young brides, Florence embarked upon matrimony with high hopes. Perhaps she even subscribed to the age-old

delusion that marriage changes a man. In any event, the honeymoon came to an abrupt end when it became apparent that
"hearth and home" were just two rather unfamiliar words in
the English language to Captain Ricardo. He was keeping
mistresses and making a cult out of the empty bottle. To
Florence, spoiled and petted, six years of violent scenes, pitying
smiles from friends and relations, and a husband's total lack of
concern over her happiness were devastating blows to her ego.
Captain Ricardo alternated between sessions with pink elephants
and fits of black remorse, and in the middle of this emotional
maelstrom, was Florence, her self-confidence shaken, her ego
badly fractured. To help soften the ugly edges, she started drinking herself. If you can't beat 'em, join 'em, seemed to be her
attitude. Let there be no mistake that Florence's drinking fell
under the proscribed limits of social drinking for Victorian
females. The sip of sherry or blackberry wine, the gulp of stronger
spirits for medicinal reasons were not for Florence. She drank
as she did everything else—whole heartedly, on the spur of the
moment, and all the way. Any self-respecting AA would un-
abashedly tip his hat to the capacity of this frail Victorian belle.

By 1870, Florence was on the verge of what would now be
called a nervous breakdown. Six years of marriage to Captain
Ricardo plus the solace of the vine was just about all an emotionally weak woman could stand. Mr. and Mrs. Campbell suggested that Florence and her captain go to Malvern, a famous
spa, to take the cure, but it was useless. Captain Ricardo had
retired from the army and was now devoting his full time and
energy to drinking, so Florence's parents insisted upon a deed of
separation. In the following April, Captain Ricardo died in
Cologne as he had lived—with a transient mistress in his bed
and the eternal bottle at his elbow. His will was unaltered, and
Florence was now set to become a very merry widow with an
income of £4000 a year to be merry on and Dr. Gully to be
merry with.

In 1842, Dr. William Gully had developed a water cure and offered it to an ailing public. Dr. Gully was no quack. He was a thoroughly trained medical man, and his water cure put the town of Malvern on the map, so to speak. Applications of water were used in every form—packing in wet sheets, compresses, spinal washes, friction with dripping towels—and his patients included Tennyson, Carlyle, Charles Reade, Bulwer-Lytton, an all-star cast from the social register, and many other water-sodden Victorian greats and near greats. Dr. Gully himself had literary aspirations. He wrote articles on medical subjects and wrote a play adapted from Dumas's *Mademoiselle de Belle-Isle,* which was produced at Drury Lane in 1839. Dr. Gully himself was sixty-two at the time Florence came to Malvern with her problem husband. He is described as handsome, if not tall, with clean-cut features and an erect bearing. He was also the possessor of a disastrous amount of personal magnetism, and a wife in her eighties whom his water cure could not help; she had been in an insane asylum for thirty years.

It was this man that Florence met when she came to Malvern. At the time she was emotionally ill, and Dr. Gully's warmth and sympathetic understanding must have been every bit as effective as his water treatments. Florence was headstrong but not self-reliant, and Captain Ricardo had proved a broken reed upon which to lean. Dr. Gully, a pillar of strength by comparison, was a welcome change from Captain Ricardo's highhanded, drunken treatment and groveling sober remorse. Florence recovered under his care. Today, when everyone nonchalantly tosses off the argot of psychoanalysis, transference is an every day word, and Gully's age was no detriment after Florence's experience with a young husband. Picture Dr. Gully, well-to-do, attractive, respected, confronted with a rampant Florence seething with devotion and flattery.

Just when Dr. Gully's bedside manner began to assume personal overtones is not clear. Florence steadfastly maintained nothing improper had occurred during her marriage to Captain Ricardo. However, early during her widowhood her parents refused to see her because of her relations with Dr. Gully and because of her continued drinking. For four years, Florence was cut off from her family and was beyond the possibility of a social circle, but she had Dr. Gully, emotional security, and her wine.

It was during this isolated, if not celibate, widowhood that Mrs. Cox entered the scene. Florence was visiting her solicitor, Mr. Brooks, and there she met Mrs. Jane Cannon Cox. Mrs. Cox was the down-at-the-heel widow of a Jamaican engineer with three sons, and through the kind offices and advice of a Mr. Joseph Bravo, who had interests in Jamaica, she had bought a small house in Lancaster Road, Notting Hill, as an investment, had placed her sons in a school for destitute gentlefolk, and obtained the post of governess to Mr. Brooks's children. Mrs. Cox, with her solid figure inclined to dumpiness, heavy-featured face, glittering spectacles, and skintight hairdo was no beauty, but she made up for it by relentless efficiency, an air of unassailable respectability, and a grim desire to please.

It wasn't long before the pretty but lonesome widow appropriated Mrs. Cox as her companion. And it was, at the time, an ideal arrangement for sheltered, beautiful Florence and plain, unsheltered Mrs. Cox. Mrs. Cox ran Florence's house, controlled the servants, and understood perfectly the comfort and elegance that Florence wished to enjoy, without exerting any effort. And Mrs. Cox had it made. She had exchanged the life of uncertainty, drudgery, and poor pay of a governess for the role of "friend of the bosom" to Florence Ricardo. They were on the footing of social equals; it was "Florence" and "Janie." She received a salary of £100 a year, clothes, and incidental expenses, and her three boys could spend all their school holidays with her.

In 1872, Dr. Gully sold his practice amid testimonials and demonstrations from the citizens of Malvern, and, wherever Mrs.

Ricardo lived, Dr. Gully's home was sure to be within spitting distance, and their friendship continued. In 1873, the pair made a trip to Kissingen, and the tangible result was a miscarriage. During this illness, Mrs. Cox attended Florence, but claimed she did not know the real nature of the trouble.

In 1874, Mrs. Ricardo moved into what was to be her permanent home, the Priory. It was a pale-tinted structure with arched windows and doorways, winding walks, flower beds, melon pits, a greenhouse, and the house was luxurious with a sparkling Venetian glass collection, a lush conservatory with ferns that cost 20 guineas each, and every expensive horror of Victorian decoration. Here Florence Ricardo settled down, with the perpetual Mrs. Cox, to enjoy life's three greatest pleasures—gardening, horses, and drinking. And Dr. Gully, whom one is tempted to nickname Johnny-on-the-spot, bought a house just a few minutes from the Priory. There were lunches, dinners, drives, and several nights of illicit bliss when Mrs. Cox was away. Dr. Gully had a key to the Priory. Then, one day in 1875, Mrs. Cox wished to call on her benefactor, Mrs. Joseph Bravo, and Mrs. Ricardo went with her. There she met Charles Bravo, the spoiled son of the house. The meeting itself was without incident, but its repercussions are now called the Balham Mystery.

In October, 1875, Mrs. Ricardo and Mrs. Cox went to Brighton and there again met Charles Bravo, a sulky handsome young man with a weak chin. He was a young man her own age and of her social position, and when Florence returned to the Priory she told Dr. Gully that she was going to break off their "friendship" and reconcile with her family because of her mother's health. Actually, Florence was, in all probability, weary of her "back street" existence. She had snapped her garter at the world, and, instead of being told she was cute, was knuckle-rapped by social ostracism. What she did not tell Dr. Gully was that she was also going to marry Charles Bravo. Dr. Gully was hurt when he found out about the engagement, but later wished

Florence happiness. Perhaps the demands of a young capricious mistress had begun to tell on the sixty-seven-year-old doctor, and the prospect of placid days and monastic nights had an attraction.

But in spite of Florence's injunction that they must never see each other again, they did. According to British law at that time, every possession and all property of a woman marrying automatically became the property of her husband, unless specifically secured to her by settlement. Florence wanted the Priory and its furnishings secured to her, but Charles sulked and muttered he wanted to sit in his own chairs or he'd call the marriage off. Florence arranged a meeting with Dr. Gully to discuss the impasse, and they met at one of the Priory lodges. Dr. Gully advised her to give in on the matter and wished her luck. As usual, Florence backed down, and "Charlie" won the moral victory of "sitting in his own chairs."

Charles Bravo was not a wealthy man in his own right and was mostly dependent on his father's spasmodic handouts, since his law practice only netted him £200 in the last year of his life. However, his future was bright. He was his stepfather's heir, and his prospects for becoming a member of Parliament were good, and here was a young, infatuated, wealthy widow, with a belated yearning for respectability and security, palpitating on his doorstep.

Charles and Florence told each other "all." He had had a purple passage with a young and willing woman in Maidenhead but had made a final settlement with her before breaking off. Florence told him about her idyll with the autumnal Dr. Gully, and Charles seems to have accepted it with equanimity. Charles was what might be called "rotten spoiled." He was charming when things went his way, extremely conscious of money, probably because he had been around it so much, yet had so little of his own. And the prospect of marrying a wealthy widow— even one with a sexual slip-up in her past—was attractive.

Certainly he was not consumed with jealousy. When he went to see Florence's attorney about the settlement, he received the lawyer's congratulations with the remark, "to hell with the congratulations, it's the money I'm interested in!"

Mr. Bravo, Sr., settled £20,000 on Charles as a wedding present, but Mrs. Bravo refused to attend the wedding. She didn't like Florence. For that matter, she probably wouldn't have liked any girl her son married. And so Florence and Charles Bravo were married and settled down at the Priory, and they might have lived happily ever after if Charles Bravo hadn't been so stingy.

They seemed like an average, happy couple. Charles brought his business associates to dinner and heartily endorsed the institution of marriage. The servants all thought the Bravos a happy, devoted couple, but Mrs. Cox was worried. Charles was cutting down on the overhead. He wanted Florence to give up her horses and her personal maid which she did, and he wanted her to dispense with Mrs. Cox. He had put together a pound here and a pound there and figured out that the genteel companionship of the widow was costing £400 a year—enough to keep a pair of horses. And Florence, who operated on an anything-for-the-sake-of-peace basis and who was charmed by her young attractive husband, decided to give up her horses and maid, and Mrs. Cox could see the handwriting on the wall. Her relatives in Jamaica had been pressing her to return, and now Mr. Joseph Bravo and his son were urging the same thing.

During this period of surface serenity, several curious events occurred. Mrs. Cox had several meetings with Dr. Gully; whether they were planned or accidental, they have all the aspects of Mrs. Cox trying to stir something up. Mrs. Bravo had had a miscarriage, and Mrs. Cox, at one encounter, asked Dr. Gully, who knew Florence couldn't take regular opiates, to send something to her house on Lancaster Road. The doctor sent some laurel water and thus laid himself open to later insinuations that he was supplying Mrs. Bravo with abortive medicines, a rather empty charge in view of the fact that a child would have been just what Florence Bravo needed to cement her newly established respectability and reconcile Charles's mother to the marriage. And then, just after Charles Bravo figured out the cost of Mrs. Cox's companionship, he was taken suddenly and mysteriously ill one morning on his way to his chambers in Essex Court. So ill, in fact, that he reported to his father he was afraid people might think he was drunk from the night before, and Charles Bravo had the digestion of an ox.

That was the situation at the Priory Easter weekend, 1876. Charles Bravo had his attractive wife and her equally attractive fortune. Florence was recovering from her miscarriage and appeared devoted to her husband, and Mrs. Cox was brooding about the imminence of a trip to Jamaica. Charles Bravo laid out a tennis court, played with Mrs. Cox's boys, who were down for the Easter vacation, and wrote to his mother that he had "loafed vigorously and thoroughly enjoyed the weekend."

Tuesday, April eighteenth, Mrs. Cox set out to look at houses in Worthing where the Bravos were planning to go for Florence to recuperate from her miscarriage and with her she took a flask of sherry to fortify herself. Mr. and Mrs. Bravo drove into town, and he went to his club at St. James Hall for lunch, while Florence returned to the Priory, after doing some shopping, for lunch, which she polished off with a bottle of champagne. Mrs. Bravo understandably spent the afternoon resting. Late in the afternoon Mr. Bravo returned home and went horseback riding. The horse threw him, and he returned home with his dignity and himself rather badly bruised. Mrs. Bravo suggested a warm bath before dinner, and then went upstairs herself to change. Mrs. Cox returned from her house hunting with a photograph of the house, and, it is presumed, an empty sherry flask. She did not have time to change for dinner, she did go upstairs to clean up a bit.

Dinner, consisting of whiting, roast lamb, a dish of eggs, and anchovy bloater was not a sparkling meal. Mr. Bravo was still smarting, both literally and figuratively, from his fall. Mrs. Bravo had dry pipes from the champagne and was trying to put out the fire with sherry, and Mrs. Cox had things to think about. Mr. Bravo drank his three customary glasses of burgundy, but the ladies put him to shame. Between them, Mrs. Bravo and Mrs. Cox polished off two bottles of sherry, and the butler later testified that he had decanted the usual amount of wine that evening.

After dinner, they retired to the morning room where again conversations languished. In about a half hour, Florence announced she was going to bed and asked Mrs. Cox to bring her a glass of wine. Since her miscarriage Mrs. Cox had been sleeping with her, and Mr. Bravo had been relegated to a guest room. Mrs. Bravo went upstairs and was followed by the obliging Mrs. Cox with a glass of wine. Mary Anne Keeber, a maid, came in to help Mrs. Bravo undress and was asked by Mrs. Bravo to bring her some wine. Mary Anne brought a tumbler of marsala and was still in Mrs. Bravo's room when Mr. Bravo entered to make the understatement of the Balham Mystery. He accused his wife of drinking too much wine and stormed off to bed. Mary Anne withdrew and saw as she left the room that three-bottle Florence had taken the count and was asleep, while Mrs. Cox sat by her bed fully dressed. As Mary Anne started downstairs, the door to Mr. Bravo's room flew open and he cried, "Florence, Florence. Water!"

And Mrs. Cox, who sat fully dressed and wide awake by Mrs. Bravo's bedside, heard nothing until Mary Anne called her. From the time of Mr. Bravo's cries for water, there began a procession of doctors and a progression of statements by Mrs. Cox. Mary Anne and Mrs. Cox rushed into Mr. Bravo's bedroom, where they found him standing by the window vomiting. Mrs. Cox ordered Mary Anne to rush for an emetic and Dr. Harrison. When Dr. Harrison arrived Mrs. Cox told him Mr.

Bravo has taken chloroform to ease a toothache, but the doctor said there was no smell of chloroform.

Mrs. Bravo was by this time aroused and sent for Dr. Moore and Royes Bell, a Harley Street surgeon and friend of the Bravo family. Mrs. Bravo threw herself down by her husband, spoke to him fondly, and promptly fell asleep and finally had to be carried to her own room. Obviously, she hadn't had time to sleep it off.

Dr. George Johnson arrived with Royes Bell, and they are told by Mr. Bravo that he has rubbed his gums with laudanum for his toothache.

"But laudanum," Dr. Johnson tells him "will not account for your symptoms." But Mr. Bravo stubbornly insisted that he had taken nothing else, no other drug.

At this point, Mrs. Cox takes Mr. Bell aside and confides to him that, while "Charlie" was vomiting at the window, he told her, "I have taken poison. Don't tell Florence."

Mr. Bravo's reply to this is "I don't remember having spoken of taking poison," and again insisted he had only rubbed his gums with laudanum. Dr. Harrison was annoyed with Mrs. Cox for not telling him about the poison. "You told me," he said petulantly, "that he had taken chloroform."

Mr. Bravo by now was in a bad way. He was frequently sick and had intense stomach pains, but he kept his wife by him, drew up a will leaving everything to her, and sent word to his mother to "be kind to Florence." Again he swears to the growing assembly of doctors that he had taken nothing but laudanum and with a trace of his old money consciousness says : "Why the devil should I send for you, if I knew what was the matter with me?"

Mr. and Mrs. Joseph Bravo arrived, and the elder Mrs. Bravo took charge of the sick room. However, when the doctors had declared the case hopeless, Florence roused herself from her despair and her hangover to take action. "They have had their way, and I as his wife will have mine." And proceeded to try water treatments and small doses of arsenicum, both approved of by the doctors, as harmless.

Then Florence calls in Sir William Gull, a physician who wore as a crown the credit for having cured the Prince of Wales of typhoid fever.

"This is not a disease," Sir William tells Bravo. "You have been poisoned. Pray tell me how you came by it."

But Bravo persists that he has taken nothing but laudanum and on Friday morning, April twenty-first, the much harrassed, much questioned Charles Bravo mercifully died.

The inquest had more of the air of a family tea than anything else. Mr. Carter, the coroner for East Surrey was informed in a note written for Mrs. Bravo by Mrs. Cox that "refreshments will be prepared for the jury," and the inquest was held in the dining room of the Priory. Mr. Carter, an experienced official, had the idea that there was something amiss and out of deference to two respectable families did not even send notices of the inquest to the papers. Test of specimens and organs revealed that Mr. Bravo had died from a large, economy-sized dose of antimony administered in the form of tartar emetic, which is easily soluble in water and tasteless. Mr. Joseph Bravo went to Scotland Yard and Inspector Clark, an expert on poisoning cases, was instructed to make inquiries to see if antimony could be traced to the Priory, because the senior Bravo suspected the story of death by accident. Both Mrs. Bravo and Mrs. Cox had medicine chests and the house contained innumerable bottles of medicine, but nothing lethal. But Mr. Joseph Bravo refused to believe Mrs. Cox's story that his son had committed suicide.

The coroner felt it was an embarrasing case of suicide, however, and closed the hearing without allowing Drs. Johnson or Moore to testify and without calling Mrs. Bravo, who was suffering from shock. Mr. Bravo even admitted to the coroner's direct question, he did not suspect foul play, but there were a lot of drugs in the house. The verdict was "that the deceased died from the effects of the poison antimony, but there was no evidence as to the circumstances in which it had come into his body."

Mr. Bravo was buried on April twenty-ninth, and Mrs. Bravo and Mrs. Cox, probably fortified by several flasks of sherry, departed for Brighton. But the end was not in sight. Charles Bravo had been popular in his circle of friends and colleagues, and they were dissatisfied with the summary verdict from the coroner's inquest. A week later, *The World* ran a provocative paragraph titled "A Tragedy?" It was done in the gossip-column style of today with no names mentioned but easily identifiable. Charles Bravo was referred to as "a rising young barrister recently married."

The following day, May eleventh, the gathering storm continued, in which the *Daily Telegraph* became more explicit, naming names and premiering the sobriquet, "The Balham Mystery." The *Telegraph* also commented on the secret and unsatisfactory inquest and called for a reopening of the investigation. The case aroused great interest, and journals and newspapers were deluged with suggestions as to how Mr. Bravo clashed head on with the antimony. Two schools of thought emerged. Either the fatal dose had been administered in his burgundy at dinner or in the water bottle which sat on his night stand and from which he was in the habit of drinking before he went to bed. Because of the time element the water jug was a 2-to-1 favorite. The doctors in the case were bitten by the literary bug. Drs. Moore and Harrison wrote for the *Daily Telegraph,* and Dr. Johnson gave a medical history in *Lancet*.

Mrs. Bravo was aware of the drift of public sentiment. She was receiving anonymous letters, and, on the advice of her father, offered a reward of £500 to anyone who could prove the sale of antimony or tartar emetic "in such a matter as would throw a satisfactory light on the mode by which Mr. Bravo came to his death."

The Home Secretary (afterwards Lord Cross) issued a statement that his office was "entirely dissatisfied with the way the inquiry had been conducted." Mrs. Bravo's consent was obtained for a thorough search of the Priory. The investigation lasted two days and every medicine in the house was tested. Nothing was discovered that Charles Bravo could have taken, but five weeks between Bravo's death and the investigation were ample time to get anything incriminating out of the way.

On May twenty-seventh a private inquiry was called, and, although Mrs. Bravo and Mrs. Cox were not asked to give evidence, they both asked to make statements. Mrs. Cox's statement, made after consultation with Mr. Brooks, her former employer and Mrs. Bravo's solicitor, dropped a bombshell. She deposed that through a misguided effort to shield Mrs. Bravo's character, she had not given full particulars at the inquest. What Mr. Bravo had actually said was, "I have taken poison for Gully—don't tell Florence." However, Mrs. Cox had to admit that Mrs. Bravo had had no contact with Dr. Gully since her marriage and characterized Dr. Gully's relations as "very imprudent" but of an innocent character. Mr. Bravo had a hasty and violent temper and four days before his death had had a violent quarrel with his wife in which he called her a selfish pig, wished he were dead, and said "let her go back to Gully." He constantly stated he hated Gully.

Mrs. Bravo's statement said that Bravo had pressed her constantly to cut down on expenses and turn away Mrs. Cox. That he was short tempered and had once struck her, that his mother was always interfering, and that he read all her mail. She had told him about her attachment to Gully, and he had told her of his kept woman at Maidenhead, and they agreed never to mention these names. Florence, in this statement, described her relationship with Gully as innocent. "Nothing improper had ever passed between us." Mrs. Bravo said that her husband had constantly harped on Gully after their marriage. The day he had taken ill they had had a fight about Gully on the way to town. Florence refused to make up. "You will see what I do when I get home." He thought she drank too much sherry, but she had given it up to please him. (Certainly one glaring untruth in Mrs. Bravo's statement.)

On the strength of this private inquiry, Mr. Clark was ordered to hold a new inquiry with a fresh jury. It opened on July 11, 1876, in the billiard room of the Bedford Hotel next to Balham Station. And if the first inquiry had been a furtive affair; the second was a field day for the public. The room was crowded with newspaper reporters and the curious, of which there were many. After the jury had viewed the exhumed body through a small piece of glass in the coffin, a grim legal formality, Mr. Joseph Bravo testified that Charles was full of life, that he was interested in forensic medicine, and that they were on intimate terms. He had never heard Charles mention Gully's name. The last three letters Charles had written to his family, just before his illness, were in the best of spirits.

Mr. Bravo said that Charles had discussed Mrs. Cox with him, that he had nothing against her, but that she cost too much. Mr. Joseph Bravo had agreed and advised Mrs. Cox himself to return to Jamaica. She said she would not return. Mr. Bravo also commented that while her husband was dying Mrs. Bravo did not "appear much grieved" in any way at the state of affairs. He did admit that his son was quick tempered.

The doctors presented a solid antisuicide wall. They said they had never heard of a case of suicide by antimony, that the time of action was variable, and they positively stated that antimony could be administered without any taste in either water or burgundy. Several of the doctors testified to drinking out of the water bottle; but admitted that in the confusion it would have been easy to either switch or clean out the water jug. Dr. Johnson testified that Mrs. Bravo overheard him mention poison to Mrs. Cox. Mrs. Bravo asked: "Did he say he had taken poison?"

"Yes, he did," replied Mrs. Cox. And that was the end of the conversation.

Rowe, the Butler, testified that Mr. Bravo drank three glasses of burgundy at his last meal and that the half-full decanter was put away. On April nineteenth he opened another bottle of burgundy. He did not remember who drank it, but the other half bottle must have been gone. With Florence around it's not surprising. He had never heard quarreling and called Charles Bravo "one of the kindest gentlemen I ever knew."

Mary Anne Keeber, the maid, said she thought Mr. and Mrs. Bravo were very fond of each other and saw no signs of jealousy or ever heard Dr. Gully's name mentioned. She had emptied and cleaned the basin Mr. Bravo had been vomiting in at Mrs. Cox's request.

Amelia Bushnell, Mrs. Joseph Bravo's maid, had heard Mr. Bravo say he had taken nothing but laudanum and testified that Mrs. Charles Bravo had been blaming his illness on something he ate at the club, cooked in a coppery pan.

John Pritchard, Dr. Gully's butler said there had been a great attachment between Dr. Gully and Mrs. Ricardo, but that, in November of the previous year, Dr. Gully had given him instructions not to admit Mrs. Ricardo or Mrs. Cox. Dr. Gully had returned pictures, presents, and key to the Priory, and Mrs. Ricardo had done the same.

Colleagues testified that Charles Bravo had no worries or cares, that he had made a special study of forensic medicine, and would never knowingly take such a painful or uncertain medicine.

Mrs. Campbell testified she was met by Mrs. Cox when she arrived during Mr. Bravo's illness and was told it was poison, while Florence was still chattering about coppery pans at Charlie's club.

Mrs. Cox, spectacles glinting, looking middle aged and dumpy in her black, said Charles Bravo had said she was welcome at the Priory, that he received an anonymous letter accusing him of marrying Gully's mistress for her money. She had seen Dr. Gully several times since Mrs. Bravo's marriage, had asked him for his remedy for ague and Jamaica fever, also something to make Mrs. Bravo sleep after her miscarriage. Bravo had asked her, "Why did you tell them? Does Florence know I poisoned myself?"

"I was obliged to tell them. I could not let you die."

Asked why she had not mentioned this conversation, Mrs. Cox replied imperturbably, "He did not wish me to." She had not mentioned Dr. Gully's name at the first inquest because it might have injured Mrs. Bravo's reputation. When she mentioned chloroform to Harrison, she was confused and meant poison. "Dr. Gully was a very fascinating man—one who would be likely to interest women very much." She said she had done everything she could to restrain Mrs. Bravo from her habit of drinking, but without much success.

Mrs. Bravo, immersed in grief and a voluminous mourning veil, testified that it was April twentieth before she knew her husband was dying of poison. Bravo harped about Gully in spite of her April sixteenth letter to Mrs. Bravo that Charles was happy as a king. At Brighton, after the first inquest, Mrs. Cox told her Charles had poisoned himself on the account of Gully. She made a full admission of her "criminal relations" with Dr. Gully, but even under a heavy barrage of insinuation, she maintained, under oath, that she was innocent of any extra-marital activities during her marriage to Captain Ricardo. But her protests of innocence were badly shaken when she was handed a letter, written by her to a woman named Laundon, who had been her maid. It was dated November seventeenth, 1870, a date that preceded Captain Ricardo's death by six months. In part the letter said: "I hope you will never allude in any way to anyone of what passed at Malvern." Asked what she referred to, Mrs. Bravo answered: "It was my attachment to Dr. Gully, but not a criminal attachment then." She burst into tears and appealed to the coroner to protect her. So much for semantics.

Then Griffiths, a former coachman to Dr. Gully and Mrs. Bravo, took the stand. He had worked for Mrs. Bravo but had been fired by Mr. Bravo for carelessness. He seems to have been a nineteenth-century hotrod and was accident prone. His testimony, however, established the presence of antimony in the form of tartar emetic at the Priory. He had bought a large amount to treat the horses. He had kept it locked in a cupboard in the stable and poured it all down the drain when he left. However, no inquiry was made as to what kind of lock was on the cupboard, and there is only Griffiths' word that after being fired, he conscientiously poured a large amount of medicine down the drain. It would seem more natural for him to go off in a huff, leaving the tartar emetic for the next coachman. But although Griffiths was called an "unreliable witness," he did establish, for the first time in the case, the presence of the poison which killed Charles Bravo.

Dr. Gully was the last witness to be called during the twenty-three-day inquest, which rivaled the Tichborne trial in public interest, if not length, when a 350-pound pretender consumed eight years and a total of 290 days trying to prove he was the long-lost Sir Roger Arthur Orton. Dr. Gully's testimony backed up Florence Bravo's contention that there had been nothing improper pass between them during Captain Ricardo's lifetime, but when asked about his relations with Captain Ricardo's widow his rueful reply was "too true, sir; too true." He swore he had nothing to do either directly or indirectly with Charles Bravo's death and told of his chance meetings with Mrs. Cox who told him repeatedly that Mr. and Mrs. Bravo were "getting along well."

The verdict turned out to be the most damaging aspect of the inquest. It concluded that "Charles Bravo was willfully murdered by the administration of tartar emetic, but there is not sufficient evidence to fix the guilt upon any person or persons." The jury significantly declined to use the standard, more familiar wording, "administered by some person or persons unknown."

And by the verdict of the jury, the Balham Mystery remains an official cipher. The suicide theory, with a nod of admiration in the direction of a lurking Mrs. Cox, does not hold up. Against the unsupported word of Mrs. Cox, there is a parade of friends, colleagues, and family who picture Charles Bravo as a happy man, contented with his career and marriage. His letters both to Florence and his family reflect Bravo's unsuicidal, rather complacent state of mind. As for Mrs. Cox's statement that "he took poison for Gully," he had known of Dr. Gully's relationship to Florence before he married her, and, according to every witness, Mrs. Bravo never saw Dr. Gully after her marriage. The only other possibility for suicide would be delayed-action remorse and jealousy, and Charles Bravo just wasn't the brooding type. His repeated denials to the doctors that he had not taken poison and his affectionate attitude toward his wife at his sick bed also lower the boom on the suicide theory. The accident theory can quickly be eliminated. The only place that antimony in the form of tartar emetic was kept at Priory was in the stables, and it is hardly conceivable that Mr. Bravo would ever dose himself in the stable on horse physic, while all medicines found in the house tested out as harmless.

Sir John Hall, considered the leading authority on the Bravo case, claims that it had to be both Mrs. Bravo and Mrs. Cox because they supported each other consistently in their statements, so at variance with all the other witnesses. But consider, Florence Bravo's actions after her husband is taken ill. Still befuddled by wine, she sends for the nearest doctor and later for specialists. She talks of food poisoning from the coppery pans at his club. The conversation between the doctor and Mrs. Cox, which she claims not to have heard, could also be the result of combined hysteria and hang-over.

Mrs. Bravo said she first heard of poison and suicide when

Mrs. Cox broke the news to her after they were settled at Brighton. Since Mrs. Bravo was in a state of shock and did not appear at the first inquest, she begins backing up Mrs. Cox only after the Brighton sojourn. So, Mrs. Bravo emerges as an upset, concerned wife, extremely fond, talking of food poisoning, and then after the trip to Brighton with Mrs. Cox she accepts and, by testimony, backs up the suicide theory and fortifies Mrs. Cox's position.

Something happened at Brighton, and everything points to a little genteel blackmail. Mrs. Cox knew her relationship with Dr. Gully was more than a harmless infatuation. She knew of her heavy drinking. She knew of the post-Kissengen illness—not hard for a woman with three sons and sickroom experience to diagnose as a miscarriage. And Florence Bravo, must above all, be considered within a specific frame of reference, that of nineteenth-century morals and manners. Within this frame, you have a woman who has made a slip and bounced from the category of "pure" to "fallen" woman. She had made an attempt at being respectable again, and Mrs. Cox knew intimately the details of the transition. Her knowledge could bounce Florence right back into the latter category. In an age when women blushingly asked for a "slice of bosom" when being served chicken and female legs were as unmentionable as four letter Anglo-Saxon words, public disgrace could assume more importance than suspected murder; and, in Florence Bravo's case, it did.

At Brighton, Mrs. Cox probably told Florence that her husband said, "I have taken poison for Gully." She told the young widow that if she would follow her lead, Mrs. Cox would protect her reputation. In view of all the public agitation, they would have to make statements. The arrangement was that Mrs. Cox would tell of Bravo's "Gully statement" but would testify that relations between Florence and Dr. Gully were imprudent but innocent and Charles Bravo was jealous of his wife's past. Florence, in turn, would tell her story of her husband's baseless jealousy of Dr. Gully. This way Florence's character would stay comparatively blameless, while Mrs. Cox's suicide theory would be reinforced. And how could Florence say no to perpetrating this half-truth, when the entire truth would mean ruin. Besides, she probably believed Mrs. Cox's story of Charlie's suicide.

So, Florence Bravo became an ex post facto accessory. By the time Mrs. Cox threw her to the wolves at the second inquest in the interest of self-preservation, Mrs. Bravo had gone so far in her statements that she was irrevocably implicated. During the second inquest, Mrs. Cox had begun to panic. She could bolster the suicide theory by admitting that Mrs. Bravo had told her of her intimate relations with Dr. Gully and that Charles Bravo knew and brooded over his wife's past sins, or she could protect Mrs. Bravo's reputation. Mrs. Cox couldn't afford to let the suicide theory languish, or she would be in a most suspicious position. So Florence's reputation had to go by the boards, and, too late to do anything, Florence realized with growing horror, that Mrs. Cox was not the friend she pretended to be, but a blackmailer consumed with some dark purpose of her own. Florence was left with no alternative but to admit her "criminal relationship" with Dr. Gully, which gave the illusion that she was still "backing up" Mrs. Cox, while in actuality these two sherry-sipping ladies had come to a parting of the ways.

Mrs. Bravo moved to Buscot to live with her mother. Mrs. Cox stopped in Manchester Street and planned to leave for Jamaica at the close of the inquiry. Florence was no intellectual giant, but she knew when she had been had.

It is the only theory that could account for Florence Bravo's opposite actions before and after Brighton. Mrs. Bravo, by herself, had neither sufficient character or motive to do the dirty deed. Nor did she have a strong enough reason to act in conjunction with Mrs. Cox. She certainly wouldn't condone the murder of her husband to keep Mrs. Cox from returning to Jamaica. The weakness of Florence Bravo's character forms the strength of her innocence. To complain, to pout, to shed a few tears was her course of action, not poison. There have been suggestions that the relationship between Mrs. Bravo and Mrs. Cox was of an unhealthy hue. But with Florence's affinity for men, about the only unhealthy thing about their relationship was the amount of sherry they consumed.

Mrs. Cox, too, falls with rigid delineation into this frame of reference. In our own era of the freewheeling career girl, it is difficult to remember that in Mrs. Cox's day a working woman was an unhappy exception, just a cut above serfdom. In most cases, a governess, a companion, or a poor relation who "earned her keep" was a step above the servants and a step below the lord and lady of the house, isolated on a lonely plateau without social contacts or standing.

When Charles Bravo showed unmistakable symptoms of snapping the purse shut and shipping her back to her Jamaican home and family, it was not simply a matter of a new job or surroundings. It was social and financial annihilation, and it was a motive. By removing Charles Bravo, she could relieve the pressure being exerted for her to return to Jamaica. She would be once again the dear friend of Florence, whom she could completely dominate, and return to the good old days when Dr. Gully's courtly charm caused a flutter under her formidable black bombazine exterior and Florence's home and funds were at her disposal.

Mrs. Cox, however, did not know her poisons as well as she knew the gentle art of conniving. By administering a large, economy-sized dose of poison, Mrs. Cox was under the impression that Charles Bravo would die immediately. She did not realize that antimony was a variable and unpredictable poison. When it became apparent that Mr. Bravo was going to linger awhile, Mrs. Cox had to come up with some quick answers off the top of her chignon, and she was in a good position. Bravo was in an incoherent state, and Mrs. Bravo, during those first chaotic hours, had a case of the hot-and-cold shakes and dry pipes, while the servants were trained to take orders unquestioningly from Mrs. Cox. It is only after the doctors agreed that it was a case of irritant poisoning that Mrs. Cox came up with the "I took poison—Don't tell Florence" statement. Only after there is a strong suspicion of murder and a second inquest is looming does Mrs. Cox add Dr. Gully's name to the statement to give the suicide theory a strong motive. And only at the second inquest, when the jury and public were taking an increasingly dimmer view of the suicide theory, did she tell of the conversation when Bravo asks, "Why did you tell them?" Only Mrs. Cox heard these three conversations with Charles Bravo. There were no witnesses except the necessarily mute Charles, and these words are the only indications of suicide. All the other testimony, all the other facts pointed to murder. Mrs. Cox may not have been telling the truth, but she was a fast girl with a cue.

But in spite of Florence's sex appeal and money, in spite of Mrs. Cox's strong, decisive character, things just didn't work out as they did in Florence's favorite romantic novels. Florence Bravo died within the year from a combination of emotional collapse, guilty knowledge, and hitting the bottle, never a healthy combination in her case. In Mrs. Bravo's will, the only mention of Jane Cannon Cox is a reference to her as the mother of three boys to whom Florence Bravo left bequests of £1,000 each. Dr. Gully, his name removed from the rosters of all medical societies, dies seven years later, full of age, if not honor. And Mrs. Cox was last heard of beside a sick bed in Jamaica, a bad place for her.

Of course, no one actually saw Mrs. Cox sneak antimony from the stable. No one saw her toying with Mr. Bravo's burgundy decanter or water bottle, but she was the only person involved in the Balham Mystery who had the character, the opportunity, the motive, and an abiding faith that the Lord helps them that help themselves.

The jury at the inquest voiced their opinion in the damning phraseology of the verdict. The man in the street borrowed some

meter from Oliver Goldsmith and circulated their own, less carefully phrased verdict.

> When lovely woman stoops to folly
> And finds her husband in the way,
> What charm can soothe her melancholy?
> What art can turn him into clay?

> The only means her aims to cover,
> And save herself from prison locks,
> And repossess her ancient lover
> Are burgundy and Mrs. Cox.

It's a little hard on Dr. Gully and Florence Bravo but gratifying to see Mrs. Cox getting public recognition for all her work
and effort.

VI

The Song of the Jabberwock

ON A FRABJOUS DAY IN 1871, a book of irrefutable nonsense, written by a gentle Oxford dean, was published. Eighteen years later, in bustling, trade-happy Liverpool, a murder trial erupted that made *Through the Looking-Glass* sound like a bit of Socratic logic. Imagine *Alice's Adventures in Wonderland* dipped in blood, with illustrations by Beardsley instead of Tenniel, and the distorted parallel fits Mrs. Florence Maybrick as snugly as the proverbial glove.

As Mrs. Maybrick sat in the prisoner's dock on trial for her life, she might have echoed Alice's words, "curiouser and curiouser." The judge had an "off-with-her-head" gleam in his eye. Her friends and relatives resembled malignant Jabberwocks with the "jaws that bite, the claws that catch," and the Queen of Hearts roaring "sentence first—verdict afterwards" was the *vox populi* of Liverpool. Mrs. Maybrick was sentenced before she stepped into the dock. The verdict was an empty appeasement to legal form.

The case of Florence Maybrick is a glowing perennial in the garden of *causes célèbres*. Just mention the name Maybrick to an avid crime connoisseur and the weather, politics, artificial insemi-

119

nation, and the world series are left in the conversational back-
field. Of all the shady ladies of crime, Mrs. Maybrick runs second
to none, and she is in illustrious, luckier company. Her com-
patriot, Adelaide Bartlett, got off free, not because the jury didn't
think her guilty of murder but because they couldn't figure out
how she did it. In America, Mrs. Maybrick too, shares honors
with Lizzie Borden, who achieved immortality with an ax and a
verdict of not guilty with her impeccable spinsterhood. And in
Scotland, there was the dashing Miss Madeleine Smith, who
wanted a permanent rupture with her lover and made sure she
got it. Miss Smith daintily eluded the hangman's noose by the
exclusively Scotch verdict—not proven. This is a legal compromise which has been accurately if lightly interpreted as:
Guilty, but don't do it again. All of these ladies protested their
innocence, but, of the distinguished group, only Mrs. Maybrick
is seriously considered to have been innocent. There is more than
a whiff of nasty suspicion clinging to the beruffled hems of the
other ladies, but while they were acquitted and released, Florence
Maybrick was the only one who paid.

In the cases of these ladies, Victorian dualism is seen as a
working mechanism. Preferably a good nineteenth-century murderess should never have a lover, since it rather muddied the pure
concept of murder with moral overtones. If she was indulging in
un peu d'amour, a lover who might be implicated or provide a
motive was literally deadly. Mrs. Bartlett's extracurricular activity
was on such a high religious plane it was acceptable to a Victorian Jury. Madeleine Smith had no problem at all since her
lover was the corpus delicti in question, and the thought of Miss
Lizzie Borden of Fall River taking a lover to her formidable
bosom is rather like picturing Whistler's mother popping out of
her rocking chair to do a hip-swinging rendition of balling the
jack. But Florence Maybrick spent three frankly carnal nights in
a hotel room with a man other than her husband, and it is to be

hoped she enjoyed herself because she paid for her pleasure right down the line. In the age of flourishing Victoriphobia, Florence Maybrick was tried on a murder charge but convicted on moral grounds. Lizzie Borden was tried for murder but acquitted because of her morals, which goes to show you could literally get away with murder in the nineteenth-century if you could cover the dirty deed with a façade of impregnable virginity, outraged maidenhood, or lofty ideals.

Florence Maybrick just didn't get the breaks. Whatever it is called—fate, predestination, the snicker-snack of the three fates, or star-crossed—Mrs. Maybrick had lousy luck. Her husband was a bustle-chasing hypochondriac, her lover was an invertebrate wolf, her friends were not the sort commemorated in friendship albums of the period; and, to put the final dark touch to this theory of disaster, the judge before whom she appeared on a murder charge was teetering on the brink of insanity. Even the heroine of a Greek tragedy or a Eugene O'Neill play couldn't ask for more than that.

Florence Chandler was born in Mobile, Alabama, in 1862 at just about the time the South was sticking out its collective tongue and saying to the obscure, newly elected President, "says who we can't secede from the Union?" Her father was a well-to-do American banker, and Florence was educated both at home and abroad. By 1881, she was acknowledged as one of the county's prettiest bits in shoe leather—one of those extremely attractive, fantastically sheltered, and completely useless young women known as a southern belle, bred for prenuptial coquetry and postmarital gracious living, a Dixie odalisque.

James Maybrick was a Liverpool cotton broker, visiting America to look over his business interests. He also looked over Florence Chandler and liked what he saw. James Maybrick was to all outward appearances a good match: he was forty-one, a bachelor, and financially well fixed. And he was an avid sportsman whose tendencies included both horses and women. There is no definite mention of the fact, but when a pretty eighteen-year-old girl and a well-to-do forty-one-year-old bachelor exchange vows, there is always a hint of older and wiser heads at work, of matches made not so much in heaven as by papa and aging suitor vis-à-vis over a glass of port, with a bankbook sticking casually out of a pocket. Anyway, in 1881 Florence Chandler, the sexy Southern belle, and James Maybrick, a bachelor at that critical age when love has a patina of lechery, took the step for better or for worse. And it certainly couldn't have been worse.

The bride and groom returned to Liverpool where they moved into a large house, well stocked with servants, and all the horrors of Victorian interior decoration. A son was born in 1882 and a daughter in 1886. But all was not well in the Maybrick household. Mr. Maybrick had relations with other women, and, probably more aggravating yet, he fussed continually about his health. And not only that, he did something about it. He was continually dosing himself. In the twentieth-century such a practice is prevalent but relatively harmless, as a nation protected by the Pure Food and Drug Act blissfully swallows, rubs on, or chews medicines guaranteed to cure everything from athlete's foot to hot flashes. But in the nineteenth century, more potent, dangerous drugs were not restricted to prescriptions, and Mr. Maybrick's medicine cabinet contained a much headier brew than Alka-Seltzer, Aspirin, and miraculously germicidal tooth pastes. He had quite exotic medicinal tastes and dosed himself with some regularity on such skull-and-crossbones items as arsenic and strychnine. Arsenic he favored as a nerve tonic, strychnine was his favorite aphrodisiac. A druggist near Mr. Maybrick's Liverpool office said Maybrick was "in and out of the shop all day long for pick-me-ups." And he must have been a nervous man because the druggist said that arsenic was present in almost all of these concoctions. Friends and relatives who knew of his curious addiction warned him about possible harmful effects. Mrs. Maybrick spoke to the family doctor about the "white powder" her husband took which worried her because it seemed to have such a bad effect on her husband, but Mr. Maybrick, impervious to advice and warnings, merrily continued his pharmaceutical orgy.

Then, in 1889, Mrs. Maybrick took unto herself a lover. James Maybrick certainly does not sound like the mate that every girl dreams of. He was the typical Victorian husband, who considered his wife a rather boring piece of property and advocated the single standard. It should be remembered that, by 1889, Florence Maybrick was a lush twenty-six while James Maybrick was nudging fifty, and even strychnine aphrodisiacs have their limitations. For eight years of married life she had to all appearances been a good wife and mother, overlooking her husband's consuming interests in women and his health and taking care of her house and her children. But now she decided to toss her plumed and ribboned bonnet over the windmill. In our society, the role of a wife and homemaker has been glorified through the years until it found its ultimate expression in twentieth-century, split-level suburbia. Most women, however, yearn for outside interests. In Florence Maybrick's time the majority of women found this expression in an active social life, works of charity, or china painting. In our own time wives may work, or there are always bridge clubs, pottery classes, or talking on the telephone, but in any age, there are a few women who either out of boredom or rebellion, go in for the triangle game, and Mrs. Maybrick was one of them. She had been carrying on a rather torrid flirtation with a young man of her own social circle called Brierley, and finally she capitulated. She told her husband that she was going to London to stay with an aunt who was having an operation, making it clear that imagination and perception weren't long suits in the Maybrick household.

Mrs. Maybrick met Brierley in London on March twenty-first, and they spent three nights of unwedded bliss in a London hotel. Brierley is the unknown quantity of the Maybrick case. He was never called to the witness stand. He made no response to Mrs. Maybrick's frantic pleas for help after her arrest, and the only words of his on record are a frosty little note he wrote to Mrs. Maybrick after the London interlude, which said, "We had better not meet again until late in the autumn," which might either be an indictment of Mrs. Maybrick's prowess as a bed-fellow or a sympton of belated caution. On the other hand, he might have just been one of those men to whom the chase is the game and the conquest the end. Brierley is like a character in a play whose name is often mentioned, who is important to the development of the plot, but who only makes a brief, one-line appearance on stage. If Mrs. Maybrick was convicted because of her morals and her affair with Brierley, then his role is an important one, but as a person he hovers wraithlike and caddish on the periphery of the Maybrick case. In many ways he is reminiscent of Madame Bovary's Leon—the young office clerk with the nineteenth century duck-tailed hairdo, who goes in for idealized love and passionate poetry but takes to his heels when Madame Bovary starts lustfully clawing at her satin bodice and making more mundane demands. Perhaps Florence Maybrick was just too much woman for the cautious, effete Brierley, and when poetry turned to prose, he just wanted out, a panicky feeling not unfamiliar to the male of the species.

With her abortive intrigue over and the chill of Brierley's note putting a damper on smouldering sparks, Mrs. Maybrick settled back into her matronly mold. Shortly after her return from London, she and Mr. Maybrick went to Aintree to watch the Grand National. There they accidentally ran into Brierley and the two men had rather heated words, evidently about the mutual object of their affections. Mr. Maybrick must have had a nasty suspicion about Florence's aunt, and the fight continued after they returned home where Mr. Maybrick violated the code for nineteenth-century cuckolds. In the lower classes a man might thoroughly beat up his wife for extramarital activities. In the middle classes, upper and lower, there were several acknowledged recourses. A verbal lashing by the husband followed by wifely shame and tears or an endorsement of the ignorance-is-bliss dictum. As for the top crust and *café* society, it was discreetly smart. But James Maybrick was no gentleman, he blacked Mrs. Maybrick's eye. Mrs. Maybrick threatened to leave home, but the family doctor and several friends persuaded the bruised and erring Florence to stay with her husband because of the children and because the disgrace might damage Mr. Maybrick's business. To close things on a sunny note, Mrs. Maybrick later revealed that she made a full confession and received entire forgiveness from her husband, but it's strictly a case of Mrs. Maybrick's word on this because by the time she made the statement, James Maybrick was very dead.

Then, what might have been the end of a domestic fracas took on more serious overtones. In the middle part of April, Mr. Maybrick became ill. He at first thought he had overdosed on strychnine and went to London to consult Dr. Fuller, who was his brother, Michael Maybrick's physician. Dr. Fuller diagnosed it as indigestion and gave him a prescription for a harmless stomach sedative.

On April twenty-second, Mr. Maybrick returned to Liverpool and began tippling on Dr. Fuller's prescription, which must have seemed pretty tame going after his own dosings.

On April twenty-fourth, Mrs. Maybrick bought a dozen fly papers from a nearby chemist, charged them to her account and had them delivered. A week later she bought two dozen more fly papers from another chemist and some face lotion. She was also known to this chemist. All of the fly papers she purchased had arsenic in them, and a servant saw them soaking in a basin in Mrs. Maybrick's bedroom. According to Mrs. Maybrick, she had a skin erruption and was unable to locate an old recipe for a face wash which contained arsenic. She was trying to approximate this by soaking the arsenic out of the fly papers to add to the face wash she had bought. She had a slight eruption, and, as she was going to a ball on April thirtieth, she was most anxious to get it cleared up.

On April twenty-seventh, Mr. Maybrick had a violent attack of vomiting. However, he went to the Wirral races and dined with friends, although he was so shaky he spilled wine all over the table. He was still ill the next day, and Mrs. Maybrick sent for their regular family doctor, Dr. Humphreys, who thought Dr. Fuller's diagnosis was correct—an upset stomach. The doctor put Maybrick on a strict diet, and his patient was so much better that he made his last call on the first of May. Mr. Maybrick returned to his office and worked May second and third, although he did have an upset stomach, which this time he attributed to some bad sherry. On the night of May third, he again was taken ill, but May fourth he improved. He took some Valentine's Meat Juice and three doses of Fuller's Solution of Arsenic, which shows he was up to his old tricks again. On May seventh, Mrs. Maybrick called in another doctor, Dr. Carter, who again diagnosed dyspepsia—upset stomach—and thought there was an irritant substance in the stomach. He, too, prescribed mild sedatives.

Now begins one of the most airtight conspiracies in criminal history. Alice Yapp, the children's nursemaid, graphically named, told two of the Maybricks' friends, Mrs. Hughes and Mrs. Briggs, about the water-soaked fly papers. Mrs. Briggs sent a wire to Michael Maybrick in London provocatively worded, "Come at once. Strange things are going on here." In the meantime, Mrs. Maybrick had sent for a nurse and Nurse Gore arrived at two in the afternoon. Another brother, Edwin Maybrick gave orders that no one but the nurse was to attend his brother.

Within twenty-four hours, on the basis of a snooping servant, meddling friends, and family discord, Florence Maybrick was a displaced person in her own house. And the way she was spied on would have made Mata Hari look like a girl scout on a bird walk. For instance, Mrs. Maybrick was pouring medicine from a small bottle to a larger bottle and was caught red-handed by Michael Maybrick. "Florrie, how dare you tamper with the medicine?" he yelled at her. She explained that there was so much sediment in the medicine that the larger bottle was more convenient for shaking. On analysis no arsenic was found in the bottle, but Michael Maybrick had his mind made up. There seems to have been an antagonism, and, by the time he arrived at the Liverpool house, the well-meaning friends had briefed him. Nurse Gore later stated that she saw Mrs. Maybrick handling meat juice in a surreptitious way. This was later found to contain arsenic, but Mrs. Maybrick insisted her husband had asked her to add a powder to the meat juice, as it would make him feel better. On May eleventh, Mr. Maybrick died, and a postmortem examination showed stomach inflammation caused by an an irritant poison. On May fourteenth, Mrs. Maybrick was arrested.

The fast acceleration of suspicion, the rapidity of the arrest can be explained in only one way: Mrs. Maybrick was not popular. Her brother-in-law, Michael Maybrick, who should have been her protector in the circumstances, turned out to be an archevil genius. He jumped to conclusions and stirred up suspicion like a fury. It is interesting to note that he was also known as Stephen Adams, successful composer of highly popular sentimental ballads. Why were two supposedly good friends willing to leap to conclusions on the gossip of a servant? What made the servant take it upon herself to talk to the two friends? The answer can be found in only one source. Mrs. Maybrick was a foreigner, the bride with different ways from another country, who is brought home to adjust to new ways and watched like a hawk to see that she does. There had to be underlying resentments, a dormant venom. Family, friends, and servants don't just turn on a person on such tenuous grounds, particularly on someone like Mrs. Maybrick, who for eight years had lived among them apparently on the best of terms. And yet within twenty-four hours, the secure wife, the fond mother, the sister-in-law, the friend is completely isolated by suspicion. There were deep roots here, not the easy overnight flowering of a tropical bloom, and it could only come from resentment against the proud, petulant Southern beauty, who as Mrs. James Maybrick had cut a swathe in sedate Liverpool. The "foreigner" had married a native son. Why wasn't an English girl good enough instead of a Colonial, with her simpering you-alls, plantation snobbery, and highhanded American ways. The foreign bride is a common enough phenomena, but seldom is she the target of such a malignant attack.

Mrs. Maybrick was arrested while she was ill in bed, taken to Walton Jail, and then removed to a hospital and, at a hearing, was ordered to stand trial. When leaving the hearing, Mrs. Maybrick was hissed by a group of ladies. There was talk of transferring her case to London because of the feeling, but her solicitors decided against it. Florence Maybrick was to stand trial for the murder of her husband in Liverpool. She was completely alone. Her family was far away, and there was no friend to say a good word for her, except one. Her defense was handled by Sir Charles Russell, later Lord Chief Justice of England, one of the all-time titans of the British bar.

The trial opened at the Liverpool assizes on July 31, 1889, to a packed courtroom and a curious nation. The prosecution used as their three big guns the arsenic in the meat juice, the arsenic-impregnated fly papers, and a letter from Florence Maybrick written to Brierley. Mr. Addison was appearing as Q.C., and Mr. Justice James Fitzjames Stephen was to preside. This judge had a brilliant mind and a distinguished career as a jurist and an essayist, but in 1885 he had had a stroke, and two years after the Maybrick trial his mind shattered completely and he was forced to retire. From transcripts of the trial, it is painfully evident that the shadows of bedlam were already closing in, obscuring externals, clouding issues.

Witnesses trooped to the stand to testify that for years James Maybrick had been in the habit of eating all kinds of harmful substances. As a matter of fact, the prosecution was having a bad time proving Mr. Maybrick died from his favorite tonic at all. Addison had stated that the prosecution would swear Maybrick died by arsenic, but on cross-examination Dr. Humphrey admitted that he had not thought of arsenic as a possible cause of death until it was suggested to him by Mr. Michael Maybrick. He would have given the death certificate as gastroenteritis.

Dr. Carter admitted that symptoms caused by arsenic might equally be caused by impure food, and that there are no post-mortem symptoms distinctive of arsenical poisoning that are not also distinctive of gastroenteritis.

Dr. Stevenson, the Home Office toxicologist stated, "There is no distinctive diagnostic symptom of arsenical poisoning. The diagnostic thing is finding the arsenic. If Maybrick was a chronic arsenic eater, he mighe have met death from natural causes." With arsenic in the system in an incidental way, three defense doctors said gastroenteritis. So when the smoke of forensic battle cleared, not only had the prosecution failed to prove conclusively that Maybrick died of arsenic, but new vistas opened up. He might have died from natural causes or he might have died from an overdose of arsenic, since it was a cumulative poison. The prosecution was in the embarrassing position of possibly having a murderess but no murder.

Dr. Stevenson, Home Office expert, had no doubt Maybrick died from the effects of an overdose of arsenic. Dr. Tidy, an equally eminent expert for the defense, negated the suggestion of death by arsenic, which recalls a familiar spectacle of the twentieth century : the psychiatrist for the defense saying, insane, and the psychiatrist for the prosecution saying, sane. Evidence was given that Mr. Maybrick's mortal coil had traces of arsenic, strychnine, henbane, morphia, and prussic acid. The one unquestionable, uncontested fact that emerged at the trial was that James Maybrick had cast-iron guts.

Dr. Stevenson also testified that arsenic is a cumulative poison that the system will retain and store up over a period of time. Since James Maybrick had admittedly been taking arsenic over a period of years, there was a very good chance that a dose, administered as the usual tonic, could have been the proverbial straw. Today, it is admitted by legal minds as well as laymen, that the Maybrick Case was one of the biggest goofs in legal history. A woman was tried for murder where murder was never proved and convicted because of her morals, or lack of them. The price for three nights of love in a London hotel was inflationary. Mrs. Maybrick, who, according to the law of time, was not allowed to appear in her own defense but was allowed to make a statement in court. Statements such as these, however, had a limited effect because the deponent was not under oath, and her statement contained nothing new.

The most damning piece of evidence was the letter written to Brierley three days before Maybrick died. As a matter of fact, Sir Charles Russell always maintained that if there hadn't been this letter, there would have been no trial. It was given to Alice Yapp to post, she dropped it and while putting it in a clean envelope, happened to read it, and then gave it to Michael Maybrick. Sir Charles Russell's cross-examination demolished her, but nothing could demolish the letter. It read :

May 8th

Dearest :

Your letter under cover to John K. came to hand just after I had written you on Monday. I did not expect to hear from you so soon, and had delayed in giving him the necessary instructions. Since my return I have been nursing M. day and night. He is sick unto death. The doctors held a consultation yesterday and now all depends on how long his strength will hold out. Both my brothers-in-law are here, and we are terribly anxious. I cannot answer your letter fully today, my darling, but relieve your mind of all fear of discovery now and in the future. M. has been delirious since Sunday, and I know now that he is perfectly ignorant of everything, even the name of the street, and also he has not been making any inquiries whatever. The tale he told me was a pure fabrication, and only intended to frighten the truth out of me. In fact, he believes my statement, although he will not admit it. You need not therefore go abroad on that account, dearest; but, in any case, don't leave England until I have seen you once again. You must feel that those two letters of mine were written under circumstances which must even excuse their injustice in your eyes. Do you suppose I could act as I am doing if I really felt and meant what I inferred then? If you wish to write me about anything do so now, as all the letters pass through my hands at present. Excuse the scrawl, my own darling, but I do not dare leave the room for a moment, and I do not know when I shall be able to write to you again. In haste, yours ever,

FLORRIE

There's no denying it's a love letter with all the tensions and misunderstandings that usually copartner such an affair, but the "sick unto death" phrase was used as one of the mainstays of prosecution's case, since doctors testified that on May seventh their prognosis had been hopeful. Russell claimed that the generally gloomy, suspicious atmosphere of the household might have preyed upon Mrs. Maybrick's nerves and led to such pessimism. There is also another possible explanation, when one recalls the letters of Mrs. Edith Thompson to Frederick Bywaters. Mrs. Thompson was a born exaggerator, a not uncommon feminine failing. In fact, Mrs. Thompson exaggerated herself right up the steps of the scaffold. Mrs. Maybrick, who is apologizing for two evidently offensive letters she wrote Brierley ("you must feel that those two letters of mine were written under circumstances which must even excuse their injustice in your eyes"), is excusing herself on the grounds that her husband is sick and she has been nursing him day and night. Naturally the gloomier she paints the picture, the sicker she makes her husband, the more excusable whatever she said in the two letters becomes. The meat juice is easily explained. For although most husbands don't ask their wives to spike their juice with arsenic, in this case it is completely believable because of Maybrick's long-standing arsenic-eating habit. The fly papers are even more believable; in a house loaded with arsenic, why would Mrs. Maybrick bother to go to two chemists where she was well known to buy it in fly paper and then go to all the trouble of soaking it in plain sight in her bedroom. After Mr. Maybrick's death, there was ready-to-use arsenic in packets, in bottles, in jars, in tumblers. Between Mr. Maybrick's nerves and Mrs. Maybrick's complexion problems, there was enough arsenic in the house to decimate the rat population of the wharves of the world.

The judge's summing up was enough to make Justice take off her blindfold and stare in horror. The judge rambled, he had to be corrected on dates by Mr. Pickford, junior counsel for the defense. He quoted from a letter that had never been admitted as evidence. He lingered over the Brierley affair and stressed it as a motive for murder. He reveled in *nonsequiturs,* and he was going to have his say. When corrected, he snapped grumpily, "There is no use in disputing whether I used one word, or another." And so Florence Maybrick waited for the jury to come back. She must have felt like the only reality in the middle of unreality. The courtroom, the expressionless jurors, the hissing women, the avid faces of the spectators watching and waiting for the pitiful fragments of her broken life to be tossed to them, the judge who continually stared at her, these were all the shadows. She was the substance in a world gone mad. After a half hour the jury filed back with the ultimate unreality, guilty. And the judge, as if thinking of something pleasant, donned the black cap and told her she must hang by the neck until dead.

But Florence Maybrick did have friends. The country was shocked by the verdict. Newspapers clamored; doctors protested; petitions were signed by the tens of thousands, and there were worried conferences in the Home Office. In Walton Gaol, Mrs. Maybrick could tick off the minutes by the hammering as they erected her scaffold. Finally, the reprieve came. Her sentence was commuted to penal servitude for life, and the words of the Home Office Secretary make just about as much sense as "'Twas brillig, and the slithy toves/Did gyre and gimble in the wabe : All mimsy . . . etc.". : "Although the evidence leads clearly to the conclusion that the prisoner administered and attempted to administer, arsenic to her husband, yet it does not wholly exclude a reasonable doubt whether his death was in fact caused by the administration of arsenic." There's not much choice between Lewis Carroll and the Home Office. It's all Jabberwocky talk. They convicted her for poisoning her husband with arsenic but aren't sure that he died from arsenic. So, Mrs. Maybrick served fifteen years for a crime that might not even have been committed, and, until his death in 1900, Sir Charles Russell never stopped fighting for Mrs. Maybrick's release and protesting her innocence.

In 1904, Mrs. Maybrick was released, but the slow erosion of routine in prison had made its impression. The unreality had become real. Crime and punishment had been her daily companions, and her sheltered, luxurious Liverpool existence had a dreamlike remoteness. She came to America where she lived for many years as a quiet recluse. Her only eccentricity was cats, her small cottage meant milk and refuge for dozens of feline vagabonds. And who is to question Florence Maybrick's preference for cats—instead of people?

VII

The Fruit of the Prophet

IN THE EARLY part of the nineteenth century, messengers of heavenly origin were unusually busy in the state of New York. A messenger of the Lord appeared to Robert Mathews in Albany, telling him that he was a reincarnation of St. Matthew and to take over the world in the name of the Lord. In New York City, an angel appeared to Mr. Elijah Pierson, in the rather prosaic confines of Wall Street, while that gentleman was riding an omnibus. Mr. Pierson was informed that he was a reincarnation of Elijah the Tishbite and to prepare for the coming of the Prophet.

In a period when the mysticism of Swedenborg and the animal magnetism of Mesmer were two of the most important European exports to America, when the thunder of Jonathan Edwards's warnings of man's damnation still echoed in the minds of eastern seaboard dwellers, and when camp meetings reached the proportions of Roman orgies, salvation of the soul was the order of the day and divine visitants were ordinary occurrences. The only thing that distinguishes the angels of Mr. Pierson and Mr. Mathews is that this combination of ethereal advice resulted in a most mundane happening—murder.

135

Mr. Pierson began his preparations for the arrival of the promised prophet by organizing a Holy Club, composed of renegades from the Methodists and Baptist churches, and the rumor went around New York that Mr. Pierson, a wealthy and respected business man, had become "a little queer in the head." Mr. Pierson, after carefully combing the scriptures, came up with the startling revelation that the first people to enter through the Golden Gate on the Day of Judgement would be the descendants of Mary Magdalene. Accordingly, he and his Holy Club opened a house on Bowery Hill where the conversion and care of the city's *filles de joie* were carried on. Cynics uncharitably hinted that the ceremonies and meetings on Bowery Hill were more of an earthly than a celestial nature, and, although there is no recorded comment on the subject, it would be interesting to know just what effect Mr. Pierson's scriptural discovery had on the "respectable" women of his congregation.

When Mrs. Pierson died, Mr. Pierson promised his flock and his dying wife that she would be resurrected, but as frenziedly as he prayed and anointed his wife's body, the mortal envelope of Mrs. Pierson's soul clung stubbornly to the "dust thou art and to dust thou shalt return" school of thought. But Mr. Pierson regarded this as a minor setback and declared that all would be well when the promised Prophet arrived. The Holy Club and Elijah the Tishbite sat back and waited for his arrival.

Robert Mathews seems to have had an earlier awareness of his impending divinity. In 1797, when he was nine years old, some sweets and fruits were distributed at school. Having either eaten or hidden his own allotment, he demanded a share of his schoolmates' booty. Quite naturally they refused.

"Then if you do not," he threatened them, "I will make the Man of the Thunder speak to you."

"Where is he?" asked the skeptical school boys.

It was a cloudy afternoon, and Robert pointed to a black

cloud in the sky. "There in that black cloud. He is my uncle."

In a few minutes there was a boom of thunder, and a finger of lightning appeared across the darkened sky. The frightened school boys were only too willing to give some of their fruits and candy to a personage with such impressive connections in exchange for his promise that he would not allow the Man of the Thunder to harm them. Although the stakes were higher, Mathews used the same technique thirty years later, with the same gratifying results.

When he was sixteen, Robert apprenticed himself to a carpenter, saying that it was a "divine trade" and worthy of his consideration. He wandered from Hudson to Albany and then to New York, plying his trade and quoting his scriptures. He would even go into churches during a service and interrupt the minister in the middle of a sermon to discuss a small point. One such embattled New York clergyman banned Mathews from his church, and, for the rest of his life, Mathews never found a good word to say about orthodox religions. During his subsequent career the feeling was reciprocal. Because of his geographical instability and his capacity for working himself into a frenzy over the discussion of religion, he became known all over New York state as "Jumping Jesus." But he finally married and gave up his wandering for a while, although he studied and argued his scripture more diligently than ever.

One day, after some years of married life, he told his wife that he was going to take the children "out into the wilderness," and, before the anxious mother could stop him, he gathered up the brood and was marching off into the woods surrounding Albany. Neither Mathews nor the children were seen for several days, and, as Mrs. Mathews' anxiety changed to hysteria, a group of sympathetic neighbors formed a posse and began a search of the countryside. They found the future prophet and his children on the verge of starvation on the border of Washington County in a cabin formed from the boughs of trees. The children were crying, and the father seemed relieved when the neighbors offered to return the children to their mother.

He decided to stay in his woodland retreat, hunger and all, and it was here that he received his divine revelation. When he returned to Albany it was not as Robert Mathews, the carpenter, but as St. Matthew, or Matthias, the Prophet. His first acts as a newly created saint were to grow a luxuriant beard, desert his family, and go forth to prepare for the Kingdom of the Lord that was to begin on earth just as soon as he could get things in order.

His tall, slow-moving figure and impressive beard became familiar as he wandered from camp meeting to camp meeting, preaching his garbled doctrine of vegetarianism, temperance, and a supreme faith in himself as the only sure means of salvation. An extensive knowledge of scripture and an even more extensive ego were the tools of his trade, and he used both of them to the limit. But his aim was not the poor farmer or the grubbing homesteader he met at camp meetings. His kingdom was to be rich in fact as well as in spirit.

New York City attracted him. He went there, and, through his street preaching, he met and impressed a wealthy New York business man, Mr. Mills, who after talking with the Prophet, agreed to finance the spiritual kingdom. Matthias, as he now called himself, gave Mr. Mills the privilege of going on a shopping spree with him. They ordered plates mounted with the lion of the tribe of Judah, two silver chalices, and some costly royal-purple robes. But Mr. Mills's family and friends questioned the divinity of the Prophet with infuriating skepticism. Matthias quoted scripture to the nonbelievers. He threatened them, but they weren't convinced. He was committed to the department of the Insane Poor at Bellevue Hospital, and Mr. Mills, on a warrant also issued by his family, was taken to the Bloomingdale

Lunatic Asylum, where eventually he came to see the error of his ways.

Matthias had become accustomed to the kid gloves, silk hose, and gold watch presented to him by his benefactor, so upon his release from Bellevue he decided to call upon a friend of Mr. Mills, Mr. Elijah Pierson. Mr. Pierson, since his revelation, must have been training his household because when the bearded, imposing stranger knocked on the door, the colored woman who opened it gasped and asked, "Art thou the Lord?"

"I am," was the unperturbed reply.

Overcome, the Negro cook, who was also a Holy Club convert, fell at his feet and burst into tears, and Mr. Pierson, after talking with the Prophet for several hours, realized that here was the saviour he had been promised. He invited Matthias to live with him and introduced him to his friends and members of the Holy Club. The supply of silk hose and kid gloves grew, and, in appreciation perhaps, the Prophet announced that the spirit of John the Baptist had entered into Pierson. Pierson, notwithstanding his horrible death, lived gloriously. What other mere mortal, in one short lifetime, has had the privilege of being the fleshly container of two such spirits as Elijah the Prophet and John the Baptist?

Through Pierson, the Prophet met Mr. Benjamin Folger, also a wealthy New York business man. Mr. Folger at first was skeptical and even warned Pierson against "the workings of false prophets," but Matthias concentrated on Mr. Folger. Within a month, Folger was enthusiastically helping Pierson order purple robes trimmed in gold and silver and a jeweled ceremonial sword for the Prophet.

In September, 1822, the Prophet was invited to visit the summer home of Mr. and Mrs. Folger at Sing Sing. Matthias liked the house, and he asked both Pierson and Folger to give him an account of their financial status, property and real estate holdings. The accounts must have satisfied Matthias, for he then told them that they must agree to support him. He, in return, would guarantee the forgiveness of all their sins and the continued blessing of God. The Prophet also decided that he couldn't establish a permanent kingdom until he had fought and vanquished the forces of the devil, and in the meantime he must have a home. Matthias must have been happy when another one of his opportune visions confirmed his home-loving tendencies. This convenient shade told him that, when Mr. Folger had purchased the house, he had been directed by the Spirit of Truth and in reality bought the house for Matthias.

Under the persuasion of promises of further blessings and threats of "almighty wrath," Folger surrendered his home. And Pierson's house on Third Street in New York with furniture, carriages, horses, and silver was deeded over to the Prophet. They gave him ten thousand dollars in cash and placed the remainder of their property at his disposal. Matthias accepted these donations with regal dignity and announced that Folger's house could be called Mount Zion and would do very well for the ninety-nine years which must elapse before he vanquished the devil and built his palace in New Jerusalem with "agate framed doors and windows of carbuncle."

At Mount Zion a holy dictatorship was established. Mr. and Mrs. Folger and their children, Pierson, his daughter, and Isabella, the colored woman who had believed Matthias to be the Lord, all lived a communal life. No one was allowed to eat, sleep, drink, or leave the grounds without the consent of the Prophet. They divided the housework and gardening among themselves, while Matthias would drape himself languidly in his robes, with perfumed beard, and allow the enlightened members of his kingdom to adore him. Sometimes, if he felt that there was any evidence of backsliding, the Prophet would rise from his dais and curse his followers so terribly that they became convinced only he could save them from the eternally blazing fires of hell. He liked to deliver long sermons at mealtimes, and often, if the "spirit" inspired him, the Prophet would talk for three to four hours. Elizabeth Pierson was the recipient of a tirade of scripture-punctuated wrath when she observed that the preaching lasted so long there was no time to wash the dishes from the last meal to serve the next one.

Another interesting feature of the life at Mount Zion was the purification ceremony. Matthias would bathe in a tub of water and then, gathering his followers around a stove in a complete state of coeducational nudity, would sprinkle them with the water he had purified. At a period when a lady's ankle was the ultimate in sex appeal, communal life at Mount Zion must have had its attractive side.

Although the Prophet, in his earlier career, had damned the institution of marriage and maintained that women were "full of deviltry," he must have eradicated the deviltry with the purification ceremony, and a situation was developing at Mount Zion that had more of Rabelais than the scripture in it. Matthias, in a "wondrously clear vision" discovered that Mrs. Folger was his soulmate and was destined to become the mother of the Kingdom—in a literal as well as a figurative sense. Mrs. Folger simultaneously had a vision in which she was told that she was Matthias's matched spirit and a virgin, a rather startling revelation for the mother of two children.

Folger, by now completely under the influence of Matthias was persuaded that his wife as well as his property were the Prophet's, although a witness reports that on the night of the informal ceremony that made "Mother Folger" and the Prophet one, Mr. Folger looked a little disconsolate as he watched the couple withdraw to his old bedroom, while he was forced to spend the night in the Prophet's room.

After this, there were uncomfortable scenes. Folger would gaze at his wife and follow her around the house, and one day Mrs. Folger's light soprano voice with a slight titter in it floated down the hall, saying "Benjamin, behave yourself!" The Prophet saw that he would have to take action for the welfare of his community. He sent Folger to Albany to bring his eldest daughter, Isabella, to Mount Zion. The inevitable vision had proclaimed that Isabella was Folger's spiritual mate.

Folger arrived in Albany, found Isabella and her mother both agreeable to the idea of the trip, but a sullen young man who hovered in the background and was referred to rather airily as Isabella's husband had to be pacified with a handsome gold watch. On the journey back, Isabella and Folger stopped at an inn for the night, and there they became "matched spirits." At Mount Zion Matthias annulled the marriage through his supreme power and pronounced the happy, if slightly irregular couple, man and wife.

Life rolled along at Mount Zion. Matthias was forced to whip his daughter with a cowhide thong for impertinence to "Mother Folger," and Isabella went back to her husband, who had, in the meantime, decided that a gold watch was a poor exchange for a wife and had issued a warrant charging Matthias with abduction. Matthias survived this outrage to his dignity and recommended the disconsolate Folger to Catherine Galloway, a lively young widow who had recently joined the communal colony.

Matthias spent the greater part of his time in discussing scriptural passages, but the intellectual atmosphere in the Kingdom was subordinated to dogma—the Prophet's dogma. In the case of an argument, he would scream at the person who was rash enough to question his opinion, "You are a devil. You cannot talk with me." He finally announced that no human could argue with him, because it was a matter of divine reason (his) against human reason.

But John the Baptist, alias Mr. Pierson, was not faring well. He had been reduced to tasks such as clearing weeds in the garden, and he had begun to suffer from epileptic fits. Catherine Galloway, the pretty young widow, had "appealed to his spirit greatly," but she had been given to Folger. Maybe Pierson thought the Kingdom of Heaven on earth was too long in arriving or perhaps his back bothered him from so much weeding, but whatever the reason, August, 1834, the month that was to prove crucial for the two saints, began with a strange request from Pierson. He wanted the lease on his house given back to his daughter. The Prophet and his premier disciple were heard having violent arguments, but for once "divine reason" capitulated to human reason. Matthias turned the house lease over to Elizabeth Pierson. Matthias by this time had become an unrestrained egomaniac, and the only thing that could explain the enforced transaction so much against the Prophet's wishes is a little blackmail in self-defense on Pierson's part. He probably threatened Matthias's security and ego by hinting that he might expose the Kingdom.

Pierson picked an unfortunate time to come to his senses. Matthias had not only been able to give his ego free play in the Kingdom; he had also reached a state of insane confidence in his ability to deal with anything or anyone who put him in personal danger. It was the same state that Dr. Pritchard reached when he gorged his wife and mother-in-law on assorted poisons with no attempt at subterfuge; and G. J. Smith reveled in the same complacency as he dunked his various brides into a tin bath tub with such fatal results. What is familiarly known as "the long arm of the law" gave these two gentlemen an efficient nudge to the scaffold. The Prophet escaped the extreme penalty, not because he was any more clever or any less guilty, but because of the slow advance of medicine.

Mr. Pierson, after his victory over the Prophet, moved to his own country home in Westchester County, but his days of newly recovered sense and freedom were numbered. Within a week, the Prophet, "Mother Folger," Catherine Galloway, and Matthias's two sons from Albany had entrenched themselves as the uninvited house guests of Pierson.

The next day, Matthias and his two sons went out to pick blackberries, a favorite dish of Pierson's. That night at the dinner table, Pierson ate two plates of the berries. Matthias abstained. "Mother Folger" tasted them, said they were bitter, and pushed her plate away, and Catherine Galloway ate one small dish and became violently ill later in the evening.

After eating the blackberries, Pierson embarked upon one of the most harrowing illnesses on record. He vomited continuously. His epileptic fits increased and a partial paralysis developed. But the Prophet gave an unsympathetic diagnosis. Pierson was "encouraging fifty devils in himself and those who nursed him or offered sympathy were guilty of harboring the devil, too."

Pierson spent all day Wednesday in bed. Thursday, Friday, and Saturday, he shuffled around the house, but he seemed to be in a stupor. When anyone spoke to him, the effort of answering would bring on a slight fit. The Prophet issued an order that no one was to speak with Pierson, as the speaker was guilty of encouraging the devil. Within three days, the sick, dazed man was effectively cut off from communication with anyone in the house.

On Sunday, Pierson was unable to get out of bed. He was left alone by Matthias's orders. On Monday, while the Kingdom was eating dinner, Catherine Galloway and "Mother Folger" heard a noise from Pierson's room, as if something had fallen. Both women started for his room, but Matthias forbid them to leave the table and delivered them an hour-long lecture on how their conduct was keeping the sick spirit in the house. After the lecture, Matthias and the women went up to Pierson's room. They found the sick man on the floor. Hoping to punish the stubborn devil who had taken up living quarters in Pierson's body, the Prophet refused to have Pierson returned to his bed and instead had some straw brought in from the carriage house to be used as a sickbed. By Tuesday, Pierson was lying on his straw pallet in a coma, and the Prophet's medicinal counterirritant for that was to slap Pierson on the face, order him to come out of that "hellish sleep," and douse his unresisting, long-suffering body in ice water.

The next day, although his visions evidently hadn't warned him, the Prophet met his eventual nemesis in the person of Mrs. Dratch. Mrs. Dratch, an elderly woman, was an old friend of Pierson's, and she came by to pay a social visit. She was met by the Prophet, who told her that Pierson was ill. She immediately wanted to send for a doctor, but Matthias stopped her with the information that he "had the power of life and death" and that Mr. Pierson would not die. Seeing that Mrs. Dratch was not convinced and having very sound reasons for not wanting a doctor on the premises, the Prophet's manner changed. He assured Mrs. Dratch that he was something of a doctor and would give Pierson treatment immediately.

If Mrs. Dratch had seen the treatment, she would have picked up her sedate skirts and run for the nearest doctor—or policeman —in spite of the Prophet's charming manner and assurances. The treatment consisted of pouring ice-cold water into the comatose Pierson's open mouth from a height of four or five feet. Even "Mother Folger" whose delicate, womanly sensibilities don't seem to have been much in evidence during the past week, couldn't stand the strange, choking gurgle and fled the room.

A few hours later, Matthias came out of the sickroom and announced that his John the Baptist had died. Mr. Folger came up from New York with a coffin. The platitudes were observed, and the Folgers and the Prophet set out for New York. Mrs. Dratch returned to her home accompanied by doubts that were to result in sleepless nights and an eventual visit to the police. The Prophet gave an interesting diagnosis of the cause of death, and, if it seemed unsound medically, it was at least colorful. He told Mr. and Mrs. Folger that as soon as he found out that his spirit had rejected the body of Mr. Pierson, he had gone into his room and made a sign as simple as "to turn the spoke of a chair," which never failed and inevitably resulted in the death of his enemies. It certainly hadn't in this instance. And, since the Prophet had sensed a certain wariness in the Folgers since Pierson's death, he informed them that they should receive the same gruesome attention if they opposed him or proved treacherous. Opposing the Prophet, as Pierson found out too late, was evidently a life and death matter.

Back in New York, "Mother Folger" was rapidly losing faith. The son she had expected turned out to be a girl, and the Prophet's assurance that he could save Pierson's life had amounted to nothing. Her faith was shaken. But Mr. Folger had lost more than faith. He had gone bankrupt. Maintaining a Prophet's Earthly Kingdom was no bargain. The next months were strange, waiting ones in the Folger household. The Prophet cursed the Folgers and tried in every way to give his waning divinity a boost. He exhorted them; he promised them eternal spiritual bliss; he threatened them with hell. But their minds were on other things; the great spiritual adventure had ended, and, in the place of religious exaltation, they were confronted by a tall man who strode through the house raving at them and frightening them.

Mr. Folger seemed to sink into a black apathy and became incapable of any action, and Mrs. Folger, realizing that the divine cause for which she had strayed from the path of virtue was not divine at all, faced the unpleasant prospect of becoming a fallen woman instead of the Mother of the Kingdom. Friends of the Folgers finally pointed out to the Prophet that in this sordid, work-a-day world the creditors had a more legal, if less holy, claim to Mr. Folger's remaining assets, and the Prophet agreed to go away for a few weeks. There is no record of where he went, but in a week he was back on the Folger's doorstep. The week had been enough for the Folgers. They asked him to please leave. Matthias could see by their attitude that his days as St. Matthew were over. He was to be relegated to a skeleton in the Folger's family closet, but he made one more attempt to regain his power. Matthias told the Folgers that if they really insisted on his leaving that "sickness and perhaps death would follow." Mr. Folger's answer was to ask him to set a date for his departure.

On the morning he was to leave, Matthias abstained from all food and even coffee, his one indulgence, saying he wasn't feeling well. He probably wasn't. Mr. Folger had been a walking checkbook and Mrs. Folger even more. He left immediately after breakfast, and his prophecy came to pass. The entire Folger family became violently ill with stomach cramps and violent vomiting fits which left them all ill and shaken for over a year. The only person to escape the sickness was the cook, who had abstained from coffee that morning.

Between violent attacks of nausea, Mr. Folger came out of his daze long enough to issue a warrant for Matthias's arrest on the charge of theft. The Prophet was apprehended in Albany, and the contents of his two large trunks were a source of amazement to the staunch officers of the law. They contained a large key which was to unlock the Gate of Heaven; two elaborate nightcaps, which Mrs. Folger had lovingly embroidered with the names of the twelve apostles; his ceremonial sword, with which to "smite the devil"; and a rod, with which to measure the bounds of paradise. He also had his ornate ceremonial robes, a gold watch, and some money which Folger claimed was stolen and the Prophet claimed was a gift. He was brought back to New

York on the steamboat *Champion*. On the boat, he stopped a gentleman passenger, and to the man's amazement and the police officers' amusement, Matthias asked the stranger peremptorily: "How long have I been on earth?"

"I have no idea," answered the astonished man.

"Well, I will tell you," the Prophet confided. "More than eighteen hundred years."

"Then all I have to say is that you're a remarkable looking man," was the stranger's socially conscious reply.

Matthias was held for trial in New York, and, even in his old age, the presiding judge must have remembered the irregular answer to the form question as to the identity of the prisoner. When asked who he was Matthias repllied: "My person is the trumpet for the Spirit of Truth."

In the meantime Mrs. Dratch had entered a complaint in Westchester County, accusing Matthias of murdering Mr. Pierson. The body was exhumed and traces of a morbid, foreign substance were found in the stomach. The legal machinery went into action, and the New York court asked Mr. Folger to dismiss his case as it would be hard to prove that the Prophet's claims were acceptable to a man of prudence and intellect and equally hard to prove them false. The court recommended further that the lesser charge yield to the graver charge. As Matthias was probably thinking, the devil has many allies on earth.

On November 11, 1834, the Prophet was delivered to the sheriff of Westchester County to stand trial for murder. As he was being escorted to the jailhouse, Matthias stopped in a nearby graveyard and asked to be allowed to address the curious crowd of people, which had been following him. He called upon the farmers to lay aside their plows and do no sowing of the earth until "I, the twelfth and last of the apostles shall be delivered from the house of bondage." To show his power to the crowd, Matthias gestured to a steep, stony hill. "I can move that mountain," he screamed and several large slabs of rock obligingly tumbled down. The people were awed and impressed. They wanted to touch and shake hands with the miracle worker, but he protested, "Touch not the Prophet of the Lord." The feeling that the age of miracles was not yet passed was slightly dampened when it was discovered that some school boys, walking on the hill and hearing the loud voice of the Prophet, had dislodged the pieces of rock by coming too near the edge to investigate the noise.

In April, 1835, the trial of the state of New York versus the reincarnaate Saint Matthew began. The self-styled saint put in an appearance that was more reminiscent of pagan times than Christianity. He was tall and thin with slow movements and gracefully graying hair. His beard was full and rippling. He wore a brown camlet cloak lined with silk and caught with a massive gilt clasp, a green frock coat with a pink silk lining, buff pantaloons, a brocade vest, gray stockings and pumps, a crimson sash, and elegant cascades of snowy ruffles. And just to make sure that no one would mistake him for an ordinary mortal, a large silver sun gleamed on the left side of his waistcoat, and silver stars sprinkled the right lapel. One court reporter from the *New York Sun* said that he was "constantly brushing his wavy hair with the hair brush he carried in his pocket, and when he had the good fortune to meet with a looking glass, he proceeds to beautify himself."

When he was called upon to face the court and hear the charges, Matthias heaped curses upon the judge, the jury, and the spectators. The judge rapped for order long and hard before the "Damned! Damned! DAMNED!" of the Prophet subsided. Mr. Martyn Paine and Dr. David L. Rogers were the first witnesses. They testified that Matthias had the "peculiar expression found in men of disordered intellect." The Prophet's brother-in-law, Andrew Wight of New York City, who had known the prisoner for twenty years, found him "partially deranged but of a shrewd bargaining disposition." Several merchants from Sing Sing rather ruefully testified to the lucidity of the Prophet's business dealings, and he was declared sane.

Jesse Bishop of Sing Sing was the first witness on the following day, April 17. He said that he had liked "old Pierson" and had attended his funeral. He testified that the corpse showed "no signs of ill will."

Moses Cheyney, the sexton in charge of the burying ground at Morristown, Mr. Pierson's last resting place, informed the court that Mr. Pierson had been buried on the eighth of August and exhumed ten days later by a Dr. Condit, who had carried away the deceased's stomach. The sexton didn't put it into words, but his expression showed exactly what he thought of dead people's stomachs being traipsed all over the country. With even icier disapproval, he told of a later exhumation by other doctors. He let it be known that he was definitely of the opinion that the dead should be left to rest in peace.

Dr. Lewus Condit testified that he had examined the stomach and found the anterior portion was inflamed. He discovered a substance resembling wet chalk or calomel, a white spot three inches in diameter on the fore part of the inner surface of the stomach, and a corresponding spot on the outside. There were other red and brown spots on the inner coat of the stomach, and the tissue under these spots was soft, pulpy, and disorganized. The second examination had disclosed that the upper part of the esophogus was irritated. There was a distinct odor of smoked herring, and the body was in an unusually well-preserved state, both indications of arsenic poisoning not known at the time.

Dr. Canfield Johns and Dr. Condit both gave a verdict that death was not due to natural causes and stated that they had reason to believe it was induced by some poisonous substance, but Dr. Torrey of New York, although he agreed with the other doctors, was unable to discover any concrete evidence of poison when he performed an analysis on the stomach. The doctors did their best, and they were right as far as they could go. They were sure there was poison in the system, but the trial took place twelve years before the introduction of the Marsh and Reinsch tests, which could chemically prove the presence of arsenic in the human body. In other words, the medical men had the right idea, but there was no way of proving it to the satisfaction of the law.

Mrs. Folger took the stand and gave information on the communal life at Mount Zion that was of interest to students of erotica but of no help legally. The judge charged the jury to remember that a diseased condition already existed that would probably have been fatal and that there was not too much evidence to prove that neglect had hastened death. It was a strangely partial charge to the jury, but the year was 1835. Arsenic was an unknown quantity. The "diseased condition" referred to was Pierson's epilepsy, and the judge had no way of knowing that epilepsy is one symptom of slow arsenic poisoning. There was no record of any epileptic seizures until after Pierson's eventually fatal meeting with Matthias. In the absence of any concrete medical knowledge on the subject of arsenic, however, it would seem that the Divine Power with whom the Prophet claimed such intimate acquaintance was on his side, and the jury acquitted him.

Nonetheless, the devil's work was not done. There was still another charge pending. Mr. Laisdell, Isabella Mathews' husband, after recovering his wife, had pressed charges against her father for assault. The judge promptly and with a great deal of satisfaction sentenced the Prophet to three months in the county jail and, just as an extra, added thirty days for contempt of court. The judge was still squirming under the memory of threats and damnations the fiery Prophet had hurled during the trial, and he delivered Matthias a lecture.

"We now tell you that the times for practicing these foolish impositions are past. We advise you therefore when you come out of jail, shave off your beard, lay aside your peculiar dress, and go to work like an honest man."

The Prophet's only answer to such heresy was a defiant, "It is not true," and more curses on the law in general and the Westchester County branch of it in particular.

The acquittal was the signal for the beginning of a bitter literary battle between two journalists. William Leete Stone, a friend of the Folgers, advanced the theory that Isabella, the Negro cook, was the "wickedest of the wicked" and that she had been a far from passive accomplice in some of the Prophet's activities. Geographically, the theory was sound. Isabella had worked for Mr. Pierson and was a member of good standing in the Holy Club. She had joined the converts at Mount Zion and then worked for the Folgers after the hegira to New York, following Pierson's death. She not only made the coffee in the morning of the almost-fatal departure; she abstained from it, following the wise example set by Matthias. Mr. Folger was convinced that there had been some rabid scripture quoting as well as some culinary sleight-of-hand in his kitchen that morning and confided to Mr. Stone that he was sure Isabella had taken part in the poisoning plot. Mr. Stone, in an effort to make the Folgers appear blameless had to compromise. He completely ignored the titillating evidence concerning Mrs. Folger's maternal connection with the Kingdom and its sovereign lord, and the purification ceremonies were never mentioned, and in order to vindicate his friends, he had to picture them as morons, once removed from congenital idiocy. But Mr. Stone does build a solid case against Isabella.

Mr. Gilbert Vale read William Stone's book, polished his

shining armor, and went forth to do verbal battle in defense of
Isabella. His case for Isabella is even less convincing than Stone's
for the Folgers. It consists of a verbatim report by Isabella on
life in the Kingdom, and it is mainly a very womanly indictment
of Mrs. Folger, who seems to have occupied more of the Prophet's
time than Isabella thought was right. Isabella was a religious
hysteric. Her entire life was a series of connections with a varied
assortment of highly questionable religious cults, and what both
men seemed to have lost sight of is that, whether or not she was
guilty of being an accomplice, Isabella was the instrument, not
the intelligence of the act. Mr. Vale also delivered a series of
personal attacks on Mr. Stone in the most ornate Victorian prose.
But the two gentlemen had one thing in common. They both had
the same indifferent attitude toward the Prophet's guilt as the
jury of Westchester County. There might be several explanations
for this. The lack of morality and all its intriguing sidelights was
probably more shocking than murder to the early Victorian mind,
and the communal bathing more interesting than Mr. Pierson's
dying gurgles.

It must have been hard for the jury to feel much sympathy for
the corpse, which is a very important element in murder trials.
A good prosecuting attorney will always emphasize the virtues of
the murderee and keep his personality a living thing for the
jurors, and a good defense attorney will always try to arouse
sympathy for his "innocent, wronged" client. And when a
prisoner begins to receive oranges, cigarettes, and proposals, the
odds in favor of acquittal go up. In the case of Mathews, while
there wasn't much sympathy for him and there is no proposal of
marriage recorded, it was equally hard for the jury to work up
any feeling of affinity with the Folgers or Pierson who had been
so easily duped by hysteria and vanity. Mathews was a freak,
regarded as not quite normal. But the Folgers and Pierson were
respected members of a demanding society; they had known its

benefits and rejected them. Their sin was more serious than
Mathews's.

Thomas De Quincey, an unquestionable authority on things
gory, has defined murder as, "Design, gentlemen, grouping, light
and shade, poetry and sentiment, are now deemed indispensable
to attempts of this nature." While the case of the Prophet does
not have the horror of the allegedly cannibalistic Fritz Haar-
mann, the unleashed blood and violence of the Borden home, or
the wholesale impact of Landru, it is a nice period piece with
neat detail work. There is grouping in the small band of hysterics,
scrambling to save their eternal souls against the solid, industrial
background of the nineteenth century. There is light and shade
in the holiness that was preached and the manner in which it was
perverted, and there is poetry of a sort in the "matched spirits"
and communal life. There is Mathews, who had the same
majestic, monotonal belief in his Right as the prophets of Biblical
times, combined with the methods and soul of a confidence man.

After Mathews was released from jail, he wandered West, but
the ghosts of the lunatic Mr. Mills, the disgraced Folgers, and
the hypothetically murdered Pierson hovered around him, giving
off an unhealthy odor of theft, fraud, illicit sex, and murder. His
claims to sainthood and his teachings were never again received
with any enthusiasm, and the rest of his life must have been a
more effective punishment than the most legal of scaffolds.

There is only one further portrait of Robert Mathews before
he drops into obscurity. He visited Joseph Smith, the father of
Mormonism. "The gilt clasp was a little tarnished, the green
frock coat a little frayed," says one biographer, but since Elizabeth Pierson had only succeeded in regaining seven thousand of
the eighty thousand dollars her father had turned over to the
Prophet, this seedy indication is either an inspired bit of poetic
license or an indication that the formerly immaculate Matthias
had let himself go. Smith talked with Mathews all night, saying

later that the man had "a brilliant intellect but a mind full of darkness." Before his death in 1837, Robert Mathews had become the saddest and most familiar of spectacles—a prophet without honor in his own country.

VIII

Confession of a Humanitarian

THE STATE OF CONNECTICUT CLAIMS the honor of the first law school, the first school for girls, and the first agricultural experiment station in the United States. It does not claim the honor of producing the first American Lucrezia Borgia with the same alacrity. Perhaps if the "state of steady habits" knew that one of its most colorful residents was essentially a humanitarian rather than a murderess, it would acknowledge her with more civic pride.

Mercy killings always have a guarantee of several columns of print in the newspapers and are almost as incendiary as politics or religion conversationwise. The intention is good, even if the actual deed is not condoned. And there have been many murderers who, while their acts do not come under the strict heading of mercy killing, have committed homicide with the most humane motives. John Blymeyer of York, Pennsylvania, killed a man, whom he believed had put a hex on him. It was, his attorneys argued heatedly, when they were not busy pleading insanity, a humanitarian act to eliminate a hex-prone character. Dr. Crippen's motive was kindly and considerate. His mistress, Ethel Le Neve, found her position as "unofficial" wife unendurable and

156

injurious to her health, so Dr. Crippen obligingly gave his current wife a concrete shroud in the basement of their house. Guiteau had the most altruistic of motives when he took a pot shot at President Garfield. He was going to save and unite the Republican party.

Perhaps one of the most interesting killers in this classification, which might be titled Humanitarians Gone Wrong, is Lydia Sherman. Her intentions were blameless, but her methods were questioned by the courts of the land. Lydia Danbury was born in Burlington, New Jersey, although Derby, Connecticut, was the scene of her more mature activities and good deeds. Her mother died when she was a year old, and her father was a butcher. Perhaps Lydia inherited some of her father's abilities, refined down to a more feminine and subtle level. After her father's remarriage, Lydia found her new step-mother uncongenial and moved to the home of an aunt in New Brunswick. There she met Edward Struck, a coachman for a wealthy New Yorker, and in 1846 they were married. Lydia was a tall, dark, and attractive seventeen, and she gazed at her new husband with flattering adoration in her eyes. Life in New Brunswick hadn't been very exciting, and as Lydia looked at Mr. Struck, who had promised her the bliss of honorable love and the bright lights of New York City, it would be hard to say which of these assets made her eyes glow more brilliantly.

The young couple moved to New York, and the fruits of honorable love turned out to be six children in seven years. But the bright lights were elusive. Lydia was urging her husband to "get on a bit." To please his wife, Edward Struck became a police officer in the upper wards of New York, and from 1857 until 1863 the family lived on One Hundred Twenty-fifth Street. Edward acquitted himself creditably as the long arm of the law, and Lydia was the perfect wife and mother. Struck's career on the police force ended obscurely. At a barroom brawl on his beat,

Struck was accused of cowardice for not arresting one of the active participants, who carried a pistol. His own account was different. Struck said he was several blocks away from the barroom, that a stage driver notified him of the fracas down the street, but when he arrived the man with the pistol had escaped.

The One Hundred Twenty-fifth Street section of Manhattan was not noted for its spotless politics in 1863, and it is probable that Struck, who was spoken of as an honest, hard-working man, had stumbled upon a little knowledge of local corruption which his superiors feared might become a dangerous thing. His actions for the remainder of the short time he had to live were those of an innocent man, misunderstood and bitter. Police Chief Hart called at the One Hundred Twenty-fifth Street apartment, but Edward refused to speak, look at, or have anything to do with his former superior officer. Captain Hart, on the other hand, made a most unethical suggestion to Mrs. Struck, and a rather unfounded one, from the meager evidence. He told Lydia that her husband was out of his mind and advised the anxious wife to send him to an insane asylum.

Edward became progressively more bitter about his lost job and prestige. One night he became so bitter, Lydia claimed in her confession, that she was forced to call a police sergeant, who lived in the apartment below, to restore peace. Now, if no one else learned a lesson from the career of Lydia Sherman, the police sergeant, when he was reading his morning paper eight years later, probably took a firm vow never again to suggest anything to a literal-minded woman. But that night, after Mr. Struck had been pacified, the sergeant called Lydia into the kitchen and advised her to "put Struck out of the way," since he was "no good to himself or anybody else." The next day Lydia purchased ten cents worth of arsenic, mixed it in a bowl of oatmeal, and the misunderstood Struck had painfully and permanently vacated this vale of tears by eight o'clock the following morning, May 26,

1864. The police force of New York City had exerted a malignant influence on the departed Edward.

A doctor was called in but he was unable to diagnose the cause of death. Neighbors uncharitably remarked that the symptoms were those of poison, but Lydia flashed her dark eyes at the doctor, told him that her husband had taken the wrong medicine, and the doctor, under the influence of the dark eyes, which must have been completely demoralizing, gave the cause of death as "consumption."

With the death of her husband, Lydia found herself an attractive widow with six children. But six children have a way of detracting from the prettiest widow's allure. So for the next two years she began replanning her life. Lydia kept the family together by working as a nurse and a seamstress, finally finding permanent employment in a sewing-machine factory on Canal Street. And within these two years all of her children died. No one knew what had happened to the rosy, healthy Struck brood —except that they all died suddenly.

It is here that Lydia, the humanitarian, begins to emerge, according to her own confession. In July, Lydia was considering her four-year-old son, Edward, and her younger daughter. She decided that the children would "be better off if they were out of the way." This was no life for them : A poor, widowed mother, no father to guide them, no opportunities in life. Why not give them a well-directed, if slightly premature, push to their Heavenly Father? Lydia finally "made up her mind" on the fifth of July. She went to the kitchen, mixed up another batch of her potent oatmeal, and "they survived only a short time," reports the efficient mother. The diagnosis of the cause of the two children's deaths was remittent fever and bronchitis, respectively.

In March, 1866, Anna, the twelve-year-old daughter, was ill from natural causes. "She made me downhearted and discouraged," said the doting mother. "She was the happiest child

I ever saw." So to put the child in a state of eternal well-being, Lydia added a little arsenic to her medicine, and Anna died the next day. The cause of death was written on the record as typhoid fever. Either the medical profession on the Eastern seaboard was alarmingly careless or Lydia's lively eyes were sabotaging the Hippocratic oath.

At the time of Anna's death, Lydia was working for Dr. L. Rodenstein, who attended the small girl and wrote typhoid fever on the death certificate. The pamphlet press of the seventies, an ancestor of the present day tabloid, later called Lydia the "Modern Borgia" and even hinted that this unspeakable woman had not stopped putting arsenic in medicine on the death of her daughter. They intimated that perhaps the patients of Dr. Rodenstein had been similarly favored. What the pamphleteers overlooked was that Lydia never killed senselessly or impersonally. There was always a kind, good motive lurking in the background whenever her dainty hands reached for the arsenic packet.

The next casualty was Lydia Struck, the younger, who was eighteen. In her confession, the elder Lydia claims that this daughter died a natural death in May, 1866, but in August Lydia again took the Godly arbitration of life and death into her hands. It was so easy to make her children well and happy when they were sick by administering a permanent cure. Her eldest son was sick with painter's colic and did not improve. So, explains the easily depressed mother, "I became discouraged and mixed some arsenic in his tea."

In the meantime, Lydia had made the acquaintance of a Mr. Curtis, who engaged her to live with his elderly mother at Stratford, about nine miles from New York. Her pay was eight dollars a month, which was a rather handsome wage. Her children were well cared for by a higher Power, and, when Lydia met Mr. Hurlburt of Huntington, it seemed that fortune was giving a benign nod in her direction. Mr. Hurlburt was a solid citizen of

Huntington. He lived quietly as a farmer and fisherman, but he was worthy of Lydia's attention, being the possessor of an attractive amount of real estate, an estimated ten thousand dollars in cash, and a frail constitution.

It was not a romantic match. Mr. Hurlburt was known in his neighborhood as "Old Hurlburt" and was obviously not in the first flush of ardent youth. However, Lydia and her mature suitor were married on November 22, 1868. Lydia professed a great fondness for her husband and met him at the door every evening with an affectionate kiss, and "Old Hurlburt" was pleased with his acquisition of the trim, dashing, cuddlesome widow. The people of the town gave a collective nod of approval and considered the union one of those autumnal romances that so often make the most bicker-free and enduring marriages. Lydia and Hurlburt made a pretty picture of marital bliss, but there were several ominous portents. Hurlburt made a will in which he deeded everything in the way of worldly possessions to his wife, and Lydia remarked solicitously that her husband was subject to "dizzy spells."

In the spring of 1870, Mr. Church, the village physician, was summoned to the home of the elderly honeymooner. "Old Hurlburt" was suffering from pains in his head and stomach and an intense burning, as if from a high fever. Consulting physicians were called in, but before they could agree on a diagnosis, Hurlburt was dead. And before the doctors could argue any more about the cause of death, the widow had hastily consigned her husband's body to the dust from whence it came.

In Lydia's disarming future confession, she firmly denied that she "gave Hurlburt anything" and stated that he frequently ate strange combinations of food which gave him acute indigestion. Now, it would be charitable to give Lydia the benefit of the doubt, but one natural death among so many assisted demises is suspect. Moreover, when her confession was written, there was a warrant against her for Hulburt's murder and a medical report which swore to the presence of arsenic in the stomach of the corpse. It was a politic denial, and it lends variety to Lydia's confession, but although indigestion has been blamed for many things, including unfavorable drama reviews and spots in the front of the eyes, it has never been claimed before or since that the scourge of the twentieth-century businessman could leave seven or eight grains of arsenic in the stomach.

Lydia now found herself in the pleasant position of a widow with pecuniary as well as personal attractions. She had married the first time to escape the monotony of New Brunswick and the second time to escape the monotony of poverty. Now she could marry for fun.

During her brief and profitable career as Mrs. Hurlburt, Lydia had become slightly acquainted with a young Birmingham mechanic, Nelson Sherman. He was the type of man who has an ever-fresh appeal for women such as Lydia. That methodical, practical women are attracted to large, irresponsible, happy-go-lucky men is one of the working hypothoses of the law of opposites. Sherman was a genial widower with four children, a real *joie de vivre* that manifested itself in an occasional spree, and no sense of responsibility. His big, handsome body and his booming devil-may-care personality appealed to the woman in Lydia, and his self-admitted little weakness in the matter of alcohol appealed to her maternal instincts—a dangerous appeal.

Lydia's confession is the only source of information on this transitional period in her career. After Hurlburt's death, Lydia said, Sherman came to her home in Derby, Connecticut, and asked if she would work for him as a housekeeper and nurse. He said his daughter and his mother-in-law, Mrs. Jones, were continually fighting, and that, if Lydia would take the job, he could ask the old lady to leave. Now, why a fairly prosperous mechanic would ask a widow with, by New England standards, an impressive inheritance to be his housekeeper is one of the many ciphers of Lydia Sherman's story, for, in spite of her apparently frank and gruesomely detailed confession, there are important points that remain as enigmatic as the writer. It sounds, under the modest evasion of Lydia's period prose, as if Mr. Sherman had made the most reprehensible of all suggestions—a proposition. Sherman and Lydia may have had an understanding before her husband's death or she may have become infatuated with the Birmingham mechanic while shopping around for the third "Mr. Lydia." She told the hopeful suitor, with none of the symptoms of outraged, crinoline-bedecked womanhood, that she would "think it over." Thus indicating to Mr. Sherman that, while she did not find the ambiguous role of "housekeeper" attractive, if he would add a few legal trimmings, she might find both Mr. Sherman and the duties of his household agreeable. From his casual approach, Sherman does not seem to have been interested in Lydia's money, but he was a man who appreciated a trim ankle and dark eyes. So he took the hint, and within two weeks he returned with a proposal of marriage.

Sherman did make one stipulation in his proposal which shows a certain amount of foresight. He said he thought they should get to know each other better, so Lydia, with his help, rented her house, and moved into Sherman's home. Unfortunately for Sherman he was slightly myopic in the matter of foresight and the "getting acquainted" period didn't last long enough. To be fair to Lydia, however, she did practice great restraint, and Sherman's four children were all alive and in perfect health at the nuptials which took place in September, 1870, at the home of Mr. Sherman's sister in Bridgewater.

The newlyweds returned to the Sherman house in Birmingham, and in two months history began repeating itself. Frank, Sherman's seven months old baby became ill, and, following the familiar pattern, "died shortly." Mrs. Jones, her job as the baby's nurse ended, moved her belongings, and the honeymooners were left in privacy with their bereavement. In December of the same year, Addie, the fourteen-year-old Sherman daughter, became ill. Several doctors were called in. They diagnosed it as a light case of typhoid fever. But Addie suddenly had a relapse and with it the symptoms which were as familiar as the pattern : pains in the head and stomach and an intense burning fever. She died on the thirty-first of December, 1870.

In the meantime, Mr. and Mrs. Sherman had adopted a way of life that is not usually advocated by brides and grooms. Mr. Sherman, perhaps sensing that all was not right, slept upstairs with his four-year-old son Nattie, and Mrs. Sherman was sleeping downstairs in a complete, if unappreciated state of chastity. Nelson Sherman was tempting a malignant fate. When Lydia didn't have what she wanted, she usually did something about it with an undeviating regularity. She had married Sherman for one reason, his sweeping virility; and Nelson was not living up to his potentialities. When a man arouses a twice-married, mature woman and then leaves her in an involuntary state of suspended animation, it is always dangerous; with Lydia Sherman it was suicidal.

On the eleventh of May, 1871, Mr. Sherman announced to his wife "in name only" that he was going to New Haven with friends for a party. It turned out to be a rather spirited party in both a literal and a figurative sense. The other members of the celebration made a pale and shaky entrance into Birmingham the next morning, but Sherman stayed in New Haven for a week.

When his father failed to return, seventeen-year-old Nelson, Jr., was worried and, after much persuasion, coaxed two dollars and fifty cents from a huffy Lydia as searching funds. The boy went to New Haven, and while one contemporary account says that the boy found his father in a "den with low people," another version maintains that Nelson, Jr., found his father walking unconcernedly down a main street of the town with nothing more depraved on his mind than a thirst for Bromo-Seltzer. They returned to Birmingham together, and, although the elder Sherman was not violently ill, he was unable to work for several days. He showed the usual quivering signs of a gargantuan hang-over. When he finally returned to his job, Sherman was depressed and refused to go home for his meals. It is possible that he had been doing some thinking as well as drinking while he sojourned in New Haven. Or perhaps his motive was less serious. Wives the world over have a universally unsympathetic attitude toward a husband with a hang-over and have been known to become screechingly voluble in their disapproval.

On Sunday night Lydia and Sherman indulged in a popular domestic pastime. They had a fight. Lydia brought up the delicate subject of her unwelcome celibacy and chided her husband for not doing his duty in the marital sense of the word. Sherman answered ominously that he knew too much about her and should "soon begin to talk out to her." He also told her that the neighbors knew as much as he did and that there would soon be trouble. But Lydia still greeted Sherman with a necessarily chaste kiss when he came home from work and that was a bad sign.

On May twelfth, Sherman consented to come home for dinner. He drank some brandy, mixed by his wife with loving and lethal care, went into town for several hours and returned home with a bad headache. The rest of the familiar trio soon followed: stomach pains and an intense, burning fever. Lydia took care of Sherman, making all the potions and soothing drinks the doctors had ordered with her own hands. On Friday, Nelson Sherman was dead. Dr. Beardsley and Dr. Kinney who had attended the sick man decided that the number of deaths in the Sherman house was diametrically opposed to the law of averages. Lydia, with the supreme confidence of so many murderers, gave the doctors permission to hold a post-mortem, and their findings justified their suspicions. They sent one-third of the liver to Professor Barker in New Haven for analysis, and in three weeks the report came back. There was enough arsenic in Mr. Sherman's entrails to transport three healthy men to a "better world." A warrant was issued for Lydia's arrest and placed in the hands of Deputy Sheriff Henry A. Blakeman for execution at the proper time.

While the authorities gathered more and more evidence and Professor Barker tested Mr. Sherman's liver, Lydia became restive. Looks from her neighbors, hints dropped on the street, and information from her neighbor, Mrs. Hubbard, that her husband's remains were undergoing chemical tests led Lydia to the inescapable conclusion that Birmingham was no longer a safe place to further her career. So, she quietly moved to New Brunswick. There, although she was unaware of it, she was under constant surveillance while the police and District Attorney Herbert waited to hear from Professor Barker and assemble enough evidence to justify an arrest.

The evidence was not slow in accumulating. Repeated successes in her chosen field had bred the familiarity of contempt in Lydia. After she left Birmingham, friends of the Sherman family had the children's bodies exhumed, and unmistakable signs of poison were found. The police found that Lydia had bought poison at the neighborhood pharmacy, and on the seventh of June Deputy Sheriff Blakeman decided to put the warrant into action. He and Detective Mitchell went to New Brunswick and communicated with Chief of Police Oliver, making all the necessary arrangements for taking Lydia back to Connecticut. They discovered that she had gone to New York on a shopping trip, but when she returned on the 10:50 train, Lydia found a most persuasive reception committee waiting for her at the depot. Blakeman and Mitchell took her to New Haven, where she was formally charged with murder on the person of Nelson Sherman and ordered to await trial.

Ugly suspicions had been revived in the case of "Old Hurl-burt's" death, and an exhumation was ordered. Poison was found in his stomach, and Lydia was in the uncomfortable position of being what is idiomatically termed a two-time loser. If she should be acquitted for Sherman's murder, there was a warrant against her from Fairfield Country charging her with the murder of her second husband. There was also a belated wave of sympathy and suspicion over the death of Mr. Struck and the six small Strucks. Lydia, in a warped sense, had cast her bread upon the waters, and now it was coming back in the form of a tidal wave.

Actually, the case against her for Sherman's murder was the weakest upon which she could have been tried. The motive, as Lydia explains it in her confession, seems altruistic but not very strong. The state would claim that Sherman was a worthless husband who had become a financial liability. But whether we accept Lydia's reason or the prosecution's reason for Sherman's death, her motive for poisoning Hurlburt was immeasurably stronger. It was the one murder of which she was suspected where the motive runs along established lines—money. And no claim was ever advanced by Lydia that she wanted to cure Hurlburt of his indigestion.

The trial opened in New Haven on April 16, 1872. The newspapers and pamphleteers were prolific in their output and prodigal with their adjectives, and a large crowd, craning to see the "Modern Borgia" and "The Unnatural Wife and Mother," strained the capacity of the small courtroom and proved the formidable power of the press. Judge Sanford was the presiding judge and with him was Justice Park of the Supreme Court, who associated with him in the trial because the law required the presence of a Supreme Court justice. E. K. Foster, State Prosecuting Attorney, with Colonel William B. Wooster and Colonel Torrance, handled the state's case, and George B.

Waterous and S. M. Gardner had the difficult job of saving Lydia's neck as the battery for the defense.

Lydia made her entrance looking very cheerful. Her appearance was very ladylike and very unlethal. She wore a black alpaca dress trimmed with silk velvet, a mixed black and white woolen shawl, black kid gloves, and a white straw bonnet trimmed with black velvet, a brown plume, and a thin lace veil. Lydia, with admirable subtlety, managed by her costume to convey the right amount of subdued elegance with just a hint of mourning about it. She was given permission to sit during the reading of the indictment, but she declined and stood calmly as the paper was read. Lydia very firmly pleaded not guilty.

At that moment there was a commotion at the door of the courtroom and Lydia's sister, Mrs. Nofey of New Brunswick, hurried down the aisle to the dock. Lydia smiled, and they kissed each other while tears flowed freely. Her brother, Joseph Danbury of New Brunswick and her brother-in-law joined Mrs. Nofey at the dock, kissed Lydia and presented a picture of family unity to the courtroom and the world.

Dr. Beardsley was the first witness called by the state. He told of receiving a call from the Sherman house on the ninth of May, 1871. When he arrived Lydia met him at the door and told him that Sherman was sick from the after effects of a spree. She said piteously that she tried to control her husband in vain and added rather peevishly that Sherman had spent between thirteen and fourteen hundred dollars of her money. Dr. Beardsley said that when he returned the next evening to see the patient he found that the soothing drinks and brandy slings he had prescribed were producing the opposite effect. Sherman's condition was agitated. Both Mr. and Mrs. Sherman assured the doctor that nothing had been administered but the prescribed drinks. Mr. Sherman, at least, was in the satisfying position of telling the truth. Dr. Beardsley found symptoms of arsenical poisoning, and even the mixed-up Sherman knew that this was no ordinary hang-over and that he was dying. The doctor described Sherman as a strong man of forty-five, who went on occasional sprees interspersed by months of abstinence.

Nelson Sherman was accustomed to refer to his hang-overs as "dizzy spells" or "old turns." On cross-examination, Mr. Waterous wanted to know why the brain hadn't been examined at the post-mortem. The doctor replied that the condition of the stomach indicated poison and he and the other doctors did not think it necessary to make a further investigation at the time. Dr. Beardsley also managed to make the statements, much to the defense counsel's chagrin, that Mrs. Sherman had said she could nurse her husband without any aid and that a second dose of poison had been administered between his visits.

Mr. Waterous gave an early indication of the line the defense would take. He tried to coax the doctor into admitting that arsenic from colored candies, green wallpaper, or certain liquors could kill a person. But the doctor denied this and also denied that there was the slightest suggestion of a green tinge to the jar in which Sherman's stomach was placed for shipment to New Haven. The defense was out to prove that the arsenic could have come from any number of likely places other than Mrs. Sherman. Had the doctor, Mr. Waterous wanted to know, told the defendant that one more spree would end Sherman? Yes, admitted the doctor who evidently had his own brand of psychology, but he often told his drinking patients that to scare them.

Q. : Was Mrs. Sherman an attentive and devoted wife?

"As far as I could see she was," answered the doctor with guarded understatement. He evidently had mental reservations about wives whose husbands had arsenic in their stomachs.

The state next tried to introduce evidence on the other deaths, and the jury was excused while the state produced a witness who had seen Addie die of the same symptoms as her father and a deposition saying that there was arsenic in Hurlburt's stomach. The defense objected to the admission of such evidence on the grounds that it was an "unjust attempt by the prosecution to prejudice the judge and the jury by proving Mrs. Sherman a dangerous woman hence capable of the crime for which she is charged." The judge overruled the request, but as the trial proceeded, the prosecution didn't need the admission of this evidence to prove that "Mrs. Sherman was a dangerous woman."

The trial resumed the next day, and the prisoner entered the courtroom flanked by her brother, sister, and brother-in-law. Another relation was present, too, but his interest was more academic. He was John Struck, a son of the ill-treated and deceased Mr. Struck by a former marriage. He took a seat quietly and watched Lydia closely.

Nelson Sherman, Jr., was the first witness. The crowd was morbidly interested in the young man. He had the glamor and automatic heroism of an escaped victim. He told the story of searching for his father in New Haven. He said his father was perfectly sober but shaky on the day of his return. He had noticed nothing unusual in his father's manner, and Monday the elder Sherman returned to work. Nelson saw his father again at 7.30 in the evening. He was watching an outdoor auction. When young Nelson came home that evening, Lydia said that his father had been sick. He testified that Lydia had had complete charge of the sick man. Under cross-examination, Nelson admitted that he had known of his father's and step-mother's odd sleeping arrangements and that he had never seen his father have spasms such as he had during his last illness, even in his "old turns."

Dr. Kinney who had been called in Thursday evening in the absence of Dr. Beardsley at the request of Mr. Sherman's mother testified that the symptoms were those of irritant poisoning. He had asked Mrs. Sherman about her husband's health, and she answered that he had been on a debauch and she expected it would kill him. On cross-examination, he reiterated his belief that the symptoms in the sick man were those of a powerful irritant poison.

Q. : What symptoms did you observe that you had not seen in other cases?

A. : It was not one symptom but the combination of symptoms.

Waterous : I don't want you to argue the case; I don't inquire about the combination of symptoms.

Kinney : Excuse me, sir. I did not know I was arguing the case.

After this verbal clash, Kinney said that he had never had an arsenic case before but that from his reading and studying of medicine he was sure that Sherman had the symptoms of arsenic poisoning.

Nelson Sherman's mother was the next witness to be called. She was a spry old lady with opinions of her own which she meant to express come hell, high water, or legal technicalities. She testified that she had been in her son's house twice since his remarriage, for Addie's funeral and her son's last illness. At Addie's funeral, Lydia had told Mrs. Sherman she would leave Nelson if things didn't change, as she had money and friends. On the second visit, Mrs. Sherman testified, the sick man's relations with his wife had seemed friendly, but she thought that one particular cup of tea brewed by Lydia had had a strange effect on her son.

Q. : What was the effect of the tea?

A. : He put his hand on his stomach and said, "Oh my God," and fainted away.

Lydia mixed a very strong brand of tea.

Mrs. Sherman said that her son asked her, "Mother, hand me my wallet from my pants pocket."

"I know he didn't want Lydia to know about it, because he

asked where she was. I told him she was in the basement and gave him his wallet."

The defense objected to Mrs. Sherman's purely personal opinion, but she was allowed to continue and said that Lydia had come into the room and Nelson had shoved the wallet under his pillow. Later Nelson gave his mother the wallet and asked her to give the money to his younger son if he died. The day following Nelson's death, Lydia asked Mrs. Sherman what she had done with the money Nelson had given her. Mrs. Sherman said that she had given it to Nattie at Sherman's request. Lydia remarked that this was strange since her husband had said she should have it. Lydia then told the boy that she was short of money and he surrendered his inheritance to her. But Lydia was feeling magnanimous. She gave him five dollars out of the one hundred five dollars for himself. The bereaved widow also confided to Mrs. Sherman: "I had about made up my mind to leave Nelson but as things have turned out I am very glad I did not."

As things turned out, Lydia might have saved herself and the State of Connecticut time and expense by following her first inclination.

Mrs. Sherman rather grudgingly admitted to Mr. Waterous that Nelson had committed his son to Lydia's care and that at the time he had seemed lucid. She also admitted with equal reluctance that when she had received the telegram about Nelson's illness, she had said to her other son with whom she was living in Brooklyn, "I know that Nelson will not get well, for he has had several of these spells and one of them will take him off." Mrs. Sherman had also talked with the family physician.

George Peck, a Birmingham druggist, said that he sold Mrs. Sherman poison for rats. He couldn't fix the exact date but he knew it was a warm, spring day in 1871.

The next day Prof. George Barker was called as the first

witness. He gave a graphic and detailed description of his examination of Sherman's stomach and liver and described the Fresenuis, Babo, Marsh and Reinsch tests by which he detected five grains of arsenic in the liver. The defense tried to implicate Dr. Kinney's bismuth prescription as a possible poison and a possible cause of death, but Professor Parker said that the bismuth in Sherman's stomach was pure and that arsenic was definitely the cause of death. Under cross-examination, he admitted that he had never seen a case of arsenic poisoning but from information received from Dr. Beardsley he had expected to find traces of some metallic poison, but not arsenic in particular. Then Mr. Waterous introduced a book which claimed to list two cases where people had died of bismuth dosage. Mr. Waterous asked if he believed it, and Professor Barker countered by asking to see the book. He looked at the book for several minutes and then answered decisively, "I do not believe it; it has been contradicted." He was then questioned about arsenic in beverages.

"I do not know about certain coloring matter, but I have heard that in beverages they can produce bad effect."

However, this scoring of a point by the defense was made less effective by Professor Barker's statement on redirect examination. He said that if the poison were taken before Friday—that is during the New Haven drinking bout—it would have acted before Monday.

William Ford, a Derby officer, then testified that he had met Sherman on Sunday afternoon and that he showed no signs of drinking.

On April 23 the trial resumed. The courtroom was filled with ladies, doctors, and ministers. By now, Lydia Sherman was public property, and so was the sobriquet bestowed upon her by the press: "The Modern Female Borgia." But in the middle of the excitement, still surrounded by her family, Lydia remained calm.

William S. Downes was the first witness of the day. He said

that he had worked with Sherman for fifteen years. Yes, all the
men at the factory knew about Sherman's "old turns," but he
was well liked and they weren't held against him. Sherman had
seemed well enough when he came back to work on Monday.
Several of the men had chipped in and bought about two quarts
of beer that day, but all five drank from the same pitcher, and
no one else was sick.

George Sherman of Brooklyn, Nelson Sherman's brother. was
the next witness to take the stand, and during his testimony the
"Horror of the Century" lost its grand proportions and degen-
erated into a familiar spectacle, domestic bickering. George
Sherman had visited his brother's home several times after
Nelson's remarriage. He had noticed that his brother and his
new wife "did not live happily together." On his second visit,
Lydia told George with unladylike directness that she and Nelson
"did not live together at all." George said he had heard them
having words about the sleeping arrangements, and Nelson told
his passionate wife that if she didn't like it she could "take what
things she brought and go." She told George that the reason for
sleeping separately was that Nelson would not let Nattie sleep
away from him. A fine paternal sentiment but rather harsh on a
bride of less than a year.

Lydia had also told her brother-in-law that she knew Nelson
did not love or respect her and was ashamed to be seen on the
street with her. She hinted at divorce and the possibility of other
women in the life of her gregarious husband. She complained
that she had been warned by friends not to marry Sherman and
that she would not have married him except that she had already
loaned him money before their marriage and he represented a
financial investment. She complained that Nelson would not
speak to her except when it was absolutely necessary and that he
served the other members of the family at the table but would
not serve her. In fact, Mr. Sherman finished his testimony rather

wearily, "she complained a great deal about him." Considering Lydia, with her effective means of solving any unpleasantness, one of the biggest mysteries of the case is why the ungallant Mr. Sherman survived as long as he did. On cross-examination, Mr. Waterous asked George Sherman about an alleged conversation he had held with Mrs. Hubbard, a neighbor of the Shermans.

Q. : Did you not say that Mrs. Sherman was a "jewel of a woman?"

A. : Never (emphatically).

The "emphatically" is that of a perceptive court reporter.

Orrin Lathrop testified that he saw Sherman on Monday night between six and seven o'clock. Sherman was pale and said he felt sick to his stomach. He did not see Sherman again until he was called to fulfill one of the more macabre duties of friendship, that of keeping watch with Sherman's corpse.

Mrs. Mary Jones, the troublesome mother-in-law of Lydia's courtship days, was called to the stand. She said she had returned to the house for Addie's funeral after receiving a wire from Sherman. Mrs. Jones testified that Lydia and Nelson quarreled frequently and that after Addie's funeral Sherman asked her to stay for the winter. He was afraid, he told Mrs. Jones, that Nattie would "be sick like Addie." Just as Sherman extended the doom-tinged invitation, Lydia flew into the room and accused Sherman of talking behind her back. "She was very angry in her manner, more so than I ever saw a person," Mrs. Jones stated. Mrs. Jones also gave the case of the state an additional boost by remarking that she had never known Nelson Sherman to be sick from drinking after a night's sleep and strong coffee or tea. Mrs. Jones was the recipient of another tragic wire when Sherman died. She again went to the Sherman house to help with the funeral arrangements. Lydia mentioned that she thought she would take in gentleman boarders. It is interesting to speculate on just how many bachelors of New England were spared

Sherman's painful fate by the prompt action of Dr. Beardsley, Dr. Kinney, and the state of Connecticut. Lydia might have gone down in criminal history as the female Landru, if her promising career had not ended so prematurely. The picture of Lydia as a genteel landlady in elegant black, mixing "strong tea" for gentlemen boarders, has a gaslight piquancy about it, with a suggestion of *Arsenic and Old Lace*.

The prosecution, anticipating the next move of the defense, recalled Dr. Beardsley to testify that had all the bismuth Dr. Kinney prescribed been taken in one dose the effects still could not have been harmful. He also stated, to counteract the innuendos the defense had been injecting into cross-examination, that the effects of arsenic are usually felt within a half hour to three hours after its entrance into the system.

Q.: You do not know the subnitrate of bismuth was not supplanted by arsenic?

A.: I did not examine it. I could not have told by looking at it.

Q.: If in the place of five grains of bismuth there had been five grains of arsenic, it would have caused death, would it not?

A.: I think it would, but he had had the symptoms of death before he took that prescription (smiles).

On the sixth day of the trial, April 24, the defense opened its case, and, unexpectedly, it closed on the same day. Only five witnesses were called. Charles and Andrew Sherman, brothers of Nelson, who had a brass foundry in Brooklyn, were in the courtroom, and Lydia must have felt slightly haunted as Nelson's two brothers and her ex-stepson watched her quietly but intently from the audience. The defense said it would prove the deceased had started drinking and had come home Sunday night in a state of "extreme intoxication," that Lydia had cared for him during his last illness solicitously and was a kind and faithful wife, and that it was impossible to say how the arsenic got into Nelson

Sherman's stomach. Mr. Waterous discredited Professor Barker's testimony and then in a *non sequitur* added that the suicide theory would be introduced. He said that Lydia and Sherman were not cohabiting because of Nattie, but that Lydia did not resent the child. In fact, claimed Mr. Waterous, there was evidence that Lydia had given lavishly to Nattie in the past and that for the state to make such a nasty issue out of her taking the one hundred five dollars from the boy was too ungentlemanly.

The aims of the defense were admirable, but somehow the witnesses failed to live up to them. Lewis D. Hubbard, who had lived in the other part of the house occupied by the Shermans for twelve years, testified that he had met Lydia in the back yard on Tuesday morning with vomit in a pan which smelled faintly of beer. Wednesday night Sherman asked to see Hubbard. Sherman said to his neighbor, "I feel as if I were going to die." Mr. Hubbard offered to help Lydia watch the sick man during the night, but she said she could get along very well alone. And she could. Thursday night, Sherman requested that Hubbard stay with him, but he preferred to have his wife mix the brandy slings the doctors had ordered. Mr. Hubbard said he had been present when Sherman entrusted Nattie to Lydia's care. Lydia, said the good neighbor, had "manifested all feelings of wifely affection for her husband during his illness." The witness was unaware of any rats that had been poisoned, except some that he had poisoned himself with phosphorous, but Mr. Hubbard did admit that in the fall of 1870 Sherman had told him he couldn't stand the rats around the house and must get some poison. He had the impression that the poison mentioned was arsenic but couldn't be sure. Lydia was also interested in rats. She told Mr. Hubbard that she was poisoning rats on the Monday that Sherman was taken ill. Lydia, from her own standpoint, was about fifty years ahead of her time in the command of popular idiom.

Reverend Leonidas B. Baldwin, rector of the St. James Episcopal Church in Birmingham, testified that he had visited the Sherman house twice on Thursday and once on Friday morning immediately following Sherman's death. "Mrs. Sherman's conduct was becoming a wife under the circumstances." This was the undeviating refrain of the witnesses for the defense. Mrs. Sherman had behaved in the accepted manner of a good, affectionate wife. The defense seemed to imply that if Lydia had really poisoned her husband, she would have fought publicly with Sherman, called him a beast in front of witnesses, and overtly seasoned his brandy slings with rat poison.

Ichabod D. Allen, who had known Sherman for fifteen years, was called to prove the defense's contention that Sherman had been in a state of "extreme intoxication." He saw Sherman Sunday evening in Captain Healy's Saloon. They had three or four drinks and walked home together. Sherman, he said, was not intoxicated but not "stone cold sober," and he said people were trying to kill him and injure him. But, Allen informed the court, Sherman talked this way sometimes after he had been drinking. Mr. Allen, however, was the only witness the defense produced to prove their contention of Sherman's Sunday-night drunkeness, and Mr. Allen's story of a few ales at Captain Healy's Saloon didn't add up to "extreme intoxication." Also, Sherman had put in a full day's work on Monday before he became ill in the evening, and, in spite of Mr. Waterous's heavy skepticism, arsenic works much faster than that.

Mrs. Hubbard testified that she was in the Sherman's part of the house during Sherman's illness and that Lydia's conduct was "uniformly kind during this trying time." Mrs. Hubbard still maintained that George Sherman had made the much debated "jewel of a woman" remark to her. She was also Lydia's best booster, saying Lydia was too kind to Nattie, that she thought too much of Nelson for a divorce, and encouraged him to keep up his activities in a local temperance lodge. Mrs. Hubbard was evidently one of those admirable women who with a grim determination see only the bright side of things.

Philip Meyers had known Sherman for three or four years and saw him at John Miller's Saloon on Sunday. He did not think from his appearance that he had been drinking.

The defense closed a shaky case with a shaky summation, suggesting that death had been caused by accident or suicide. Lydia wept a little as her lawyer made glowing references to her wifely virtues, and the tears flowed freely when Mr. Gardener was dwelling on her efforts to interest Sherman in a temperance league and "lift him to a higher plane of manhood." Perhaps she was touched that Mr. Gardener understood her so well. She certainly had lifted Nelson Sherman singlehanded to a "higher plane." The fact that Sherman had entrusted one of his two surviving children to Lydia was the strongest point for the defense, and it was utilized fully.

Colonel Wooster summed up for the state. He remarked with acumen that the only thing both sides seemed to agree on was that Sherman was dead. He pointed out that, while the defense had hinted at suicide and accident, had refuted the state's medical testimony and intimated switched stomachs, bismuth poisoning, colored candy, and green wallpaper as the cause of arsenic in Sherman's stomach, that no positive testimony had been offered for the defendant, not even that Sherman had been intoxicated on Sunday night.

Mr. Foster then gave a scholarly dissertation of what it would take to convict. The jury must be satisfied that Sherman had died; that he had died of poison; that the poison had been administered by his wife and with felonious intent. When a well man takes food from his wife, sickens, and dies, Mr. Foster pointed out, there is at least room for suspicion. Lydia, a contemporary reporter said, looked meditative during the state's

summing up. She was probably considering asking Mr. Foster to
have tea with her one day soon.

On Friday, April 26, the jury was charged. Judge Park made
no secret of his conviction of the prisoner's guilt but pointed out
to the jury with what must have been painful fairness that it was
possible to find the defendant guilty of murder in the second
degree, murder which indicates ill will but where murderous
intent is not established beyond a doubt. The state had asked for
a verdict of guilty in the first degree.

The jury was out fifty minutes and came back with a verdict
of guilty of murder in the second degree. Lydia pressed her hands
to her head for a minute and then began talking with friends
and relatives who had crowded around her. She was taken to an
open buggy and driven back to the county jail, where she
swooned, wept, and expressed great disappointment over the
verdict. However, she apparently recovered her native common
sense, and the following notice appeared in the *New York Times*
on January 11, 1873 :

"It will be remembered that this woman in a fit of remorse,
no doubt brought about by the gloom of her cell, not long since
restrained her counsel from making further attempts for a new
trial, declaring she was satisfied with the verdict already
obtained."

It was while Lydia was waiting to be sentenced that she wrote
and released her confession. Her crime and trial were worth
page-one space in the *New York Times,* but the notice of her
confession appeared on a back page under a column titled
"Minor Events." "The gloom of her cell" and "remorse" may
have prompted the confession, but the literary style is more
reminiscent of entries in a business ledger than the prose of a
remorseful murderess. The confession throws some light on the
happenings in the Sherman household, but it makes bigger
mysteries of other things. In her confession Lydia says that after

she and her third husband had been married two months, Sherman said he wished the baby would die so that the old woman (Mrs. Jones) would not have an excuse to stay in the house. Sherman, like the police sergeant in New York, didn't realize that Lydia was so highly susceptible to suggestion. "I was full of trouble after he told me this," says Lydia. But again her sense of wifely duty triumphed over minor scruples. Mrs. Jones had bought arsenic for the rats, so with a terse economy of words, Lydia goes on "I put some in the baby's milk."

When Mr. Sherman "took to drink" Lydia claims she supported the family for six months, but it is her word against an abundance of evidence that showed Sherman to be a steady worker, except for brief and infrequent lapses. While Addie was legitimately sick, Mr. and Mrs. Sherman had a quarrel over Mr. Sherman's very human little frailty of purloining the bulk of Addie's medicinal brandy. "That made me so mad I decided to do as I had done before." Knowing that Addie was Sherman's favorite child, she dropped a little arsenic in the girl's tea "to even the score." But Lydia reaches her greatest heights in both literary and humanitarian talents when she explains why she poisoned Nelson. "When he returned home Monday night, I put arsenic in a pint of his brandy. I did not mean to kill him. I only wanted to make him sick of liquor."

Lydia's motives were unimpeachable. Who can blame a brave little woman for wanting to cure her children of sickness and to remove her assorted husbands from the disgrace and discomfort of insanity, indigestion, and drunkenness? Her motives were certainly more worthy than those of Mrs. Whiteling, who removed a husband and two small children for three hundred dollars worth of insurance, or Mrs. Lucretia Chapman, who fed her husband dainty but lethal bowls of soup while her handsome Latin lover stood by offering incentive and moral support. The confession of

Lydia Sherman is the confession of a humanitarian who strained the quality of mercy.

The confession, like so many other things in the nineteenth century, was an acceptable camouflage for unmentionable facts. Lydia couldn't face reality, and where other people in the same position have turned to fantasy, vegetarianism, and hypochondria, Lydia found escape in a pinch of white powder. There was no reason to be burdened with an uncongenial or unsatisfactory husband or the responsibility of children. When situations became unpleasant or uncomfortable, Lydia could eradicate them instead of facing them. And, combined with her subjective attitude toward problems, she paraphrased the most famous of Machiavelli's subtleties, along with many other murderers. The means is murder; and the justified end is gratification of a self.

Nelson Sherman's actions are still a mystery. He had some suspicions about Lydia, but his dependence on her during his illness and his act of entrusting Nattie to her dubious care are puzzling. But Nelson Sherman was a simple man with an eye for a pretty woman. He probably, during his last illness, had his suspicions blunted by Lydia's wifely nursing and solicitude. It is also highly possible that he didn't question the cause of his death, because he had taken Dr. Beardsley's warning seriously. And above all Nelson Sherman was more generously endowed with brawn than brain. He probably never knew what hit him.

Lydia Sherman was sentenced on the eleventh of January, 1873, to life imprisonment in the state prison at Wethersfield. The road to Wethersfield, for her, was paved with good intentions, and the hardest part of Lydia Sherman's punishment must have been that at Wethersfield, among so many suffering and unhappy women, arsenic was not an item available to prisoners.

IX

The Lady Is Not for Spurning

IN THE VIOLENT kilt-and-claymore era of fifteenth-century
Scotland, the peers of the realm objected to scholarly, muddle-
headed James III's indiscriminate elevation of lowborn favorites.
"Heed not. I will bell the cat," the Red Douglas assured his
fellow noblemen. He gave all the lowborn favorites a Highland
necktie party and earned for himself the Aesopian nickname of
Bell-the-Cat. In the more tranquil 1850's, Miss Madeleine
Hamilton Smith of Glasgow, who was rumored to be a remote
kissing cousin to the ducal Douglas family, carried on the family
tradition in her own modest way. Aside from wool, golf, and
whiskey, Madeleine is Scotland's most popular export. Perpetually enigmatic, eternally fascinating, she is the Mona Lisa of
crime.

Murder knows no age, but its motives and methods light up
the sky of specific cultures or periods. The methods vary from the
Renaissance glitter of the Borgia's poisoned rings to the glint-on-
metal highlights of our present-day guns. Motives change with
the times, too, ranging from business to politics to the personal.
The household pet of the Tudors, the Bill of Attainder, was
political murder to effect elimination with a nice, healthy cut

of swag for the crown. The lynx-eyed Countess of Somerset's culinary horrors were predicated by a world that revolved around court favor. The advent of insurance companies gave impetus to such men of gambling instincts as Dr. Palmer and Dr. Lamson. Jeanne Raies, a Swiss nurse who strained the quality of mercy around 1880, polished off twelve people for a small kickback from the local undertaker. Dr. Crippen eliminated his wife for the most personal reasons: she nagged him. The modern, Chicago-inspired school of slaughter is reflex conditioned by the prosaic need for protecting business interests. And for a fun thing, there's the aesthetic motive of Thomas Griffiths Wainewright, who slipped his sister-in-law a lethal dose because "her ankles were too thick."

Madeleine Smith was an old-fashioned girl, and her motive was typically Victorian—elimination for respectability. Since poison was enjoying a popular revival in the nineteenth century, many people uncharitably believe that she used this rather sneaky method to straighten out her personal life.

In the nineteenth century, Glasgow was the industrial center of Scotland's central Lowlands with shipyards, docks, and warehouses sprawling for twenty-one-miles on the man-dredged banks of the River Clyde. Within the industry-based hierarchy of Glasgow society, one of the most conspicuous and attractive component parts was Madeleine Smith, the daughter of a prosperous, established Glasgow architect. Madeleine had a well-formed figure, which in those days meant a formidable bust measurement and an infinitesimal waist, brunette good looks, and a fine contralto voice, and she was a popular, sought-after member of Glasgow's ruling middle-class society. It is true the younger women gave her calculating looks over the giddy tops of their painted fans and murmured the word "bold" behind their gold-stoppered scent bottles, while turbaned matrons, jealous of their own entries into the matrimonial sweepstakes, referred to

Madeleine in saccharine overtones as "just a wee bit too forward." But the low-cravated, pomaded gallants, with one eye on the card room and the other eye on the main chance, thought Madeleine dashing, fascinating, and heiress to a rather nice fortune.

Madeleine was an exceptionally competent young lady, too. At the age of nineteen, she had the care of an invalid mother, four younger brothers and sisters, and the job of running two full-scale establishments for her father—the Glasgow House, and their country home, Rowaleyn, on the Forth, near the Bridge of Allan. But the responsibility of running two large homes, the care of a vaporing, helpless mother, and the demands of a growing family were tiring Madeleine. The constant round of quadrilles, small-talk compliments, and digestively staggering midnight suppers of jellied meats and elaborate ices was beginning to pall. The capable, popular Miss Smith was heard to remark with pettish ennui, and perhaps an understandable trace of indigestion, that there was altogether too much entertaining and she was getting tired of having so many friends to look after.

In 1855, Madeleine Smith met Pierre Emile L'Angelier. L'Angelier was an operator. He had seen Miss Smith, and he knew a good thing when he saw it. L'Angelier confirmed the elegant swish of her skirts and the expensive tilt of her hat by roundabout inquiries. He discovered that she was a young lady of financial and physical attractions, so he arranged a casual, on-the-street meeting with the bonnie lassie through a mutual friend, Robert Baird. They went for walks together unchaperoned, and they began their historic correspondence which started with the correct "Dear Friend" and "Your Esteemed Servant" but ended up with the purely courtesy salutations of "Dear Husband" and "Your Loving Wife." Only a few of L'Angelier's letters survive, but he kept hers, a dangerous devotion as things turned out. Mr. Smith very understandably objected to this relationship and felt that L'Angelier was socially impossible and a fortune hunter, which, in view of L'Angelier's history and his irregular meeting with Madeleine, was not an unreasonable assumption.

L'Angelier had a spicy tang of the gutter about him, a nasty hint of sex appeal measured in pounds and shillings. Women were fair game to him, and he vultured after them. He had been brought up in Jersey, the largest and lushest of the Channel Islands, where his father was a market gardener. Either L'Angelier found no inspiration in fruits and vegetables or he was something of a black sheep. He had held a variety of undistinguished jobs in both France and Scotland and had only two claims to glory. He had served in the French National Guard during the Revolution of 1848, which ended in the Orleanist obituary. His motives were probably mixed and consisted of a melodramatic patriotism and the gilt lure of a uniform. His bedside manner was flawless, and he had a way with women.

L'Angelier liked to talk about both. When he and Madeleine met, he was twenty-nine and had drifted back to Scotland, where he was working for the seed firm of Messrs. Huggins. for the sum of princely two pounds a month. No wonder he was classed as "socially impossible." Such a salary wouldn't have kept a girl like Madeleine in corset covers. But L'Angelier was a good-looking, little bantam of a man. He had a Gallic swagger, and the exaggerated version he gave of his part in the Revolution gave him the glamour of faraway places. Madeleine fell fast and hard. L'Angelier was sex with a personal glint in his eye, different from the proper young men she knew, whose lives were circumscribed by the limits of propriety and property. L'Angelier was completely uninhibited; he had neither. Her friends had noticed that she showed signs of finding her life tedious, and to her the little French clerk represented an escape hatch. And like all escape mechanisms, the secretive atmosphere made these snatched, isolated meetings glow, and letters underlined and punctuated the world apart. This apartness and contrast colored gray routine, spiked the flatness of every day, and promoted an egg-in-the beer attitude toward life in general.

She wrote to L'Angelier : "Papa was very angry with me for walking with a gentleman unknown to him. I told him we had been introduced and saw no harm in it." Although Madeleine was nervous about her father's reaction and realized that L'Angelier was impossible socially, she continued to see him in any nook, cranny, or corner and to write voluminously. Because of the composite position she occupied as chatelaine and maiden, she had acquired a certain amount of independence, and a little independence, like a little knowledge, can be a dangerous thing.

However, Madeleine seems to have had occasional flashes of sanity. In April, 1855, she wrote L'Angelier from Rowaleyn and suggested their relationship should cease because of her parents' disapproval. In the summer of 1855, she again tried to break with L'Angelier because of the risk and parental disapproval. L'Angelier may have not been long on money, but he wasn't short on ideas. He saw the estimable Miss Smith with all her pecuniary and pyhsical charms slipping from his grasp and arranged for a middle-aged spinster friend, Miss Mary Perry, to entertain them both at her house. It was a constructive step in those days when it was extremely difficult for lovers to meet unobserved or uncriticized. Motels and drive-in movies had not yet materialized to smooth the rocky road of love. Miss Perry is a shadowy supporting player, but she and L'Angelier had one of those ambiguous relationships that lonely older women and enterprising young men form. The woman gives, the man takes, and friendship is an unhealthy euphemism, rather that a statement of fact. During this time, another nasty little trait of L'Angelier's manifested itself. He wrote to Madeleine, in one of his few surviving letters, begging her not to break off their relationship and adding ominously, "Think of what your father would say if I sent him your letters for perusal."

The meetings were arranged at Miss Perry's with the help of one of the Smith's maids, and from this time on Madeleine existed in a sensual torpor, taking the attitude that she had virtuously tried to break off the relationship and dismissing L'Angelier's playful attempt at blackmail as a lover's desperation. Now, she reveled in unleashed enjoyment. Her letters were tropical and determined. She talked of a secret marriage, an elopement, anything to be with her Emile, adding with seething abandon that she would be happy with him anywhere, obviously forgetting the inelastic qualities of ten shillings a week. But L'Angelier was a realist. He knew that Madeleine was completely dependent on her parents for her reticule money and held out for their consent or at least their conditional approval. He wanted Madeleine the heiress, as well as Madeleine the woman.

During the autumn and winter of 1855–56 Madeleine and L'Angelier seemed to have each other at emotional stalemate. She wanted marriage under any condition. He was holding out for some crack in the icy wall of disapproval that would make him acceptable to the Smith family. They corresponded, they met at Miss Perry's house, and sometimes, Madeleine was able to smuggle him into the Smith's house for passionate interludes. In April, 1856, the Smith family adjourned to Rowaleyn, but this time Madeleine made arrangements for L'Angelier to meet her not far from the Smith country home. By now Madeleine was obsessed with the idea of marrying Emile, and L'Angelier was worried by her reckless passion. He begged Madeleine to speak to her parents. But Madeleine was in a turmoil. She could not let her parents know how far she had gone or how much she had been seeing L'Angelier against their wishes. Madeleine, however, had a low boiling point, and, during their meetings in the heather, nature took its course to judge from Madeleine's letter written at five o'clock Wednesday morning : "Tell me pet, you were not angry for letting you do what you did. Was it very bad of me. We should, I suppose, have waited till we were married. I shall always remember that night." L'Angelier's answer was a little rigid for a French gallant : "I was not angry at you for allowing me, Mimi, but I am sad it happened. You had no resolution. We should indeed have waited till we were married. It was very bad indeed. I shall look with regret on that night."

It was a strange note in many ways. If this was the woman he wanted, he should have been delighted at her capitulation. Instead, he blames her for her weakness, says they should have waited until they were married, and yet has ignored her importunities to a secret marriage. It certainly shows that he was still holding out for marriage with parental approval, and there is also a hint that the romps in the heather will not continue until sanctioned by law. After all, Monsieur L'Angelier would hardly be acceptable to Smith *père* if there were indications that he was a father before he became a bridegroom.

Scotland must have enjoyed a long, mild summer in the year of 1856, because the Smith family was still bucolically entrenched at Rowaleyn in September, when a visitor arrived who unwittingly became part of an unpleasant eternal triangle. Mr. William Minnoch was a well-to-do Scottish businessman from Glasgow. He was thirty-five, slim, with finely-drawn features, and was generally considered a "good match." And Madeleine had had it. She had defied her parents' wishes, she had given her all, and L'Angelier still refused to marry her. In other words she was piqued, and she led Mr. Minnoch on, probably to show Emile just what she thought of the way he had acted. Her first glandular rapture had exhausted itself against L'Angelier's insistence on family approval of their marriage, and commonsense certainly would indicate a marriage to a prosperous Glasgow businessman rather than an unsanctioned union with a two-pound-a-month clerk. That tortuous pattern known as feminine psychology was shaping up. She had begged L'Angelier to marry her, but he had hesitated, and he was lost.

Love is a lonely hunter, and when the heart finds an object for its affections, there is often a sliding scale of emotions, a conflict in nuances. Two people may be locked in a passionate embrace, agreeing unanimously that they "are in love," but they may also be worlds apart semantically. When these differences in context crystallize, they may result in anything from a mild case of heartbreak to murder. The ego has its own set of defenses, and what cannot be rationalized must be eliminated. The result varies. There's the hen-pecked husband, the nagging wife, the gay divorcee, the social drinker who's gone over the hill, or the murderer. Love to L'Angelier was the only way he knew to financial security; love to Madeleine was the royal road to romance. They were both disillusioned hunters.

In November, 1856, the Smith family returned to Glasgow and took a house at Number 7, Blythswood Square, next door to Mr. Minnoch's residence. With a prosperous, socially acceptable son-in-law looming literally and figuratively on his doorstep, Mr. Smith took a belated stand and put his paternal foot down. Madeleine was forbidden to go roaming in the gloaming with L'Angelier. But Madeleine was still up to her backstairs tricks. She was seeing L'Angelier in all the old familiar places. Their correspondence continued on the old torrid note, but now Madeleine had an object in mind other than matrimony. As a woman scorned, she was doing a slow burn, but she wanted her letters back from L'Angelier before she loosed her extensive vocabulary on him. She was going to be a respectable matron one way or the other, and L'Angelier, who had once represented this goal, was now a threat to it. He had threatened to use them against her once. Now there was a two-way threat. He could send them to her father—or to Mr. Minnoch. But Madeleine was an incurable optimist. In January, 1857, Mr. Minnoch proposed, and Madeleine, with the proper amount of maidenly fluttering, accepted him. In February, she wrote to L'Angelier: "As there is a coolness on both sides, I think our engagement had better be broken." She also asked for the return of her picture and letters. Evidently the strain of being engaged to two men at the same time was too much even for the competent Madeleine. But L'Angelier had heard rumors of the engagement and seeing his heiress evaporating, he evidently wrote a rather nasty letter, because on February 12 Madeleine answered desperately, "Emile, write to no one, to papa or any other. On Wednesday night, I shall open my shutter and then you shall come to the area gate. When I ceased to love you, believe me, it was not to love another. I am free from all engagements at present. Emile, for God's sake, do not send my letters to papa."

But L'Angelier was a talkative soul. He was caddish enough to kiss and tell. "I shall never give up the letters," he told a friend, Tom Kennedy, adding with deadly accuracy, "She shall never marry another man as long as I live."

Madeleine's letter evidently did the job. Her sweet Emile told Miss Perry he was to see Madeleine on February 19. That night he left his lodgings, taking the pass key as he always did when he intended to be late. The next morning his landlady found him writhing on the floor. His diary for February 19 cryptically records, "Saw Mimi a few moments. Was very ill during the night." At 4 A.M. on Monday, February 23, L'Angelier rang for the landlady, who found him suffering from a similar attack. His diary records "Sunday 22 Feb. Saw Mimi in drawing room. Promised me French Bible. Taken very ill."

Madeleine sat in her stanchioned basement window on a side street leading off Blythswood Square, waiting for Emile to come to her, using the window sill as a post office for impassioned pleas, and offering him heady brews of hot chocolate through the

window. The beckoning fair one had finally come to the conclusion that an ounce of cocoa was worth a pound of lure.
L'Angelier told Miss Perry, "I can't think why I was so unwell
after getting coffee and chocolate from her." He told a friend,
Towers, that he thought he had been poisoned twice after taking
coffee and cocoa, probably using the word "poisoned" inter-
changeably with "unwell." However, Madeleine had a dietary
explanation. "You did look bad on Sunday night and Monday
morning. I think you get sick with walking home so late and the
long want of food, so the next time we meet I shall make you
eat a loaf of bread before you go out."

Prior to L'Angelier's first attack, Madeleine made an unsuccess-
ful attempt to buy some prussic acid. Madeleine wanted it for
her hands. On the day before the second attack, Madeleine
bought from druggist Murdock one ounce of arsenic "to send to
the gardener at the country house." As a brief aside on related
selling, on March 5, L'Angelier wrote demanding the truth about
Minnoch, and on the same day Madeleine purchased from druggist Currie a second ounce of arsenic to kill rats in Blythswood
Square. There was ample testimony at the trial that Blythswood
Square was as rat-free as a sinking ship.

On March 6, Madeleine, seeking fresh air, a breathing spell
from rats, or a respite from L'Angelier, went with her family and
Mr. Minnoch to the Bridge of Allan. The wedding was fixed
for June. On March 16, Madeleine wrote to Mr. Minnoch who
had returned to Glasgow :

My Dearest William :

It is but fair, after your kindness to me, that I should write
you a note. The day I part from friends I always feel sad. But
to part from one I love, as I do you, makes me feel truly sad
and dull. My only consolation is that we meet soon. Tomorrow
we shall be home. I do wish you were here today. We might
take a long walk. Our walk to Dumblanc I shall ever remember with pleasure. That walk fixed a day on which we are to

begin a new life—a life which I hope may be of happiness and long duration to both of us. My aim through life shall be to please you and study you. Dear William, I must conclude, as Mama is ready to go to Stirling. I do not go with the same pleasure as I did the last time. I hope you got to town safe, and hope you found your sisters well. Accept my warmest kindest love and ever believe me to be,

Yours with affcn., MADELEINE

I'Angelier was on sick leave in Edinburgh, but on the nineteenth of March he followed Madeleine to Rowaleyn. Madeleine had already returned to Glasgow on the seventeenth, which suggests a fallen-off correspondence. On March 18, Madeleine bought another ounce of arsenic from druggist Currie. "The first was so effective," she told the druggist succinctly. On Sunday, March 22, L'Angelier returned to his lodgings. A letter forwarded to him from Glasgow brought him home. He looked well and happy, and, after a hasty meal, hurried out saying he might be late.

At 2:30 A.M., L'Angelier's landlady was awakened by the ringing of the doorbell. She found L'Angelier doubled up on the front doorstep, writhing in agony. A doctor was summoned, and, although L'Angelier took a very dim view of his illness, saying, "I am far worse than the doctor thinks," he said nothing as to the cause of his illness nor did he indicate any suspicions. He remarked, "If I could only get a little sleep, I think I should be well." He asked to see Miss Perry but was dead when she arrived.

A letter was found in his pocket which read: "Why, my beloved, did you not come to me. Oh, beloved, are you ill. Come to me sweet one. I waited and waited for you but you came not. I shall wait again tomorrow night same hour and arrangement. Do come sweet love, my own dear love of a sweetheart. Come beloved, and clasp me to your heart. Come and we shall be happy. A kiss fond love. Adieu with tender embraces ever believe me to be your own ever dear fond Mimi." It was postmarked Glasgow, 21 March. It is interesting to compare Madeleine's letter of March 16 to Mr. Minnoch with the letter dated March 21 found in L'Angelier's pocket. Her veracity might be questioned but never her versatility.

L'Angelier's friends went into action. Among his effects they found the "Mimi" half of the correspondence. An examination of the body pointed to poison, and a post-mortem showed a confirming and staggering eighty-eight grains of arsenic.

Monsieur LeMean, the French Consul at Glasgow and a friend of L'Angelier's, visited Madeleine and warned her of the unkind things L'Angelier's friends were saying. He questioned her four or five different times about when she had last seen L'Angelier. "I swear to you," answered Madeleine, "Mr. LeMean, that I have not seen L'Angelier, not on that Sunday only, but not for three weeks." And that is the crux of the case. No one was able to prove otherwise. Monsieur LeMean asked Madeleine why she had continued her correspondence with L'Angelier when she was engaged to another, and she answered—perhaps the frankest, most truthful statement of Madeleine's on record—that she wanted to get back her letters.

But Madeleine's letters, the eighty-eight grains of arsenic found in L'Angelier's body, plus the unkind suspicions of the dead man's friends were causing rumbles. Mr. Minnoch took Madeleine to a dinner party, and whether she was received with out-of-focus glances, polar coolness, or barbed remark, the next day Madeleine took a steamer for Rowaleyn. Mr. Minnoch found her on the steamer and brought her back to Glasgow. Within a week, she was arrested for the murder of L'Angelier.

On June 30, Madeleine Smith's trial began in Edinburgh and was fondly and repetitiously referred to as the nine-day wonder. Such current topics as Franz Liszt's conquests, in both the concert hall and the boudoir, and the blazing Indian mutiny were temporarily forgotten while Auld Reekie collectively held its breath waiting to see whether a prosperous lady of genteel up- bringing could possibly "do a Lady Macbeth."

The prosecution was headed by Lord Advocate James Mon- crieff, a most formidable opponent. The famous Dean of Faculty John Inglis took upon himself the task of saving the fair Mad- eleine's skin, or more specifically her neck. The judge, Lord Justice-Clerk John Hope, was credited with unjudicial interest in a well-turned ankle, so Madeleine was advised to tilt her crinoline accordingly, and Madeleine was a girl who knew how to tilt her crinoline.

Inglis's opening statement is still widely quoted as a graphically gripping, powerful description of a capital trial. "Gentlemen, the charge against the prisoner is murder, and the punishment of murder is death; and that simple statement is sufficient to suggest to you the awful nature of the occasion which brings you and me face to face." His handling of the case was emotional tour de force, crawling with sentiments calculated to get through to the jury. "Was it possible," he thundered, "that a gentle loving girl passes at once into the savage grandeur of a Medea or the appall- ing wickedness of a Borgia? No gentlemen, such a thing is not possible." It is a forerunner of Governor Robinson's defense of Lizzie Borden, which reached a *non sequitur* peak when he roared to the New England Jury, "Does she look it?"

Madeleine may not have had the over-life-size proportions of a Medea or the epic swing of the Borgias, but she and her Caledo- nian predecessor, Lady Macbeth, did share a hardheaded Scots attribute of "getting down to business."

Moncrieff's approach was strong, restrained, and convincing. Most poison cases run true to an undeviating form legally and are as predictable as a bishop's gambit opening. The prosecution must prove that the deceased actually died of poison and then that the accused not only obtained poison but had the motive and

the opportunity to administer it. The defense has more latitude.
They usually try for a convincing case of suicide or accident. But
the prosecution had two giant stumbling blocks. There was no
proof of the meetings before each attack. There were, of course,
stories current that L'Angelier had been seen in the vicinity of
Blythswood Square at the crucial times, but no witness ever came
forward to take the oath and make the statement. The crown's
case gave a forensic wheeze when L'Angelier's scrappy diary,
oddly covering only the period February 11 to March 14 of the
fatal year, was ruled not admissible as evidence. The ruling on
L'Angelier's diary was made on the grounds that if a dead man's
diary is read in court and is permitted to prejudice the case
against an accused person, it would lead to undesirable con-
sequences in other cases; it certainly would have in Madeleine's.

Mary Perry was a surprising and damaging prosecution witness. Surprising because the role she had played as a romantic
liason officer between L'Angelier and Madeleine surrounded her
name with a faint bordello aroma and put her in a class where
"Madame" need not have been a courtesy title. She turned out
to be a lace-mitt-and-lavender type of little old maid, wearing
a neat black bonnet, spectacles, and a brown dress that aspired to
nothing higher than being a decent covering. Miss Perry testified
L'Angelier had told her he had had attacks after drinking hot
chocolate and coffee with Madeleine but had added, "If she were
to poison me, I would forgive her." A terse cross-examination
reduced this accusatory statement to one of those convertible
remarks where voice inflection and context can make it either a
joke or a serious charge.

Again the prosecution was balked by lack of concrete proof.
There was absolutely no proof that Madeleine had had arsenic in
her possession at the time of L'Angelier's first attack. But this
was checkmate, because the defense made several hollow attempts
to prove that L'Angelier was an arsenic eater but could never

prove his purchase of arsenic during the years he lived in Britain. The defense also tried the theory of suicide on the installment plan, but the spectacle of a man making two extremely unpleasant and painful attempts to take his life, reconsidering it for three weeks, and then trying it again just wouldn't stick. As to the arsenic Madeleine had purchased, the defense, faced with nonexistent rats, put forth the theory that Miss Smith was gilding the lily and had bought it for cosmetic use. The fact that the arsenic contained soot and indigo made it unsuitable as a beauty aid. Soot and indigo were absent in the post-mortemed remains of L'Angelier, but medical testimony made it clear that water would wash these ingredients out of the arsenic, which still left the matter of arsenic a fifty-fifty proposition.

The defense and the prosecution seemed to agree on one point, since they both referred to the rumor that L'Angelier was seen at 7 Blythswood Square the night of his death. The defense claimed that L'Angelier had fallen into bad company. So did the prosecution, but they named names. Some of Madeleine's letters were read in court and created a sensation. They were frankly sexual, and she called a spade a spade. She knew quite a few other terms of direct reference, too, and didn't hestitate to use them. But her contemporaries could not distinguish between genuine passion and calculated pornography. Edith Thompson ran into the same literary problem almost sixty-five years later.

L'Angelier had come rushing back from the Bridge of Allan when Madeleine's forwarded letter reached him, but Madeleine said he never kept the appointment. One of L'Angelier's last remarks before he died, "If I could only get a little sleep, I think I should be well," is certainly not the observation of a man who has the remotest suspicion that he is being systematically poisoned. The defense gave the jury meaning looks as it hammered home these points.

Mr. Minnoch, the long-suffering fiancé, deserves a word of praise. He testified with a businesslike brevity. A slight cough and frequent sips from a glass of water being the only signs of nervousness, Mr. Minnoch had declared his intention of still marrying Madeleine after her arrest. He contributed five hundred pounds to her defense fund, and he gave up his business to come to Edinburgh for the trial. His testimony added nothing, but his presence was a tremendous psychological boost for Madeleine. The letters to L'Angelier read at the trial must, however, have been too much even for Mr. Minnoch's iron composure. His relationship with Madeleine ended abruptly after the trial. Mr. Minnoch, at the end, must have taken a dim view of Madeleine's avowals of love and promises of the good life. L'Angelier had received vows of enduring love and letters predicting a rosy future from Madeleine, too, and look what happened to him.

Through all this Miss Madeleine Smith conducted herself with cool poise, a ladylike relish, and a suggestion from words dropped here and there by contemporary journalists that she was even enjoying herself. She wore an elegant, brown silk dress. A small, white straw bonnet trimmed with ribbons topped masses of brown hair, dark gray eyes, and strong features. Kid gloves, a handsome brooch, and a filigree smelling-salts bottle completed a picture of what the well-dressed young lady should wear in the dock, circa 1857. Even Godey's fashion illustrations couldn't have improved on it. Then, as now, the metamorphosis a trial effects on a person is nothing short of miraculous. Contemporaries describe her in the pretrial days as "pretty," "beautiful," "dashing," and "possessed of a fine contralto voice." But during the trial such phrases as "hawk-like aspect," "fox-like countenance," and "cunning and deceitful" kept cropping up. Madeleine would pass from her cab to the cell below the dock with the air of a belle entering a ballroom. She ascended the narrow staircase leading into the dock with a jaunty air, her veil pushed back, and a smile so perpetual and empty it was almost the beginning of a snarl. The same kind of a smile won an American co-worker of Miss Smith's the accolade of the "Tiger Woman." During the luncheon recess, she insisted on sitting in the dock—something like a current-day movie star, who has such an oversupply of ham that she doesn't know whether the klieg lights are on or off.

During the Lord Advocate's speech, Madeleine remained composed. She studied the reaction to the speech; she glanced at different faces in the gallery, but even Madeleine had her Achilles' heel. Whenever Moncrieff used the word "arsenic," she looked directly at the speaker. Prosecution appealed to intellect, although it was shaky on legal proof. Inglis was at his brilliant emotional best in one of the finest defense speeches ever heard in a Scots court. The judge, in summing up, had to admit that legal proof was somewhat lacking and to the cheers from the audience, the jury brought in a verdict of not proven, which meant maybe she did and maybe she didn't, but they couldn't be sure. The gate of the dock opened for the last time, and Madeleine Smith made a final sweeping exit to the congratulations of friends, relatives, and well-wishers. But one voice, one warm handclasp was missing. Dean of Faculty Inglis, remained seated at the defense table in the well of the court, his head sunk in his hands. He neither looked up nor smiled. Perhaps he was just tired. On any level of communication with Madeleine Smith, the male of the species found it strenuous going.

The public reaction was all for Mimi. The public opinion of the day was "if she didn't poison him, she ought to have done it," which seems a little hard on a young man who was just trying to make his way in the world. After the trial Madeleine returned to her family at Rowaleyn. After her return home, in a letter of thanks to the matron of the prison, Miss Aitken, she wrote : "I think I must have had several hundred letters, all from gentlemen, some offering me consolation and some their hearths and homes. My friend, Mr. Minnoch, I know nothing of. I have not seen him. I hear he has been ill, which I don't much care. If you ever see Mr. C. Combe [the foreman of the jury] tell him that the 'panel' was not at all pleased with the verdict. I was delighted with the loud cheer the Court gave."

Her letter to Mr. Rose, the prison chaplain, shows variety of literary style : "I found Mama far, far from well but I trust she will soon be convalescent. . . . I see a different feeling pervades our family circle already. I am so glad that they all view it as an affliction sent from God for past errors and crimes, and if this be the means of drawing family to the feet of Christ, I shall not grumble at the pain that sad event has cost me. I may live to hear the family exclaim that it was the most blessed day of their life—the day I was cast into prison. . . ." This shows a fine spirit of Christian fortitude, but seems a little hard on the rest of the Smith family.

In the year of the trial, Madeleine Smith married a surgeon, Tudor Hora, and emigrated with her husband to Australia. She lived quietly in Melbourne until her husband's death. The records do not say how he died, but if the good doctor did nothing to aggravate his combustible little wife and she kept her lace mitts out of his medicine bag, chances are he died of natural causes. She returned to England and married George Wardle on July 4, 1861. He was a talented artist and one of the first members of the social democratic club in London. Madeleine did not sip her pleasures sadly. She circulated in literary and social circles in London and was last heard from when she died at the age of ninety-two in America in 1928, where it was rumored Hollywood had approached her on a film treatment of her case.

Even with the verdict of not proven, the Mystery of Blythswood Square and the secret of the stanchioned windows remains unsolved. But there are clues in the people and their period. In looking backward, it is pointless to view the nineteenth century through the revealing microscope of the twentieth. It is important what these people of the nineteenth century thought and felt, how the world appeared to them. The living ideals of yesterday are often the embalmed memories of today, and applying present-day standards to the past makes period pieces out of people. The abysmal lack of medical knowledge made the nineteenth century a real Indian Summer for the poisoner. A digestive upset could mean anything from an injudicious pistachio ice to arsenic. Upset spleen, bilious attacks, palpitations were prevalent but were dosed instead of diagnosed. It is really distressing to think of the number of people buried with cipherlike death certificates reading "acute gastroenteritis" or "digestive inflammation." It is equally distress-ink to think of the almost idiotic trust with which the nineteenth-century poisonee guzzled or gobbled the lethal brew. The list is endless. Dr. Palmer's family and friends, Sarah Jane Robinson's beer-drinking victims, Mrs. Carew's unsuspecting husband, Lydia Sherman's victims who are legion, and Carlyle Harris's bride. In our own age of atomic skepticism, people aren't so trusting. They literally have to be hit over the head. But L'Angelier's singular lack of suspicion was part of the nineteenth-century poison pat-tern. He suspected his Mimi of a romantic reshuffling but never seriously voiced any suspicions that she might be a Caledonian Borgia. Even at the agonizing end, he knew he was sick, but his diary made complete *non sequiturs* of his meetings with Madeleine and his subsequent bouts of illness. So, Madeleine felt safe in spiking L'Angelier's hot chocolate. Although murder was no way to get the letters back, it would silence the person who threatened to use them. But her plans went "agley." L'Angelier liked to kiss and tell, so that many of his friends knew who the "Mimi" of the letters was, and Madeleine did not know of the existence of the diary.

The mystery of Blythswood Square is best approached through the character of Madeleine Smith and the period that framed her. It was a time when refined families displayed Tennyson's *Idylls of the King* on the parlor table and hid *Madame Bovary* in a back cupboard. In 1856, the first installment of Flaubert's novel was published, and both author and publisher were hauled into court for portions that were considered obscene. Fortunately, the book ended on a properly gory moral note, so the charges were dismissed. Madeleine Smith herself was something of an actress. There are some people who need an audience to give them existence. Left to themselves, they remain psychologically a shapeless blob until an outside stimulus comes along to imprint shape and shading on the mass. They lead a reflected existence, compulsively playing the role that is expected of them by other people. This thread of a jigsaw personality runs strong and clear through what might loosely be termed Madeleine's courtships, trial, and the aftermath. Depending upon whom she was with, Madeleine was a perfect daughter, a social butterfly, a romantic mistress, a virginal fiancée, the brave prisoner in the dock. At her trial she was described as entering the dock like a belle going to a ball. Madeleine was playing to the biggest audience she would ever have. Even her letters point up her necessity for play acting. Her letter to Miss Aitken was crisp and correct. She wrote to L'Angelier like a passionate nymph, but Mr. Minnoch's epistles were properly watered down. To Dr. Rose she breathed religious penitence. In other words, Madeleine always obliged by giving her current audience the kind of performance they wanted, and she was a girl who got a lot of mileage out of her roles. And L'Angelier had spurned her in her star part of the woman who gives up all for love. He was dangerously slow in picking up cues. L'Angelier's potential threat as a blackmailer would have destroyed Madeleine's make-believe world. If her father or Mr. Minnoch saw her letters to L'Angelier, two of her best roles would be destroyed—the dutiful daughter and the unsullied prospective wife. Throughout the known part of her life, Madeleine lived in a world of illusion, and the person who destroyed any facet, one role, was a threat. Such a conception, carried far enough, might even lead to a verdict of self defense in Madeleine's case. No wonder Hollywood was beckoning at the time of her death. It was twentieth-century make-believe calling to the nineteenth-century mistress of illusion.

..

The theories are endless. The verdic confirmed the shadow of a doubt. So, to the figurative skirling of the bagpipes and an ectoplasmic nod of approval from Bell-the-Cat Douglas, Madeleine Smith managed to "cheat the wuddy" and prove that while virtue may be its own reward, a cup of chocolate is sometimes more effective.

X

Come Live with Me and Be My Love

TODAY WHEN NEWS MAGAZINES have elevated terse descriptions to one of the lively arts, Maria Marten, who lived during the shank of the nineteenth century, might have been condensed into "affectionate, perpetually pregnant Maria." In her own day, however, Maria Marten rated more than a pithy, one-line description. Her name was as famous as that of "Bet" Canning, whose disappearing act and stolen stays had been toasted in London pubs and village inns almost seventy-five years before. The Red Barn attracted as many sensation seekers as Rudolph Valentino's funeral. In the strictly Victorian sense, Maria Marten was to nineteenth-century crime what Wagner was to atonal music, Cézanne to abstract art, or the Tennis Court Oath to the French Revolution. She was a sounding note of things to come, a sneak preview of future concepts.

Maria Marten started life in Polstead, a village of nine hundred inhabitants and 3,300 acres of fertile farming land in the rolling hills of Suffolk in 1801. Rural communities have always been relatively casual in their approach to the fundamentals, such as conception and birth. Horses will foal and pigs will litter, regardless of the current proprieties, and such niceties as pure love or the stork are apt to show cracks around the edges of their gentility. Rural courting, dances, and games are more direct in approach than their urban counterparts, while country thinking is much more shockproof in dealing with the facts of life. So, fortunately, or unfortunately, for Maria Marten, she was chronologically and geographically situated where her frequent forays into the realm of motherhood did not bring down local wrath upon her head or the scarlet A on her receptive bosom.

Maria's father, Thomas Marten, was a mole catcher in the preradiant-heat, prechemical days when mole catchers and chimney sweeps were still a vital part of every community. Her mother, Grace Marten, was such a frugal and industrious housewife that the Martens' simple home with the pegged-down roof became known as the "Cottage of Content." At an early age, Maria was placed in the home of a clergyman, where she assisted in the nursery, but her mother's sudden death brought Maria back home. At the age of ten, she was her father's housekeeper and a mother to her four younger brothers and sisters. For several years, Maria tracked in the path of her mother's admirable footsteps. She was an excellent housekeeper, a good shilling stretcher, and her younger brothers and sisters were healthy and always displayed well-wiped noses. In her extra time, Maria educated herself, so that she was more than par for the course for a mole catcher's daughter in social graces and cultural know-how.

Mr. Marten brought a new bride to the "Cottage of Content" when Maria was about fourteen or fifteen years old, and that rather upset the balance of power. Maria, at a sensitive age, found herself usurped as pro-tem housekeeper and honorary den mother. It left her with time on her hands, and a clamoring desire to be needed. All of Maria's fleshly seekings have the symptoms of a soul in search of affection. In her relationships with men, she was a one-man woman—one man at a time. She was not promiscuous, but she was certainly a pushover in every sense of the word for any young man who strayed up the path with an anguished I-need-you vibrato. And, since Maria had grown into a remarkably pretty, well-stacked girl, with a smile full of promise and beautiful white teeth, there were several local swains who really felt they did need her. She was a familiar type—the woman who seeks emotional security in the act of sex and finds only a thundering echo of her own insufficiency. There was never any question of money. To the bloody end, Maria maintained her amateur standing.

Thomas Corder was one of the frequent masculine callers at the Marten's cottage. The son of a wealthy farmer, he was a respectable, nice-looking young man, and it was rumored that his proposals were of the altar-and-ring variety. But Maria, at seventeen, was impetuous. Because of an irresistible combination of Suffolk moonlight and promises of marriage, she romped into a haystack relationship with Thomas Corder that had a predictable sequel nine months later. Although he made Maria an allowance for the support of the child, Mr. Corder illustrated the law of diminishing returns. He called less and less frequently, then not at all.

Maria accepted the termination of her affair with Thomas Corder philosophically and resiliently. She found another neighboring gentleman who assured her he needed her, with the proper note of need in his voice. Mr. Peter Matthews became a frequent caller, and Maria was left with a tangible memory of their brief but fruitful liason in the form of a bouncing baby boy. Mr. Matthews also made liberal arrangements for his son's support and removed himself from the calling list at the "Cottage of Content."

Maria's next essay at romance shows that she was a creature of habit or maybe there was just something about the Corder boys. She and Thomas Corder's young brother, William, started "walking out together." Both she and her father pressed the latest Corder applicant for Maria's favors to make an honest woman of her. It seemed almost wishful thinking for the mole catcher and his daughter to insist on marriage with a man of good family and excellent prospects. After all, Maria had been around the pool a few times.

William Corder was born in Polstead in 1803. His father farmed three hundred acres of fertile land and was admired equally for his industry and prosperity, but Mr. Corder's death, in 1825, was the entrance cue for a malignant fate to take a personal interest in the Corder family. Thomas Corder, Maria's ex-affiliate, took over the management of the farm but met an icy end crossing a frozen fish pond on his property. Two other sons, James and John, died from fast-paced consumption, so that within eighteen months Mrs. Corder lost her husband and three sons. That left William, which was pretty hard on Mrs. Corder and the three hundred acres.

William had attended an academy at Hadleigh. He was considered a bright boy by his instructors but had acquired a reputation as a "sneak," not being above a little petty pilfering and blurring the hard lines of truth with some fine shadings. He probably wrote the answers to test questions on his cuffs, too. William's disposition was not of the sunniest. He was inclined to alternate between a sullen moroseness and priggish virtue. Physically, he doesn't sound too prepossessing. He was about five feet four inches tall, with a stooped posture that probably knocked off another inch. He had a pale, freckled complexion, sandy hair and a nearsighted squint. He took an avid, prying interest in everybody's business and still had the on-the-sly air that had earned him the name Foxey Corder among his school fellows. Family integrity to the contrary, he was not above perpetrating petty frauds upon his father, such as selling his father's pigs and slithering the proceeds into his own pocket. In fact, at the age of twenty-three, William Corder wasn't a strong contender for any popularity poll. However, he had one trait that was regarded as a virtue and that was his sobriety. He was never seen in a state of intoxication, which, as things turned out, leaves a lot to be said for the grape.

His intimacy with Maria Marten blossomed around March, 1826, but "Foxey" Corder kept it a secret until history repeated itself with fecund regularity, and Maria had to start letting out her skirts again. He then became a frequent visitor at the Marten home and boasted around the village that she was his mistress and the expectant mother of his embryonic heir. Corder's mother did not share her son's public enthusiasm. She took the attitude that no matter how pretty, well-educated, and fertile Maria was, William could certainly do better than a mole-catcher's daughter with several lapses in her past. William, to escape the maternal pique, took Maria to neighboring Sudbury to have the baby. About a month later, Corder brought Maria and the child home in a gig. It must have been quite a homecoming with Maria, a picture of proud, if redundant, maternity and Corder sporting the proprietary air of a man with his first son and the fancy trappings of the hired gig. The people around Polstead, overlooking the irregularities of the situation, conceded that Maria "had done herself well." But Mrs. Corder took umbrage on her three hundred acres and told William in no uncertain terms what she thought about his conduct in general and her status as an illegitimate grandmother in particular.

The child died several weeks later, and the unceremonious velocity with which Corder whisked the body away in a box gave rise to some very unpleasant rumors. He gave two reasons for this rather furtive post-mortem activity. He said he did not want to embarrass his mother by reporting the death to local parish officers in Polstead, which seems a rather belated concession to his mother and respectability. He also explained he wanted to bury the baby in Sudbury where it had been born. It was later disclosed that the child never received Christian burial at Sudbury or anyplace else on the chartered map.

By now, the course of true love was not running smoothly.

As it must come to all romantic couples, the moment of truth came to Maria Marten and William Corder. He was up to his unpleasant tricks again, and they had a rousing argument about Corder's appropriation of a five pound note sent by the faithful Mr. Matthews for the support of his son. Mrs. Corder was making life very unpleasant in the family farmhouse with rumbling threats about William's inheritance, and Maria was making life equally hard in Polstead with hysterical demands for a wedding. William Corder really had a tiger by the tail, or, more accurately, two tigresses. His mother wanted him to take Maria Marten off his Christmas card list, and Maria was pressing for wedding invitations, and pressing a little too hard.

So, in his own way, William Corder arbitrated the fang-and-claw conflict with a bloody compromise. On May 18, 1827, Corder went to the Marten's cottage and told Maria and her family that he would take her to Ipswich where they could make everything legal. However, he warned them that it must be kept a secret. He didn't want his mother to know, and he clinched this with a master stroke of strategy. He told the Martens that there was a warrant out against Maria for bastardy, and they were going to "take her up about her children." With the secretive melodrama he loved, Corder gave Maria an old suit of his brother's and told her to disguise herself and wait for him until dark in the Red Barn. Maria's stepmother helped her pack a brown Holland bag, whose contents included a black velvet reticule, two pairs of black silk stockings, a black silk gown, a black cambric skirt, and several other articles of dress. Even if it wasn't large, the color of her trousseau was appropriate. Corder took the bag away with him, and Maria put on the men's clothes—a brown coat, striped waistcoat, and blue trousers. Under these she wore a flannel petticoat, a pair of white stays, an Irish linen chemise, and two handkerchiefs around her neck. One was green and she planned to pull it over her face, like a highwayman, for disguise when she left the house. Her shoes were made of Denmark satin with leather foreparts. She also wore earrings and several combs in her hair and carried a leghorn hat with black ribbon trimming. Mr. and Mrs. Marten, her younger sister, Ann, and a stepbrother, George, all saw her leave by the back door. She must have made a rather odd-looking and bulky gentleman with her formidable array of lingerie under the suit, her hair combs and earrings, coquettish Denmark satin shoes and leghorn bonnet. But for Maria the time for comedy was over. She walked out the back door and stepped into legend. Corder left by the front door. He was rather sharp with Maria and wore a brace of pistols, a rather strange attitude and even stranger equipment for an elopement. As Mrs. Marten stated in her testimony, "I never heard from Maria since that day."

After Maria's flight, Corder returned to Polstead alone. He visited the Martens, delivering messages from Maria, explaining that she could not write because of a lame hand. He told them she was staying with friends of his since there had been some trouble about the marriage license but promised Mr. Marten that he would marry her at Michaelmas. Corder explained that he could not do so any sooner because he had to superintend the gathering of his mother's harvest. To anyone born and bred in rural Polstead, this was not an evasion but just good business and a substantial reason for postponing a marriage. After all, Maria had waited this long.

Now a most active chapter began in the life of William Corder, a juggling of words, both fact and fiction. The management of the farm now rested on William's slightly stooped shoulders. He proved himself a competent farmer, and, because of the high mortality rate in the Corder family, he was considered a rich man. Polstead natives conceded that young William was "shaping up," and they were ready to forget the rather gamey atmosphere of his youth. He had just one small eccentricity during this upright period. He kept the key to the Red Barn in his pocket and the door locked. After the wheat and corn had been harvested and stored in the Red Barn, the door swung wide. The harvest had been fruitful, and the Red Barn was loaded to the rafters. But Mr. Corder was worried about his health. He was very ill, he said and feared that he would follow his two brothers to a premature and consumptive grave.

On September 29, he left Polstead for Seaforth, a watering place on the Isle of Wight. And he really did leave for his health because William Corder had been talking too much. He told Rachel Burke, who lived in a Polstead farmhouse, that Maria would not be his mistress as she had gone over to France in a steam packet. To William Marten, Maria's first cousin, Corder imparted the information that Maria was not living in Sudbury, but he could see her at any time he pleased. In September, he confided to William Pryke, his mother's farming bailiff, that he had not seen Maria since May. Phoebe Stowe, a rather prying farmer's wife, at harvest time had asked Corder if Maria was likely to have any more children. William Corder's answer was "Maria Marten will have no more children," which in view of Maria's past record should have sowed a few seeds of suspicion. Mrs. Marten saw Corder with an umbrella that Maria had taken with her when she left, but his explanation was he had borrowed it from Maria. All in all, it seemed like a good idea for William Corder to get out of town.

After his departure in September, William Corder went to some pains to see that Maria and her family kept in touch. He sent soothing, chatty letters to Mr. Marten reporting that Maria was well and happy, but Maria was a procrastinator at writing letters or they had bad luck in the mail. He said Maria's letter must have been lost, that her hand was bad again. There were many excuses but no letters. On October 18, the Marten family received happy tidings from William Corder. "I just arrived at London upon business respecting family affairs," wrote the considerate Corder, "and am writing to you before I take any refreshments, because I should be in time for this night's post, as my stay in town will be very short—anxious to return to her who is now my wife and with whom I shall be one of the happiest of men. I should have her with me, but it was her wish to stay at our lodgings in Newport in the Isle of Wight, which she described to you in her letter, and we feel astonished you have not answered it, thinking illness must be the cause. . . ." Corder also asked two or three times that the letters from Peter Matthews, containing the five pound support allotment for his child, be forwarded. Finally, Mr. Marten sent Maria a sharp letter, saying he was surprised at her long silence and that he could not afford to maintain Mr. Matthews's son much longer unless she sent at least part of the support money. By return mail, Corder sent a sovereign for the child's care.

By now, Polstead was a town divided. There were two schools of thought. Either Corder had established Maria somewhere as his mistress, or he had actually married her. However, in November, Corder had established himself in London at an inn appropriately named Bull Inn and was carrying on in a most unattached, bachelor-type fashion. On November 13, he advertised in the Morning Herald for a wife and received forty-five replies. An ad in the *Sunday Times* of November 25 for a life's companion brought fifty-three additional letters, which speaks well for Mr. Corder's prose and the circulation of the *Times*. The replies ranged all the way from genteel twitterings to alluring financial statements from the hopeful, probably desperate, applicants. It was a Miss Mary Moore who caught the brass ring and became Mrs. William Corder. There was a strong story current at the time that Miss Moore had met Corder rather informally at a watering spa and that her brother, in whose house she lived, would not have approved of such an impromptu acquaintance. So, she, her mother, and Corder, arranged to run the matrimonial ad and invite Mr. Corder to the house to meet her brother. How this put-up job would seem more respectable than a pick-up seems like hair splitting, but it must have worked as Mr. Moore gave his blessings to the marriage. Mrs. Corder then opened a school for young ladies at Brentford. Corder held up his end of things by doing a little teaching, and here they settled down into a long-range marital rut. It is rather evident that Mrs. Corder would be a rather superfluous bride in Polstead. Mrs. Corder idolized her husband, and he, within the narrow processes of his rather limited nature, seems to have returned the affection. The only drawback to wedded bliss was that William had bad dreams. His moanings and loud, but uncomprehensible, shouts even disturbed the boarders, not to mention the bride.

William Corder wasn't the only dreamer. Mrs. Marten was having dreams, too. Her dreams are one of the factors that have made the case of the Red Barn immortal. In the days before dreams were *double-entendre* pitfalls, they enjoyed the supernatural fascination of the unknown and a primitive witch-doctor infallibility for revelation. Dream books ranked second only in popularity to such volumes as the *Home Medical Advisor* and were consulted with the same faith and frequency.

The Marten family, after Corder's departure for reasons of health, became increasingly alarmed about Maria. She could write a good hand; family ties were strong; she loved her little boy. They had received nothing but second-hand greetings and vague excuses about a lame hand or lost letters through Corder. Now the fact that a girl could vanish from her home and village for a period of ten months seems rather incredible today. But, in the first place, communications were not streamlined. Many rural towns and farming communities stayed almost as isolated as they had in the heyday of feudalism. Then, Maria's character lent itself to all sorts of speculation as to why she had left home, the favorite being that she had moved elsewhere to become Corder's mistress.

But Maria's step-mother, who was evidently very fond of the girl, was magnificently obsessed with the Red Barn. She constantly suggested that Mr. Marten examine the Red Barn. Finally her husband pressed her, and she replied: "I have frequently dreamed of Maria, and twice before Christmas I dreamed that Maria was murdered and buried in the Red Barn." So, presumably to stop this nagging nonsense, Mr. Marten, with the assistance of Mrs. Corder's bailiff, Mr. William Pryke, investigated the Red Barn. One part of the floor did not seem as solid as the rest, and, after digging for about a foot and a half, they discovered a sack containing the putrid caricature of a human body. A green silk handkerchief protruded through the opening of the sack, and when Mr. Marten returned home he was informed that Maria had worn a green silk scarf or handkerchief around her neck on the day she left home.

Mr. Marten, crushed with the certainty that the rotting thing in the Red Barn was his daughter, faltered his way to the local authorities. An identification was possible because of a wen and the still intact and beautiful teeth that had made Maria's smile so alluring. A coroner's jury, after viewing the decomposed body and hearing the statements of Mr. and Mrs. Marten and Maria's sister, Ann, quickly arrived at the conclusion that Mr. William Corder might have the answers to some questions that needed answering. Corder was apprehended at his wife's boarding school for young women, a touch that M. de Maupassant or O. Henry would have appreciated. Like so many other murderers, Corder overrated his own intelligence and underestimated the world's. Murderers are so sure of their cleverness, their plausibility, their perpetual immunity. Their ego insulates them against the possibility of failure or a chance meeting with the executioner. Their judgment is short-circuited by a colossal sense of personal importance and a distorted idea of themselves in relationship to the world. It is as if they surveyed the universe, people, their victims, through the wrong end of a cosmic telescope, so that everything is reduced to small, remote entities, incapable of any force. Murderers feel themselves as giants among pygmies, towering above the law and petty conventions. Their ego forms a hard shell which the screams of their victims, the blood, the midnight terrors, and the suspicions of other people cannot crack.

G. J. Smith followed his pattern of immersing his brides with such regularity that he defied the law of averages. Dr. Palmer acted as if strychnine were sarsaparilla, which he could dispense endlessly if he went to church and smiled genially. Eugene Marie Chantrelle actually believed he could make the authorities swallow a tale of gas poisoning, after his wife had swallowed opium. Mary Anne Cotton of Durham was lulled into an understandable sense of false security because she had done away with her mother, fifteen children, three husbands, and a superfluous lodger before people got suspicious, but she pushed her luck too far, even in an age of boundless faith. The list is endless. Even that notable exception that proves the rule, Jack the Ripper, probably would have been caught if he'd continued his Whitechapel pranks. One fine night, he would have been caught literally redhanded as he was making off with a kidney or ovary as a sort of gory remembrance of things past. At any rate, William Corder possessed all the abundant ego and callous stupidity of his genre. It is interesting to speculate on what would have happened to his wife after the honeymoon was over and she started nagging him about taking the garbage out.

During the journey back to Polstead, Corder either joined in, or laughed at obscene conversation about the murder, although as they passed his mother's home he became solemn and spoke of the way his family had been cut off by death within the last few months. After listening to the testimony of witnesses and the medical evidence, which gave a bullet wound in the head as the cause of death, William Corder was charged with willful murder and taken to Bury Jail to await trial. At six o'clock that evening the tolling of the church bell announced that Maria Marten was being buried for the second time, with relations and hundreds of friends following the coffin. But in death, as in life, Maria knew no serenity. Five weeks after she was buried in the Polstead churchyard, her body was disinterred, and in addition to a hole in her head caused by a bullet, there was evidence that she had been stabbed in the side. Wide cuts in her chemise and stays had been found. The stabs had not been discovered at the first investigation because of the rather glutinous condition of Maria's mortal remains. There were wounds between the fifth and sixth ribs made by a sharp instrument, such as a well-honed knife, and a puncture at the back of the right ventricle. These wounds corresponded to the slits in the stays and chemise. Stab wounds were also found in the neck under the tightly drawn handkerchief. And Maria's heart, which had made the grand tour during her lifetime, was jugged in spirits to be produced at the trial.

The trial was set for August 7. An epidemic of visitors filled the inns, so that many had to pay a guinea for a bed, and there was a complete representation of the curious, from a baronet's heir to Suffolk peasants who had left their fields. A mob surrounded the court on the morning of the trial so that His Lordship, the Chief Baron Alexander, probably breathing smoke and fire, was twenty minutes late. A crowd at the back entrance awaited Corder's arrival in the gaol cart, chanting at intervals, "He's coming, he's coming." Even Corder appeared to be gratified at his reception. The courtroom was so jammed that several of the counselors had their wigs knocked askew and one was actually ungowned, while laymen paid their debt to curiosity by losing their hats, pocketbooks, and even the lapels of their coats.

The prisoner was brought to the bar for the reading of the indictment and presented a very natty appearance, from a new surcoat with velvet lapels to silk stockings and pumps, and he pleaded not guilty to three-way homicide since the indictment accused Corder of shooting, strangling, and stabbing the unfortunate Maria.

Mr. Andrews, counsel for the crown, opened with understandable deliberation and assurance. The prosecution tied up all the loose ends into one damning package. Maria's dream-ridden stepmother testified that she had heard Maria tell Corder that if she were sent to prison on bastardy charge, he would go too. Maria's and Corder's child had died of some sort of a fit in her arms. Ann Marten, Maria's youngest sister identified the underclothes, combs, earrings, and a leghorn hat with black ribbon trimmings as things Maria had worn on the day of her departure. When these items were produced, Mrs. Marten satisfied the sensation-hungry crowd by fainting.

George Marten, age ten, told the court in a proudly piping voice that he had seen his stepsister leave the house to join Corder at the Red Barn and how later the same day he had seen Corder coming from the barn with a pickax. Phoebe Stowe, whose farmhouse was located near the Red Barn, said Corder had borrowed a spade from her on the day Maria left home. Robert Offord, a cutler at Hadleigh, related that the first part of April the prisoner had brought him a small sword "which I wish to be ground as sharp as a carving knife for to be used as such." Mr. Offord identified the sword found in Corder's trunk when he was arrested as the same one he had sharpened, and Mr. John Baalham, constable at Polstead, in precise tones made it understood that there never had been a warrant to apprehend Maria Marten and that he had never told the prisoner he had received such a warrant to serve, and he shot Corder a look which showed exactly what he thought of people who misrepresented the law for their own devious purposes. Corder just smirked.

The prosecution had spiked just about all the conceivable guns of the defense, but the medical evidence was the clincher. John Lawton, surgeon, testified that the handkerchief around the deceased's neck had been drawn tight enough to cause strangulation; that there were stab wounds in the neck, under the handkerchief; that a bullet had caused injury to the right eye and right side of the face. In his opinion, the bullet wound would not have caused instant death, but it would have in conjunction with the strangling and the stabbing. The stab wound which penetrated the heart would have been sufficient to cause death alone.

John Charles Nairn, a chirpy little man who described himself as a surgeon, twittered his agreement with Mr. Lawton that Maria might have survived the bullet wound, and then produced the sensation of the trial when he happily announced, "I have the head right here," whisked it out of his little black bag and proceeded to illustrate his testimony regarding the bullet wound. The skull was placed on a table facing Corder and the beautiful teeth which made Maria's smile so come-hither during her lifetime, seemed to be grinning in derision at Corder. Corder just smirked back.

The defense made a rather anemic attempt by scraping up a few character witnesses and bringing out a cross-examination that Mr. Marten had used his mole spade when digging up the body in the Red Barn, the inference being that the mole digger had accidentally caused the stab wounds. This paved the way for Corder to read his defense from a quarto, blue-covered copy book. Corder adjusted his glasses and, with a courtly bow to the judge, began to read his account of what had happened in the Red Barn. He started out with a literary flourish by pointing out that his life supported the theory that "truth was sometimes stranger than fiction." He told of his relationship with Maria, of the death of the child whose body he buried in the fields to keep its death off the parish records. He claimed that Maria had stolen his pistols in a light-fingered moment. His monotonous voice droned on. There was a fight when they met in the barn. He decided that a girl with such a temper would make a very shrewish wife and belatedly told her he wouldn't marry her. He turned to leave the barn, heard a pistol shot, and came back to find the girl dead. He panicked and buried her. It was a nice, clean-cut suicide the way he told it. But Maria must have been in an absolute suicidal frenzy because according to all the evidence, she shot herself through the eye, stabbed herself in random places, and then, just to make sure, she tied a handkerchief around her neck and tried to strangle herself.

Crowds seethed around the courthouse, jammed the court-room, and even climbed on the courthouse roof to peek through the skylight, and the jury retired to deliberate. There was no doubt that Maria Marten had been thoroughly butchered in the Red Barn, and their verdict left no doubt as to who, in their opinion, had done the dirty deed. They found William Corder guilty, and the judge pronounced a particularly harsh sentence.

> Friday, August 8th, 1828
>
> William Corder, this day attainted of the willful murder of Maria Marten. Let him be hanged by the neck until he be dead, on Monday next, the eleventh day of August, instant; and let his body be delivered to the Surgeons of the Hospital of Bury Saint Edmund's to be dissected and anatomized pursuant to the Statute (reduced to a skeleton for use of medical students).

If one could forget Maria's crumbling, mutilated body in the Red Barn, William Corder's last days might be considered edifying. He got religion and requested a bible and a prayer book, and his long-suffering wife, who had moved to Bury to be near him, exhorted him to penance and brought him such books as *The Companion to the Altar* and Blair's *Sermons*. He wrote his mother that his predicament and disgrace were due to Satan "who set snares in his way," and the prison chaplain gratifyingly reported that Corder "addressed the Throne of Grace morning and night."

To his wife he wrote: "May Heaven bless and protect you throughout this transitory veil of misery and when we meet again may it be in the regions of bliss." Either he was an incurable optimist or Foxey Corder had figured out some way he could sneak through the pearly gates. On the day before his execution,

Corder made a confession, probably going on the theory that it was good for the soul and his soul could use a little help where he was going. The confession is more interesting for what it leaves unsaid than what it says:

> Bury Gaol, Aug. 10th, 1828
> Condemned Cell
>
> I acknowledge being guilty of the death of poor Maria Marten, by shooting her with a pistol. The particulars are as follows : When we left her father's house we began quarreling about the burial of the child, she apprehending that the place wherein it was deposited would be found out. The quarrel continued for about three quarters of an hour, upon this and other subjects. A scuffle ensued, and during the scuffle, and at the time I think she had hold of me, I took the pistol from the side pocket of my velveteen jacket and fired. She fell, and died in an instant. I never saw even a struggle. I was overwhelmed with agitation and dismay—the body fell near the front doors of the floor of the barn. A vast quantity of blood issued from the wound and ran on to the floor and through the crevices. Having determined to bury the body in the barn (about two hours after she was dead) I went and borrowed the spade of Mrs. Stowe, but before I went there I dragged the body from the barn into the chaffhouse and I locked up the barn. I returned again to the barn and began to dig the hole, but the spade being a bad one, and the earth firm and hard, I was obliged to go home for a pickaxe and a better spade, with which I dug the hole and then buried the body. I think I dragged the body by the handkerchief that was tied round her neck—it was dark when I finished covering up the body. I went the next day and washed the blood from off the barn floor. I declare to Almighty God I had no sharp instrument about me, and that no other wound but the one made by the pistol was inflicted by me. I have been guilty of great idleness and at times led a dissolute life, but I hope in the mercy of God to be forgiven. W. CORDER

"Corder the Murderer" was the lionized figure of the day, and the life and death of Maria Marten and Corder's trial and execution were to a breathless public what next Saturday night's "Gunsmoke" is to a humdrum, weary person of the twentieth century. Puppet shows, cartoons, ballads were sure of an audience, and thunderings even came from the pulpit about the crime. The Red Barn became a mecca to the curious. Had not a guard been posted, it would have been completely demolished. Souvenir hunters had already hacked away at its boards and timbers. The *Times* estimated that over two hundred thousand people had craned their necks under its roof, traveling from distances of fifty miles and over. And a bid was made by an enterprising snuffbox manufacturer for wood from the Red Barn to make souvenir snuff boxes.

On the morning of Corder's execution, a crowd of eight or nine thousand, not counting those who climbed trees and roof tops, gathered to see justice done. Corder was paid a rather unenviable tribute. Foxton, the peer of executioners, was summoned from Newgate to Bury to ply his trade. The noose, the drop, and the hangman, tugging at his waist to expedite matters, plunged Corder, it was hoped by the more charitable, directly to the "Throne of Grace." Foxton was satisfied with his days work. It was reported that he sold pieces of the rope for a guinea an inch. He did not commit himself, but modestly admitted "that was a very good rope." The body was taken to Shire Hall, where the last part of the sentence was carried out. It was dissected and skinned to be used as a skeleton for medical students. One piece of Corder's skin proved of immediate utility. Mr. J. Curtis of the London *Times* covered the Polstead murder and trial most thoroughly. His attention to minute details and graphic reporting was rewarded by the prison officials, who gave him a large piece of Corder's skin to bind a copy of his account of these rural doings. This ghoulishly bound book was to serve as a moral reminder to others to avoid the pitfalls of William Corder and Maria Marten.

That is the story of "poor Maria" and "wretched William" as the contemporary penny pamphlets dubbed them. While there is no actual mystery surrounding the actual *fait accompli,* several question marks hover over the Red Barn. The motive is indicated but needs clarification. Corder, in his confession, tries to carry it off as an impromptu scuffle following an argument. However, the facts point to premeditation. The story about the bastardy warrant to get Maria away from her home was proved untrue, and a brace of pistols is not *de rigueur* for an elopement.

The crux of the matter is Maria's remark that if she went to jail, Corder would go to jail, too. There are the mysterious arrangements following the death of their baby, and, even in his confession, Corder admits there was an argument about the baby. The baby, according to rather cryptic testimony, "died in Mrs. Marten's arms," but no effort was made by the defense to establish in cross-examination how or from what the baby died, even though Corder complained about the ugly rumors circulating. It was a case of leaving well enough alone. Corder had no need to kill Maria Marten for the usual clichés to cover up his seduction or unsanctioned parenthood. It was common knowledge. He could have dropped Maria at any time; in fact according to him, that is what his friends and family were urging him to do. And if the baby had died a natural death, why not leave it to Maria and her family to make burial arrangements as they had done with Thomas Corder's child? But assume William Corder murdered his child to relieve social stigma or to be free from a drawn-out financial burden. Maria went with Corder when he took the baby's body away for burial. She knew the truth and used it in a not very subtle way to goose Mr. Corder to the altar.

Maria was almost twenty-six and had very sensibly decided that it was time to forego illicit pleasures for the more respectable rewards of matrimony before the dew was completely off the rose. If Maria was insisting on marriage as the high price of silence, then it becomes the old story of the second murder to cover the first murder. Even to the end of his life, Corder refers ambiguously to the baby as being buried in the fields or "she [Maria] apprehending the place wherein it was deposited." Maria knew how the baby had died and where it was buried, but why should she "apprehend" the place where it was buried unless discovery meant suspicion or proof of dirty work at the crossroads. There is probably some truth in the statement in Corder's confession that "they fought about the baby and other things." When they met at the Red Barn, Maria might have reminded Corder that there had better be no delay in the marriage or she would reveal where the baby was buried and how it got there. And as she heard the click of the pistol cocking and saw the withdrawn look on Corder's face, Maria knew for one age-long moment that she had lost her hold on Corder and on life.

The whole thing was in keeping with Corder's character. Two murders to save money, avoid an unwelcome marriage, and keep up a sanctimonious front. As to his confession, that leaves so many ciphers. It is Foxey Corder's favorite blending of truths with half-truths. He never admitted using the sword or pointed weapon. He never admitted premeditation and was vague about the actual reason for killing Maria. In other words, he, along with many people, believed that he would never be executed, that his sentence would be commuted. Notice that he admits the shooting but only on an accidental basis and adamantly refuses to acknowledge use of the sword. According to the medical testimony at the trial, the bullet in the head was not likely to be fatal, but the combination of the stab wounds *and* the shot would have caused death. So, William Corder reached a happy, characteristic compromise in his confession. He provided an accidental shooting that might not even have been fatal, in case some earthly tribunal wished to reconsider, and a partial confession of guilt if his case went to a higher court. When questioned about obscure points in his confession, he evaded the issue: "Oh, spare me; the public must be satisfied with what I have confessed." He was confessing enough and concealing enough and always had his best foot forward.

As to the popularity of the case, it was a matter of timing. The "romantic" back-to-nature movement, with its frank approval of "instant sex," was drawing to a close. The Regency period, with the edifying spectable of the "First Gentleman of Europe" flaunting his extramarital loves while he hounded his Queen, Caroline of Brunswick, for a divorce on the flimsiest grounds, had given way to the inept reign of George IV, or rather of his ministers. It would be another nine years before Victoria, with one-track righteousness, took up the tattered, downgraded reigns of government, but already the inflexible morality that would characterize her era was shaping up.

To the casual observer, the period looks like a social and cultural hodgepodge. Actually, it was a time of action and reaction, a time of transition. The roots of the past and the seeds of the future were clamoring for a re-expression of essentials through different forms and new symbols. Blatant sexuality would give way to subversive seduction, just as the clinging, hide-nothing robes of the Directoire would be replaced by the impregnable crinoline. And the rural idyll of the Red Barn contained elements of both the past and the future: Maria's uncensored stroll down the primrose path; Corder's rather unethical battle for respectability. It was good timing and even better box office.

As to the contemporary absorption in the Red Barn Mystery, there can be no quibble. On the evening of Corder's execution, Macbeth was being presented at a town not far away from Bury. A gentleman who had witnessed the execution decided to attend the theater performance, because he was being pestered on all sides by friends wanting to know about the execution. He finally found sanctuary in the theater and was taking his seat just as the fourth act was beginning. Duncan spoke his usual line, "Is execution done on Cawdor?" The harassed gentleman, sick of the whole subject and too upset to make fine distinctions in English diction, heard the question from the stage. Said the gentleman in a loud voice to a stunned on-stage Duncan and a laughing audience: "I saw him hanged this morning, and I'll not answer any more questions about it."

Since 1828, Maria Marten has had her ups and downs. She dropped into obscurity during the more complex era of the Mesdames Bravo, Bartlett, and Maybrick. For a while Lizzie Borden and the dripping hatchet prempted Maria's popularity. Then she came into vogue again when her story was immortalized on celluloid. But in spite of the fluctuation of time, regardless of competition in the annals of crime, Maria enjoys one undisputed, unchanging claim to fame. Of all the ladies, she is the most alliterative: Maria Marten, the mole-catcher's daughter.

XI

To Sleep, Perchance to Scream

CRIME HAS ITS OWN POETRY, from the epic meter of William Palmer to the jukebox rhyming of the Black Dahlia. It even has its own Ballad of Dread Ladies. For the murder addict, Lizzie Borden, Edith Thompson, or Madeleine Smith have all the plaintive lure of Villon's lost ladies, and Adelaide Bartlett is a contender for poetic honors.

Morally speaking, Adelaide Blanche de la Tremouille started life in an awkward position. She was born on the wrong side of the blanket. Her mother was French with comme ci, comme ça attitude toward benefit of clergy. To atone for his Continental lapse, her father, a well-to-do-Englishman, brought her to England to be educated.

On April 9, 1875, Adelaide was married to Edwin Bartlett in the parish church of Croydon. It was an arranged marriage. The couple met only once before their encounter at the altar, and the crisp rustle of pound notes could be heard over the soaring strains of the wedding march. Adelaide's father settled no money on Adelaide but paid a considerable sum to Edwin Bartlett, who was willing to overlook the cloud on Adelaide's paternity for cash on the line to expand his business. The bride was nineteen. She was petite with large dark eyes, coquettish curly hair, and was equally talented at music, needlework, and the piquant art of rustling her bustle. Edwin Bartlett at thirty was an ambitious grocer and provisions dealer, with the in-condition physique and blonde, well-scrubbed gloss that passes for good looks. The bridegroom had some strange ideas, as things developed, but one of his most provocative was on the subject of how to spend a honeymoon. The marriage was not consummated, and Adelaide, an involuntary virgin, was sent to school for twelve months at Stoke Newington, then spent nearly two years in a convent school in Belgium. Obviously, Edwin Bartlett was a fanatical exponent of education.

At the end of 1877, Adelaide finally joined her husband at Herne Hill, Station Road, where he lived over his shop. A few months later, there was an addition to the family, although not the anticipated kind. Bartlett's mother had died, and his father came to live with them. Bartlett, Sr., was not a lovable character, and his two outstanding characteristics seemed to be a talent for nosiness and a real genius for troublemaking. He hadn't been established at Herne Hill long when he accused Adelaide of improper relations with her brother-in-law, Charles Bartlett. Bartlett, Sr., had not approved of the marriage, had not been invited to attend the wedding, and did not even meet his daughter-in-law until she returned from Belgium. So, the accusation was probably his own vicious brainchild, fathered by an out-of-joint nose. However, the old man had evidently done so much talking that Edwin sent for his solicitors and compelled his father to sign a sweeping document of apology and retraction. In spite of this tempestuous beginning, Bartlett senior lived for five years in comparative peace with his son and daughter-in-law, and even he had to admit that they were always on affectionate terms, which, for a married couple, is something of an accomplishment.

In 1881, there was a stillborn son, and Mr. Bartlett would not allow a doctor, although the frightened nurse, Annie Walker, pleaded for one. He probably had strange ideas on the subject of childbirth, too. Adelaide almost died and determined never again to run the risk of motherhood. She made it abundantly clear to Mr. Bartlett, in French and English words of one syllable, that although the hand that rocked the cradle might rock the world, it definitely wouldn't be hers.

In the meantime, Edwin Bartlett's business had prospered, thanks to Adelaide's money and his hard work. He now had six shops and a partner. At the end of 1883, Mr. and Mrs. Bartlett were able to move from their living quarters above the shop to a house called "The Cottage" at Merton Abbey, near Wimbledon. The diminuitive name of their new home indicates malice aforethought. Bartlett *père* did not come with them.

At Merton Abbey, the Bartletts attended a small Wesleyan chapel in High Street for their spiritual needs. In the gray, wet winter of 1885, the Reverend George Dyson, a popular, up-and-coming graduate of Trinity College, Dublin, came to take charge of the flock. He was twenty-seven, handsome in a restrained way, and a devout cad. In the line of duty, he paid Mr. and Mrs. Bartlett a pastoral call. Both the husband and wife took an immediate liking to the new minister. Edwin admired his intellect, and just what Adelaide admired is a little more nebulous. The minister became a frequent visitor, and Mr. Bartlett's raving mania for education asserted itself again. He arranged for Mr. Dyson to give his wife lessons in Latin, history, and mathematics, and, with this encouragement, the friendship gained altitude rapidly.

Mr. Bartlett had some rather quaint conversations with the minister. "I want you to be Adelaide's guardian," he told Dyson. "I know you'll be a friend to her when I'm dead." Mr. Bartlett was a good business man but a bad judge of character. During one of Dyson's visits, Bartlett asked whether it was not consistent with Biblical teaching that a man should have two wives—one for educated, intelligent companionship, and one for "usage." Mr. Dyson's parochial opinion is not on record. However, at the trial the judge asked Dyson: "Did it not strike you as an unwholesome sort of talk in the family circle?" To which Dyson replied: "Not coming from him, My Lord; he was a man who had some strange ideas." It might have been Edwin Bartlett's epitaph!

Before the end of summer, the teacher-student relationship crossed new frontiers. Dyson and Adelaide were in love. At the end of August, when the Bartletts were leaving for a month's vacation at Dover, Mr. Bartlett pressed Dyson to visit them, offering to pay his expenses and asking him to write Mrs. Bartlett. During the Dover vacation, Dyson went down six or seven times spending the days alone with Mrs. Bartlett, while her husband went to London daily to attend to his business.

On September 3, Mr. Bartlett made a new will. By the existing will, his widow would forfeit everything if she married again. By the new will, he left absolutely everything to Adelaide with no strings attached. Mr. Dyson and his solicitor were appointed joint executors. A few days later, Mr. Bartlett went to see Mr. Dyson at his lodgings in Putney. He told him of the new will and that he wished the intimacy to continue. "If anything happens to me," said Bartlett, "you two may come together." Bartlett was willing things all over the place, including his wife. Dyson, in a last desperate claw at virtue told Mr. Bartlett that he was growing attached to his wife. It was disturbing his work, and he thought the friendship should be discontinued. But Mr. Bartlett asked, "Why?" Mr. Bartlett really elevated the role of the complacent husband to a dizzy, new height and seemed to relish his horns.

A letter written during the Dover period by Bartlett to Dyson supports the otherwise incredible statements made later by

Adelaide Bartlett and George Dyson concerning Bartlett's let-George-do-it attitude:

> 14 James Street, Dover, Monday
>
> Dear George—Permit me to say I feel great pleasure in thus addressing you for the first time. To me it is a privilege to think that I am allowed to feel towards you as a brother, and I hope our friendship may ripen as time goes on, without anything to mar its future brightness. Would that I could find words to express my thankfulness to you for the very loving letter you sent Adelaide today. It would have done anybody good to see her overflowing with joy as she read it whilst walking along the street, and afterwards as she read it to me. I felt my heart going out to you. I long to tell you how proud I feel at the thought I should soon be able to clasp the hand of the man who from his heart could pen such noble thoughts. Who can help loving you? I felt that I must say two words: "Thank you," and my desire to do so is my excuse for troubling you with this. Looking towards the future with joyfulness,
>
> I am yours affectionately,
>
> EDWIN

So now it was "Edwin," "George," and "Adelaide." The Bartletts and the Reverend Dyson seemed to be establishing a rather unhealthy forerunner of "togetherness." At the end of the Dover vacation, the Bartletts took furnished lodgings at Number 85, Claverton Street, in Pimlico. Their quarters consisted of a living room and a bedroom connected by folding doors, and Mr. Bartlett had stipulated with landlord Doggett that a second bed be moved in. Mr. Bartlett gave Dyson a season ticket from Putney to Waterloo and cartes blanches visiting privileges. A lounging coat and slippers were kept at the lodging for Dyson, and things got really clubby. When Dyson called, the parlor curtains were pinned together, and Mrs. Bartlett was seen with her head at various times on Dyson's knee or shoulder by the servants. She was not only conjugating *amo* with Mr. Dyson, she was perusing Squire's *Companion to the British Pharmacopeia*. She told Dyson that Edwin suffered from a secret, recurrent illness which made him think he would not live long. Bartlett confirmed this in a roundabout way when he told Dyson : "I have no doubt that you will take good care of her." Adelaide spoke of a Dr. Nichols, who said Bartlett would die within twelve months, and mentioned Annie Walker, who had attended her during her confinement, used to bring what medicines were needed for Mr. Bartlett's mysterious malady. But within the Bartlett circle only Edwin, Adelaide, and George seemed to know of this secret illness. Mr. Bartlett's father and business partner thought him strong and healthy. He had not been sick for many years, and in 1880 he passed an insurance examination with a medical rating of "first class life."

During October and November, 1885, life paced along as usual at Number 85, Claverton Street. Mr. Bartlett went to business at 8.30 and arrived home at six o'clock. Three or four times a week, Mr. Dyson called and spent the day with Adelaide, had lunch with her, took her out, and sometimes stayed for dinner. Evidently, wearing out his welcome was a possibility that never entered the minister's handsome head.

Early in December, Mr. Bartlett complained of not feeling well. On December 10, the couple called in Dr. Alfred Leach, a neighborhood practicioner, unknown to the Bartletts, but conveniently close. Dr. Leach found the patient prostrated by extreme nervousness, severe diarrhea, and his teeth were in bad condition. In fact, Dr. Leach thought the gums suggested an excessive dose of mercury. Mr. Bartlett surprisingly admitted he had taken a large pill that had been sent to him as a sample at one of his shops without knowing what it was. It is interesting to note that mercury was used as one of the earliest treatments of syphilis, but Mr. Bartlett stuck to his story and denied any such connection. A few days later, Mr. Bartlett was worse. He suffered from insomnia and mental depression, had fits of crying, and thought he was going to die. He told Dr. Leach that his friends and relations were not kind to his wife, and Adelaide, who evidently didn't believe in beating around the bush, said: "Doctor, Mr. Bartlett's friends will accuse me of poisoning him if he does not get better." And Mr. Bartlett asked Dr. Leach to bring in another doctor for consultation "for the protection of my wife." Dr. Leach called in Dr. Dudley, a nearby physician, who was a stranger to the Bartletts. He found Bartlett in a depressed condition, complaining of sleeplessness and saying he had been overworked physically and mentally. There were no signs or symptoms of any disease, so the doctors prescribed a sedative, a tonic, and fresh air for Mr. Bartlett. Dr. Leach also advised Mrs. Bartlett to get some rest. "What is the use, Doctor, he will walk around the room like a ghost. He will not sleep unless I sit and hold his toe." One of the strangest insomnia cures on record. But the doctors could not persuade Mr. Bartlett to imbibe fresh air. He said he liked to "lie still and feel happy."

Bartlett had more teeth extracted, and there was a slight improvement. Then on December 23 he was found to be suffering from worms. A complete pharamcopia of purgatives was futile. After santonine, epsom salts, sulphate of soda, and two globules of croton oil, which he said made his stomach feel "warm, pleasant and comfortable," the literally immovable Mr. Bartlett claimed that worms were wriggling up his throat.

On Saturday, December 26, Mr. Dyson came back from a Christmas visit with his family and spent several hours at Claverton Street. He came up again from Putney on Sunday, the twenty-seventh, after his evening service, and Bartlett asked Mr. Dyson if he thought it possible for a man to be weaker than he was without passing away. During this visit Dyson also walked

Adelaide to the post office to deposit some letters. Adelaide told him she wanted chloroform to soothe Edwin and give him sleep. She assured him she had used it before sprinkled on a handkerchief. Since it was so volatile, she wanted a whole medicine bottle full and gave George a sovereign to pay for it. Dyson asked her why she didn't get it from a doctor. Adelaide told him the doctor did not appreciate that she was skilled in drugs and medicines and would not entrust her with chloroform.

Evidently Old Bartlett had been the instigator of all the "friends and relations" talk, because on this walk she had mailed a letter to Edwin's father which indicated he had been shooting off his mouth again.

Sunday night

Dear Mr. Bartlett :

I hear that you are a little disturbed because Edwin has been too ill to see you. I wish, if possible, to be friends with you, but you must place yourself on the same footing as other persons—that is to say, you are welcome here when I invite you, and at no other time. You seem to forget that I have not been in bed for thirteen days, and consequently am too tired to speak to visitors. I am sorry to speak so plainly, but I wish you to understand that I have neither forgotten or forgiven the past. Edwin will be pleased to see you on Monday evening any time after six.

Mr. Bartlett senior arrived on schedule Monday evening and found his son in a dressing gown on the bed. He told his father he was feeling better and planned to go to the country the following week.

On Monday, Mr. Dyson performed his errand of mercy in installments. He went to several chemists in the neighborhood of Putney, two of them being members of his flock, and at four different shops he bought one ounce of chloroform "to remove grease stains from his coat." He transferred the contents of the four small bottles to one big medicine bottle and pasted the "Chloroform, Poison" label which he had taken off one of the smaller bottles. If his subterfuges do not show guilty knowledge, they at least hint that Mr. Dyson thought Adelaide "was up to something."

On Tuesday, December 29, Mr. Dyson went to Claverton Street. He found Mr. Bartlett up, dressed, and apparently better. He then took Adelaide for a walk on the Embankment and gave her the bottle of chloroform, which she demurely tucked in her muff. At supper, Adelaide told Edwin and George that friends were saying unkind things about her not giving her husband full nursing service. It was very unfair, as she had not rested properly for two weeks and had slept fitfully on the sofa or in the chair— presumably holding Edwin's toe. Mr. Dyson suggested that she get a nurse to help her, and Adelaide snapped at him, "You don't trust me." Mr. Dyson apologized, although he probably wondered for what.

On December 29, 30, and 31, Dr. Leach said that the jaw symptoms had become alarming. On Thursday, December 31, Edwin was bundled up and taken to the dentist by his wife and Dr. Leach. Another tooth was extracted. On the way to the dentist, Mrs. Bartlett talked of their happy marriage and tried to keep up his spirits. Dr. Leach administered nitrous oxide gas while the dentist performed the extraction. They noticed that the bone was decayed in all four sockets where teeth had previously been extracted. In Mr. Bartlett's hearing, the dentist told Dr. Leach, "This looks very much like necrosis setting in."

The thought of necrosis did not seem to affect his appetite. Mr. Bartlett had oysters for lunch, a jugged hare for dinner, and for those who are interested in the "virility-through-oysters" theory his supper consisted of more oysters, bread and butter, mango chutney, and cake. He seemed much more cheerful. Perhaps it was the New Year's Eve atmosphere. He said he was feeling better and ordered a large haddock for breakfast the next morning, telling the maid, Alice Fulcher, he should get up an hour earlier at the thought of having it. Mrs. Caroline Doggett, the landlord's wife, came in, and Mr. Bartlett also told her he was feeling better and mentioned he was going to the seaside. But Adelaide had other things on her mind. She asked Mrs. Doggett whether she had ever taken chloroform and was it a nice or a pleasant feeling. She said Mr. Bartlett was in the habit of taking sleeping drops and that while ten drops was a strong dose, she did not hesitate to give him twelve. This evidently referred to the small bottle of chlorodyne found the next day. At 10:30 the maid took fresh coals up to the Bartlett sitting room and then went to bed. The Doggetts were splitting a few pints of cheer with a few friends in their own quarters and retired around 12:30. Silence descended on 85 Claverton Street until 4.00 A.M., and what happened during those three and a half hours is still referred to as "The Pimlico Mystery."

At 4.00 A.M. Mrs. Bartlett knocked on the door of the maid's room. "Alice, I want you to go for Dr. Leach. I think Mr. Bartlett is dead." Adelaide then called Mr. Doggett, who was conveniently at the registry for births and deaths in the district, and when Mr. Doggett and the doctor entered, they found a good fire in the room, but the body of Edwin Bartlett was cold, presumably from being dead two or three hours. The expression on his face was natural. There was no sign of a convulsion or a struggle. There was no smell detectable on the lips, although there was a slight moisture smelling of brandy on the chest as if someone had tried to pour brandy down the dead man's mouth. Dr. Leach pronounced Edwin Bartlett dead. Mrs. Bartlett was crying bitterly. She said she had heard the Doggett's guest leaving and the locking of the street door. Mr. Bartlett was asleep, and she was in the easy chair in which she usually slept these days with her left arm around his foot—toe-holding as usual. She awoke once and heard him snoring in a peculiar way but dropped off to sleep again. She awoke later with a cramp in her arm and noticed that Mr. Bartlett was in an uncomfortable position with his face buried in the pillow. She rose to turn him over and found him cold. She rubbed his chest with brandy and tried to pour it down his throat, but getting no response she called the maid. "What can he be dead of, Doctor?" asked Mrs. Bartlett. "I don't know," replied Dr. Leach. "Could he have got prussic acid?" But Mrs. Bartlett uttered one of the crucial statements of the case. "Oh, no. He could have got at no poison without my knowledge."

Dr. Leach and Mr. Doggett searched the room carefully. The head of the bed was close to one corner of the mantel shelf. Anyone in bed, by raising up slightly and stretching out an arm, could reach anything on the shelf. There was a wineglass three quarters full of brandy, but having the smell, according to Mr. Doggett, of ether or some other drug. On a small stand, out of reach of the bed, was a small bottle labeled "chlorodyne." Dr. Leach and Mr. Doggett were both positive that there was no bottle of chloroform on the mantel or in the cupboard they searched. And Adelaide stuck to her story. "I have given him nothing." She said he had rubbed his gums with the chlorodyne but did not swallow it. She urged for a post-mortem and told Dr. Leach to get any assistance he wanted and to spare no expense. "We are all interested in knowing the cause of death," she told him.

Dr. Leach telegraphed Dr. Green, an eminent pathologist at St. Thomas's Hospital, but he could not come until the next day. Adelaide pouted at the delay. The next day Dr. Green and his assistant, Dr. Murray of Charing Cross Hospital, arrived and were met by Dr. Leach and Dr. Dudley. Telegrams had been sent to old Mr. Bartlett, Mr. Baxter, Mr. Bartlett's business partner, and the Rev. George Dyson. In the meantime, Bartlett, Sr., had been literally sniffing around. He kissed his son's lips to see if he could detect the smell of prussic acid, but smelled nothing. He engaged a Dr. Cheyne to represent him at the post-mortem and sat back, expecting the worst and hoping for disaster.

Mr. Dyson, Mr. Baxter, Edwin Bartlett's father, relatives, and the widow assembled in a room below during the post-mortem. Dr. Green compared the freshly opened stomach to a freshly opened bottle of chloroform so strong was the odor, and some inflammation of the stomach was found. Generally, the body was that of a healthy, well-nourished man in his prime, and the doctors announced that they were unable to discover any natural or obvious cause of death. However the pungent smell from the stomach suggested further investigation. The rooms were locked, sealed, and handed over to the coroner. An inquest was called, and the inner man of what had been Edward Bartlett left Claverton Street in jars and bundles, bound for the Home Office and a little further analysis.

Adelaide Bartlett, with a bag and cloak, was ready to leave for the home of friends, the Matthews in Dulwich, but she was not allowed to take the bag. Bartlett senior, with snoopy malice, had searched her cloak and found no pockets so she was allowed to take that, and Mr. Bartlett even kissed her good-bye. Neither Mrs. Bartlett's abandoned bag nor the drawers in the bedroom were ever searched. Four days later, Mrs. Bartlett visited the rooms and found the bottle of chloroform still in the drawer where she later claimed to have put it. On her return trip to Dulwich, she threw the bottle out the window.

Mr. Dyson, however, was getting nervous. When he escorted Mrs. Bartlett to Dulwich after the post-mortem, he asked if she had used the chloroform he got for her. She told him no, that the bottle was there as he gave it to her and not to worry her about it and to forget it himself. The next day, Mr. Dyson threw away the four small bottles at different places on Wandsworth Common as he went to preach a sermon at Tooting. At Dulwich, there was an angry scene in which Dyson showed all the twitchy symptoms of wanting off the hook. He demanded the return of some verses he had written for Adelaide. She complied by tearing them up and giving him the pieces, but nastily announced she had either copied or memorized them. One such effort was:

> Who is it that hath burst the door,
> Unclosed the heart that shut before
> And set her queen-like on its throne,
> And made its homage all her own?—
>
> *My* BIRDIE

Whether Mr. Dyson was worried about Mr. Bartlett's unexplained death, or the calfish quality of his poetry is a moot point. He had good cause to worry about both. He again asked Adelaide about the chloroform, and she must have found him a little tiresome, because she stamped her small foot and said, "Oh, damn the chloroform."

On January 26, Dr. Leach told Mrs. Bartlett that chloroform, not a secret poison, had been found in the body, and the doctors found that Mr. Bartlett had died from swallowing liquid chloroform. To which Mrs. Bartlett replied: "I wish anything but chloroform had been found;" and then proceeded to make her famous statement to Dr. Leach. It was Balzac tainted with the sweet smell of chloroform or Boccaccio's ribald laughter distorted into a furtive leer. Mrs. Bartlett's twenty-sixth January statement to Dr. Leach was recounted both at the inquest and the trial. After her marriage, Mrs. Bartlett stated, she was induced to enter into a compact that the marital relations of the pair, in deference to certain peculiar views held by the husband, should be of an entirely platonic nature. There was one specific breach due to her desire for motherhood. After the death of her baby in 1881, their former platonic relations had resumed with her husband's full consent, and they lived on the most amicable terms. He liked to surround her with male acquaintances and was delighted with the admiration and attention she gained. It was Mr. Bartlett who threw her and Mr. Dyson together. He requested them to kiss in his presence and gave her to Dyson. At a later period, Bartlett wished to renew marital relations, but she told him with an assiduous regard for the properties, "Edwin, you know you have given me to Mr. Dyson. It is not right that you should now do what during all these years of our married life you have not done." He agreed she was right, but in December, when he was getting better, he again became urgent. She got chloroform to sprinkle on her handkerchief to soothe him to sleep. However, she did not have occasion to use it. On New Year's Eve her conscience troubled her. She got the bottle out, gave it to Bartlett and told him why she had procured it. Bartlett was not angry. He put the bottle on the corner of the mantelpiece and turned on his side pretending to sleep.

The rest, she said, happened exactly as she told it to Dr. Leach and Mr. Doggett. She said the chloroform bottle was on the mantel until she put it in a drawer in the back room at breakfast time. She did not examine the bottle to see if her husband had taken any of the contents. This statement was used at the inquest, so there was no need for Mrs. Bartlett to testify. On February 11, the Rev. George Dyson, going along with the tenet that confession is good for the soul, told all. He quoted Mrs. Bartlett as saying in reference to the chloroform, "If you do not incriminate me, you may be perfectly sure I will not incriminate you." His testimony caused a sensation. "Then, I am a ruined man," he told her.

After Dyson's evidence, to which Mrs. Bartlett listened with frosty composure, the inquest jury recommended the arrest of Mrs. Bartlett, and when the inquest closed on February 18, the verdict was willful murder against Mrs. Bartlett, with George Dyson indicted as an accessory before the fact. Reverend Dyson sank into a chair almost fainting, while a group of his Wesleyan friends, including several ministers, stood around him registering varying degrees of sympathy, shock, and suspicion.

The trial opened on April 12, 1886, to standing room only. Special tickets of admission were needed. Extra seats were built, and Mr. Gladstone's career-killing Home Rule Bill was temporarily pre-empted by the Pimlico Mystery. The case was tried at the Central Criminal Court before Mr. Justice Wills. The formidable fighting Irishman, Sir Charles Russell, who three years later was Mrs. Maybrick's defender, led for the crown. Sir Frank Lockwood appeared for Mr. Dyson, and the Horatio Alger of the bar, Sir Edward Clarke, was briefed for Adelaide Bartlett. Sir Edward had established his reputation nine years before when he defended Patrick Staunton, the more unpleasant of the two Staunton brothers, at a trial where everything hinged on the medical testimony. And here was history repeating itself.

The first unexpected move came when the attorney general stated that no case would be submitted to the jury on which they could properly be asked to convict Mr. Dyson. Mr. Dyson and Mrs. Bartlett were sitting together in the dock like disinterested strangers. After this announcement, Mr. Dyson scurried from the dock with mercurial, if not commendable, speed. Suddenly, the dock loomed bigger, and the prisoner looked smaller and very much alone.

Sir Charles Russell, in his opening statement for the crown, emphasized Edwin Bartlett's good health. He said the deceased had died from the effects of chloroform and the question was: How did it get there? There were three alternatives. Suicide, accident, or administration by another party. Taken with the intention of committing suicide or taken by accident, the pain would have been so acute there would have been contortions and outcries. Such a reaction would also be expected if it were administered to him by another person, unless it were preceded by some external application. It was the contention of the crown that Mrs. Bartlett administered the chloroform first by inhalation for partial or complete insensibility then poured the fatal dose into Edwin Bartlett's mouth.

Clarke hinted at the defense's battle formation in his opening. The defense would show that administration of liquid chloroform was extremely difficult, for the medically unskilled virtually impossible, and would seek to prove that Mrs. Bartlett's January 26 statement to Dr. Leach was extraordinary but substantially true. He added that suicide was not unfeasible.

Bartlett, Sr., loaded for bear and out to get his daughter-in-law, made an unconvincing witness because of his obvious maliciousness. His main preoccupation was to dispute his son's last will as a forgery, although he knew there were witnesses in court to testify that they had seen it properly executed. He lingered over the old scandal of Adelaide and her brother-in-law. Even the judge felt constrained to point out to the jury that "very little depends on the evidence of the senior Bartlett."

Mrs. Matthews testified as to the scene between Mr. Dyson and Mrs. Bartlett at her home in Dulwich. Mr. Matthews said that Mrs. Bartlett said her husband's death was due to mercurial poisoning and moving things in the warehouse looking for rats. She also told him there was no poison in the house and said that Dr. Leach told her it would have been impossible for her to have given Edwin chloroform by inhalation without it showing in the brain, and she could not have given it to him by mouth or he would have raised the house with his outcries. Dr. Nichols made a brief appearance to state flatly that he had never seen Mr. Bartlett, Mrs. Bartlett, or Annie Walker.

Thomas Nichols was a graduate of medicine in New York, but had no degree to practice medicine in Britain. He was responsible for the issue of the English edition of *Esoteric Anthropology (The Mysteries of Man): A Comprehensive and Confidential Treatise on the Structure, Functions, Passional Attractions and Perversions, True and False Physical and Social Conditions, and the Most Intimate Relations of Man and Woman*. The Bartletts had a copy of this book with the self-explanatory title.

Annie Walker said she attended Mrs. Bartlett during her confinement, but that chloroform was never used, discussed, or procured to her knowledge.

Tom Ralph, an officer on the Metropolitan Police Force, told of searching the rooms on Claverton Street and said that in the pockets of the deceased's clothes he had found certain articles of foreign manufacture not consistent with Mrs. Bartlett's version of their marital relationship.

Dyson, as a witness, sounded like a broken record. "I did what she wanted . . . she told me . . . she asked me," was his whining refrain. Mrs. Bartlett gazed into space. There are worse things in life than a death sentence. Mr. Bartlett's peculiar view on the subject of marriage were brought out during Dyson's cross-examination. "He made statements which left no doubt in my mind but that he contemplated Mrs. Bartlett and myself being ultimately married." He admitted he had seen Bartlett put his hand to his side and complain of some compulsive pain; on more than one occasion when his wife was present Bartlett told him he was not the strong man he once was, attributing it to overwork. He had seen Bartlett depressed and crying and had a strong impression Bartlett thought he would not recover. There's nothing like a murder trial to separate the men from the boys. Mr. Dyson flew from the witness box and from Adelaide Bartlett, probably vowing never to go near another married woman, even if she were offered to him on a silver platter like John the Baptist's head.

Dr. Alfred Leach, of Charlwood Street, made a self-conscious witness. He took the witness stand with a zealous determination to do his duty and notes in every pocket to prod his memory, and before the ordeal was over, he longed for the obscurity of Charlwood Street and the simplicities of croup and childbirth. He was told by the judge to calm down. "It detracts from the value of what you have to say." And Dr. Leach had a lot to say. He repeated Mrs. Bartlett's January 26 statement.

On cross-examination he said Mrs. Bartlett was a devoted wife and nurse. Her own health was suffering. Clarke started blocking in the picture of a man not mortally sick but of one who wanted to die. Dr. Leach testified that Mr. Bartlett was practically an hysterical patient and his wife petted him very much. On the twenty-third, he passed a worm and felt worms wriggling up his throat. Bartlett was sure that he and his wife had been mesmerized by friends. Bartlett told the doctor on the twenty-sixth, "I could not sleep. I was nervous and restless. When I saw my wife asleep in the chair, I got up and went and stood over her like this." The doctor held up his arms in dramatic demonstration. "I was like this for two hours, and I felt the vital force being drawn from her to me. I felt it going through my fingertips, and after that I laid down and slept." Such a thing could not have been imagined by an unpretentious neighborhood practicioner. Dr. Leach testified, "My patient was one of the most extraordinary men I ever had to deal with—though a very pleasant and nice man."

"Did you actually suspect him of insanity?" Clarke inquired crisply.

"At one time I did, and I tried to find the key to it." Dr. Leach gave a hopeless shrug. When Dr. Leach left the stand he remarked weakly, "It was like a college examination under oath."

The crown's medical star was Dr. Thomas Stevenson, Professor of Medical Jurisprudence at Guy's Hospital, toxicologist of international repute, and leading consulting physician of his day. He had performed the analysis of Edwin Bartlett's remains at the request of the Home Office and found $11\frac{1}{4}$ grams of chloroform in the stomach as the cause of death. Clarke's cross-examination brought admissions that there was no case recorded anywhere of murder by the administration of liquid chloroform. Dr. Stevenson stated the brain appeared normal. There was some fencing, but Dr. Stevenson finally conceded if chloroform were inhaled, an odor in cerebral ventricles of the brain would prob-

ably be apparent. Since medical evidence was the crux of the
case, it was up to Clarke to demolish the crown's chief medical
witness. It was a forensic masterpiece of verbal annihilation.

Q. : You say there is a particular point in the process of
chloroforming at which the patient would be able to swallow,
though he was sufficiently under the influence of chloroform not
to suffer from the pain.

A. : I do.

Q. : How would you yourself ascertain that that time had
arrived.

A. : By the reflex of the eye. I would not like to pour down
the throat if the reflex had been abolished.

Q. : How would you test it :

A. : By touching the eye and watching for the closure of the
eyelid.

Q. : Would you mind touching your own eye; just showing
us how it is done?

A. : Like this. You separate the eyelids, see? And . . . just
touch the conjunctiva.

Q. : I am much obliged. That is the test to ascertain if the
sensation of pain has gone.

A. : Yes.

Q. : Suppose you had to deal with a sleeping man and it was
your object to get down his throat without his knowing it, a
liquid which would cause great pain; do you not agree it would
be a very difficult and delicate operation.

A. : I think it would be an operation which would often fail;
and might often succeed.

Q. : Would you not look on it as a delicate operation?

A. : Yes, I should look on it as delicate. I should be afraid of
pouring it down the windpipe.

Q. : If the patient got into such a state of insensibility as not
to reject it, it would go down his windpipe and burn that.

A. : Some of it might.

Q. : If it did so, it would leave its traces?

A. : I should expect to find traces.

Clarke had really nailed Dr. Stevenson. Chloroform would have left burns if it had been administered after the victim was unconscious. It had been admitted there were no such traces. Prior to insensibility, there would have been loud screams. There had been no such screams. So Sir Edward Clarke had whittled down the time when Mrs. Bartlett might have safely administered chloroform to her husband, without noise and without burning traces, to an almost impossible few seconds, which even Dr. Stevenson admitted would be a "delicate operation" for him.

Just before the summing up, Annie Walker was recalled by Clarke and he probably wished he had left well enough alone.

Q. : At the time you nursed Mrs. Bartlett in her confinement, did you become aware of anything she said to you with regard to its having been the result of a single act?

A. : Yes, sir.

Mr. Justice Wills : What was it?

A. : That it happened only once, on a Sunday afternoon.

Q. : She said so?

A. : Both of them; that there was always some preventative used.

Mrs. Bartlett could not give evidence at her own trial, according to the existing law, so her statement to Dr. Leach was her only representation. She could have made voluntary statement from the dock, but she wisely refrained. Three years later Mrs. Maybrick made such a statement and just barely escaped "being turned off."

The defense called no witnesses, and Sir Edward Clarke began his six-hour closing speech. His lucid organization of the facts, the persuasive melody of his voice were almost hypnotic. He pounded home the medical evidence and the amiable relations between husband and wife. He dismissed the false excuse given by Mrs. Bartlett to Mr. Dyson for the chloroform as reticence due to the delicate nature of the problem. He argued that Mrs. Bartlett's story was supported by Bartlett's odd views on marriage and the letter to Dyson. It was suicide brought on my an unsound mind, bad health, and Mrs. Bartlett's confession about the chloroform. Sir Edward sketched a graphic picture. "He drank it off quickly . . . there were no burns in the mouth and throat . . . no vomiting or outcries . . . Mr. Bartlett went to sleep peacefully . . . Here was no scientific miracle worked by a grocer's wife. . . ."

The crown in its final reply made a desperate, last minute attempt to introduce the line that Mrs. Bartlett had administered the chloroform in brandy, but Clarke jumped up with violent objections and the judge ruled it was too late to admit the new theory as evidence. By limiting itself to the proposition that Bartlett had died from a combination of inhalation and oral administration of liquid chloroform, the crown was faced with the embarrassing fact that its whole case was based on a near impossibility.

The judge's summing up was fair and thoroughly covered all the points. "If you take the evidence on either hand alone, you would say the thing could not be done. Yet it has been done and one of the two impossible theories is right." The case had all the fascination of the murder-in-a-locked-room classic.

The jury went out at a little before three, and it was five o'clock before the word circulated that they had reached a verdict. The gas jets were lit in the court, and the only sounds were the steady drip of rain on the windows and the speculative buzz of the crowd. The judge was a scarlet exclamation mark as he resumed his seat. The sheriffs in their gold chains of office and violet costumes, the black silk robes of counsel, the white wigs, all punctuated the slender figure in widows weeds, as Mrs. Bartlett was half carried with eyes closed to the front of the dock, sagging against two women warders.

"Although we think there is the gravest suspicion attaching to the prisoner, we do not think there is sufficient evidence to show how or by whom the chloroform was administered," and they pronounced Adelaide Bartlett not guilty. With their verdict, the jury handed Adelaide Bartlett her life and liberty but not her character.

The prisoner gasped. The court erupted, and Sir Edward Clarke put his head in his hands and cried for the first and last time in fifty-years of practice. Adelaide Bartlett was the topic of the day, and Sir Edward Clarke was the hero of the hour.

On April 24, in a letter of graceful Victorian phrasing and ambiguity, Mrs. Bartlett wrote to Sir Edward Clarke:

Dear Sir:

Forgive me for not earlier expressing my heartfelt gratitude to you. I feel I owe my life to your earnest efforts, and though I cannot put into words the feelings that fill my heart, you will understand all that my pen fails to express to you.

Your kind looks towards me cheered me very much, for I felt that you believed me innocent.

I have heard many eloquent Jesuits preach, but I never listened to anything finer than your speech.

My story was a painful one, but sadly true; My consent to my marriage was not asked, and I only saw my husband once before my wedding day.

I am much gratified that Dr. Stevenson has written to say that he concurs in the verdict. He wrote so kindly of Miss Wood who has been a true friend. I received great kindness at Clerkenwell, from the Governor to the lowest.

Assuring you that I shall ever remember you with feelings of deepest gratitude, I am sincerely yours

ADELAIDE BARTLETT

So often the victim in a murder trial is an abstract that is the topic of much conversation but never emerges as a whole personality. Mr. and Mrs. Borden were no more than a specified number of hatchet gashes. Mr. Seddon grabbed the limelight while Miss Barrow's arsenic-impregnated stomach was a haggling point between the prosecution and defense. There's the impersonal jigsaw of bone splinters that had once been Miss Emily Kaye or the grouplike personality of Jack the Ripper's hollowed-out victims. But in the Bartlett case, the corpse played a dominant part. Mr. Bartlett was the primary source, the instigator of the circumstances that culminated in the Pimlico Mystery. He set the pace for the relationship between Mr. Dyson and his wife. Both Mr. Dyson and Mrs. Bartlett admitted they had reached the stage where Mr. Bartlett's death and Dyson's succession were freely discussed. Eighty-five Claverton Street was not a place where a God Bless Our Happy Home sign could hang unblushingly.

Mr. Bartlett was obviously not himself, or, in modern parlance, he was some kind of a nut. His attitude toward his wife and Dyson, the wish of a perfectly healthy man to lie still and feel happy, worms wiggling up his throat, a friend hypnotizing him, standing two hours over his sleeping wife rather selfishly extracting vital forces from her would all indicate a one-way street to the happy house. There is always the possibility of suicide during an unbalanced period or an accidental swig of chloroform for insomnia, if Mrs. Bartlett had produced the bottle of chloroform and the blushing confession as she claims in her statement. In either case, Mrs. Bartlett would have had good reason not to mention the chloroform. If the question of suicide ever came up, Bartlett, Sr., would be just around the corner, like opportunity, waiting to claim that an unsound mind automatically invalidated his son's will.

But there is still another alternative that supports the whole exotic history of Edwin Bartlett's marriage and death. His actions plus his rather peculiar mentality suggest the impotent male. At the beginning of his married life, Bartlett gained a large sum of money and an attractive bride. He grabbed the money but shipped the cuddlesome Adelaide off to school for three years. After she came to live with him there was a lapse of almost four years before the stillborn son. Annie Walker's testimony on recall only refers to what happened prior to 1881. Perhaps there had been a few fumbling attempts to play the man, but the general pattern of the Bartletts' marriage was that of the impotent husband. He humored, spoiled, and defended his wife, while she responded with an indulgent, easygoing affection. Although Adelaide Bartlett was educated, she was not too bright. She was one of those agreeable, emotional women who let the moment dictate and the situation dominate with passive affability. She was a convent-bred girl who didn't know much about life, and the rather futile attempts of Mr. Bartlett to play the husband, plus the devastating ordeal of motherhood, probably left Adelaide with an aversion to all facets of procreation and a let-well-enough-alone attitude.

Then, Mr. Dyson came along. Dyson does not come off well. He was a gospel-spouting opportunist, who had learned his Victorian catechism well : be proper, be respectable, be repressed. Even his attachment to Mrs. Bartlett was an emasculated emotion. He was all form and no content. The trend of events in the Bartlett menage suited him admirably. Here was a beautiful woman and a comfortable inheritance, plus the righteousness of Mr. Bartlett's blessings on him as his successor. The whole arrangement, although a little unusual, was technically spotless and sin free. Mr. Dyson was a knight errant in the lists of pure and chivalrous love, but while he was probably a knight *sans reproche* in his relations with Mrs. Bartlett, it was painfully evident that, in his relations with the world, he was not a knight *sans peur*.

Things might have had a less harrowing, if less respectable, ending if Adelaide Bartlett had decisively settled for the nuptial bed, the illicit couch, or both. Then Mr. Bartlett complicated things by coming home with his pockets full of suggestive goodies and caddishly insisted on his marital privileges. In view of the Bartletts' tepid marital record, his sudden and belated interest in things of the flesh would be another indication that Edwin Bartlett was going through some sort of mental tempest. Adelaide was morally outraged. She believed Edwin was not long for this world, that she was really Mr. Dyson's, and she had been reading up on chloroform. Mr. Bartlett had become a superfluous husband and was hoisted by his own petard. Her statement to Dr. Leach has the ring of truth, even if she took a few understandable liberties. She did not tell Dyson the real reason she needed the chloroform out of reticence. But Edwin Bartlett's strange reaction to medicine indicates that pouring chloroform on her handkerchief and waving it under his nose would have about the same effect as rose water.

So, she decided on the more drastic measure of mixing brandy and chloroform to cure his insomnia. Adelaide Bartlett did not realize that a normal person would have cried out or screamed, but when one considers that Edwin Bartlett only had a warm comforting sensation in his stomach from a couple of economy-size doses of croton oil, the theory that if he swallowed chloroform while conscious, he would have screamed or cried out, rather pales. There are also form of hysteria in mentally disturbed persons which create a complete insensitivity to pain. Knowing Edwin Bartlett, he probably downed Adelaide's brandy and chloroform panacea for insomnia in one lusty gulp and remarked that it settled his jugged hare and oysters. The facts fit the theory. Adelaide really thought her husband would die soon, so why should she put herself in jeopardy. Her husband certainly confirmed her fears, or her hopes. For a healthy man, he certainly was preoccupied with the grim reaper and went through some morbid motions. Her use of chloroform was simply to gain time and ward off Mr. Bartlett's urgings for something a little more intimate than toe-holding.

When she woke up and found him sleeping in an uncomfortable position, she had no idea he was dead, so she stirred up the fire and tried to get him in a more comfortable position. Only then did she discover his sleep was permanent. The three-quarters full brandy glass and the smell of brandy on his chest indicate that she told the truth about trying to rouse him, but the other smell of ether that Mr. Doggett and Dr. Leach noticed in the glass would have been a hang-over from the original draught Adelaide had given him. Neither Dr. Leach or Mr. Doggett could be jarred loose from their original statements that there was no bottle on the mantelpiece, only the wineglass. While Mrs. Bartlett clung with equal tenacity to her hiding the bottle at breakfast version. In relation to this, it is interesting to recall the Merrett case, where in an age of scientific deduction, the police themselves offered conflicting testimony as to the geographical location of the crucial gun after it was fired. The atmosphere immediately following violent death is not conclusive to cool logic or infallible memory. Her insistence on a post-mortem would indicate that she was convinced that Edwin had some fatal illness that would explain his death. She unhesitatingly closed off escape by stating there was no way he could have obtained poison without her knowledge and casually shoved the chloroform in a drawer and waited for the results. It was only after the post-mortem when an inquest was called and the authorities took over that she got rid of the chloroform. Only after chloroform was established as the cause of death, did she make her statement to Dr. Leach. But she very wisely failed to mention that she had given Edwin the fatal cup for obvious reasons. The whole relationship of the Bartletts and Dyson was based on the supposition that Bartlett would die in the near future, and Adelaide was guilty of little feminine stalling. When it became clear that death was due to chloroform and that there was nothing wrong with Edwin Bartlett, except possibly his head, the time for truth was past. She had means of death in her possession, and a pretty fantastic story. But then the Bartletts and Mr. Dyson were pretty fantastic people.

The accidental death of Edwin Bartlett would plug many of the gaps in the Pimlico Mystery, and it distills the essence of Victoriphobia. There was the public picture of a devoted couple receiving pastoral calls from their minister, the horsehair, and the cozy sanctity that the Victorians loved and applauded. But there was the private distortion of sex life definitely not in orbit, overtones of impotency, highlights of insanity. It was an outgrowth of ingrown instincts, a sort of moral flatulence, a murderous burp.

After the trial Sir James Paget, a distinguished surgeon, stated the case succinctly when he remarked: "Mrs. Bartlett was no doubt properly acquitted, but now it is to be hoped in the interest of science she will tell us how she did it."

Adelaide Bartlett was either very wronged or very lucky, or maybe both, because the operation was a success, but the patient died.

XII

The Girl of the Golden West

LAURA FAIR HAD A BAD TRACK RECORD with men and matrimony. It wasn't that she didn't try. In fact, that's how she got into trouble. Laura had the natural equipment, blond hair, blue eyes, and undulating proportions. She had the natural inclination and four marriages to prove it, but happiness eluded her like pay dirt shunned a hungry prospector. Love was a poke of gold dust that always turned into sand.

Laura was born in Holly Springs, Mississippi, in 1837. At the age of sixteen, she married William Stone, a New Orleans liquor dealer, who was overly fond of his own product and died from cholera the following year. Laura picked up a few pertinent pointers from her next husband, Thomas J. Grayson. Grayson had two hobbies—drinking and shooting. The bedroom wall of their honeymoon cottage was riddled with bullet holes, and, when he wanted more stimulating target practice, he headed for the chicken coop and "murder most fowl." Laura had learned all about marksmanship and was worried that she might wind up as a target someday, so she took off for San Francisco with her mother, Mrs. Mary Lane. From this safer vantage point and out of bullet range, Laura divorced the trigger-happy Mr. Grayson.

Her next try was Col. William D. Fair, a moderately successful lawyer. After two years of wedded bliss, and for reasons of his own, the Colonel ended it all with a Colt six-shooter accurately aimed at his head. Guns always did play an important role in Laura's life. To his widow Colonel Fair bequeathed an estate of three hundred dollars from the sale of his law books, and a one-year-old baby girl, called Lillias Lorraine. Laura didn't have an easy time. She tried to run a boarding house in Sacramento, but lodgers were elusive and a brief fling at the stage was a financial and artistic "turkey." She made the Metropolitan Theatre in San Francisco as Lady Teazle in *School for Scandal*, but, even in the undemanding days before method acting, she didn't rate SRO signs. But while Laura struggled for survival, great things were shaping. The Sierras were spitting silver. Every down-at-the-heel, low-on-cash dreamer was headed for Virginia City, Nevada, and Laura, with her mother, child, and a three hundred dollar grubstake, hit the trail. With her borrowed capital, she opened the Tahoe House. It might not be the International House on A Street with ironwork balconies, plate-glass mirrors, and crystal chandeliers, but her sheets were clean, her rooms neat, and the landlady was attractive, so within a very short time Laura was doing fine.

Even at the top of Sun Mountain, sympathy and interest over the North and South were bitter, and Laura was a real sympathizer. Tahoe House became the gathering place and political forum for the rather dust-bedecked flower of Southern chivalry in Virginia City.

In the early sixties Virginia City, Nevada, was pay dirt and pandemonium. The big bonanza—the Comstock Lode—had struck it rich in 'fifty-nine, and the rush was on. Within a year, Virginia City sprawled and spurted along the side of Sun Mountain, the home of 30,000 silver-hungry souls. A. B. and C. Streets staggered up this slope of the Sierra Nevadas, as if laid out by the hand of a city planner with too many shots of "tangle-leg" under his belt. C Street was the main street, spawning rooming houses, livery stables, hurdy-gurdy houses, saloons, restaurants, assay offices, and gambling houses. Above C Street were the residences of merchants, mining officials, and the respectable element of the town. Below C Street was the Chinese section and the wickiup huts of the Washoe and Piute Indians. And, apart from everything, in a moral and topographical quarantine, clustered rows of white cabins with no curtains, the windows a wooden frame for the commercial charms within.

Twenty-four hours a day, C Street erupted with sights and sound. There were veteran forty-niners, secessionists, poets, painters, river rats from the Mississippi, Yankees, merchants, lawyers, gamblers, swindlers, Chinese coolies with pigtails and bundles of wash, explorers in buckskins headed for the Snake and Bitteroot country to the north, Mexicans with jangling silver saddles and spurs, miners in red shirts and blue jeans. Everybody who could breathe, crawl, and dream of El Dorado, came to Virginia City. The streets might not be paved with gold, but it was the next best thing to heaven. "Blue dirt"—silver—could be shoveled right out of the loose ground.

Oxen in harness creaked up the side of the mountain with supplies. The Wells Fargo Pony Express thundered around the corner, loaded with bullion for San Francisco. Mules, or Washoe canaries, toted hopeful prospectors out to their claims. And camels made their majestic way through Devil's Gate, bringing salt from the desert for the busy amalgamating pans. An excited miner rushed up the street. He had struck pay dirt. He recorded his strike at the assay office and then started "selling feet." Girls from the faro tables and hurdy-gurdy houses promenaded on C Street, but Julia Bulette, who had made her house a home for the "boys," took the air in a brougham with an enameled escutcheon on its door. Sam Clemens of the *Territorial Enterprise* surveyed the scene and decided to sign his next article "Mark Twain." Eilley Orrum Bowers, the Queen of Washoe, was telling an awe-struck audience about the silver doorknobs in her mansion. Langford Peel, the professional gunslinger, explained the secret of his shooting skill to a group of aspiring badmen. His personal golden rule was "Do unto others as they would do unto you, only do it first." Charlie (Baron) Fairfax, after his fifth whiskey, was asserting with alcoholic fervor and frequency that he didn't want to go back to England as Lord Fairfax. He preferred a bar stool in good old Washoe to a seat in the House of Lords. Fortunes were made and lost as frequently as the swinging doors on the Young America Saloon squeaked open and shut. Road agents lounged against the frame buildings and kept a practiced eye on the Wells Fargo Express. Music tinkled and blared from the saloons and hurdy-gurdy houses. Steady pounding thudded from the mills that were crushing silver ore and quartz. Ore wagons rumbled, and the muffled blasting boomed from the guts of the mountain. The Washoe Zephyr, depending on its moods, playfully ruffled the feathers of a strolling lady or viciously bowled over an outhouse. "Stand up and deliver" in the patois of stagecoach robbers wasn't a request for an after-dinner speech, and when someone said "draw," it had nothing to do with art. "Tarantula juice" was sold for twenty-five cents a shot, and barrels of it were guzzled every day. Champagne was twelve dollars gold per bottle, and, if the customer wanted to drink out of a slipper, that cost extra too. This was Virginia City. It was lusty, loud, and hard-living and could have fit, without any apologies, onto a twenty-one-inch television screen.

In the line of business, Laura Fair met Alexander Parker Crittenden. Mr. Crittenden, of the Kentucky Crittendens, had graduated from the West Point Military Academy in 1836 and chalked up ten years of successful legal practice in the Bluegrass State. In 1849, that booming, brawling year in California's history, he came to San Francisco. When Crittenden arrived, he was riding the fiery tail of the Gold Rush, and the rallying cry of "To the Gold Fields" had one of the greatest impacts since the crusaders' "Deus Vult." From all over, men with a dream or men with an angle answered the call. They came into San Francisco Bay in anything from Chinese junks to full-rigged ships. They came overland in prairie schooners and on horseback or foot. Crittenden lived and practiced law in exciting times. He watched the activities of the Committee of Vigilance, exercising stern justice and parading to the strains of martial music with nosegays attached to their muskets. He was there during the bloody chaos of the murder of James King of William, the crusading editor if the *Daily Evening Bulletin*. He turned out with the whole town for King's funeral, following the black-plumed hearse to Lone Mountain, the pioneer cemetery, a journey he was to repeat a few years later.

Crittenden was elected to the state's first General Assembly, had one of the most successful corporation practices in the state, and oozed political and social assurance. San Francisco was three hundred miles from Virginia City, but, after the Comstock Lode came in, there were close business ties between the two towns. Silver and gold were disgorged from the mines of Nevada, but market traders in Comstock silver stock plied their brisk trade on the streets and in the banking houses of San Francisco. Charlie "Baron" Fairfax was a courtroom and barroom acquaintance, and when Crittenden asked him, over a convivial snort, "Where to put up," the Baron took him from his bar stool to the Tahoe House, the home base of "secesh" sympathizers in Virginia City. Crittenden was as Southern as a frosted julep. Mrs. Fair was a real fetching lady from the right side of the Mason-Dixon line, and, all in all, the Baron was happy for his friend and pleased with his own bottle-born perspicacity.

There were widespread lawsuits over mining titles and legal skirmishes to get possession of rich ledges, and Mr. Crittenden's business took him to Virginia City, where he became a leading and frequent figure at the Washoe Bar. He was forty-six, sternly handsome, and surprisingly virile. He had seven children, a coming crop of grandchildren, and there was the sweet smell of success and expensive bay rum about him. When Crittenden and Laura Fair met, probably as he signed his name on the guest register and she handed him the key to his room, it marked the beginning of seven years struggle that, in its own small way, was as action-packed and harrowing as that other seven-year epic, the French and Indian war. Both Laura and Crittenden were firm advocates of the institution of matrimony. Laura wanted Crittenden to marry her. Crittenden wanted to marry her, but unfortunately there was a very-much-alive lady who had staked a previous claim to Crittenden's bed, board, and name. He wanted to stay married to her, too.

Crittenden was not a cad. He was not a wolf, and he was not a despoiler of women. He was just overly domesticated. With him it was a matter of capacity. When he was in San Francisco, he lived amicably with his wife in their Taylor Street mansion, with its impressive dimensions, big-name guest lists, and top-level social life. There were moonlight parties on the bay, candle-lit cotillions. It was an enjoyable champagne-and-oysters-on-the-half-shell kind of life. When he went to Virginia City on business, Crittenden liked to prowl down the hall of the Tahoe house to Laura's room where, after a discreet tap on the door, he entered into the soft domestic glow of Laura's pretty hands on her embroidery, Lillias Lorraine playing and prattling on the floor, and Laura's mother, Mrs. Lane, reading aloud from Jane Porter's *The Scottish Chiefs* or a dime novel, a recent and lucrative innovation of Mr. Erastus Beadle's. Crittenden had no yen for the fleshpots nor the glass-clinking sociability of the barroom. He was a family man, whose home was his castle. He just had too many castles.

In a more rigid society, the chance of a relationship between a prominent lawyer and the keeper of a rooming house would have had long odds, but in Virginia City such things were dismissed with a democratic wink. And Laura was no frontier trollop, trailing her feathers and finery in the C Street dust. She was a shrewd business woman, who made a success of her boom-town boarding house and, over the years, parleyed a few holdings in the Comstock to 45,000. But she was too prodigal with her southern hospitality.

One night Laura perched on Crittenden's knee full of purpose and languishing sighs and asked him when would they get married. Mr. Crittenden soothingly patted her gold curls and told her it would be within the next few months, just as soon as he got some business deals straightened out. His was really a sin of omission. He neglected to mention that one of the "business deals" was the current Mrs. Crittenden.

At this time, word reached Virginia City of President Lincoln's inaugural address. The *Territorial Enterprise* hit the dusty streets with an "X-tra" edition. Northern sympathizers ran up a thirty-foot banner on the summit of Sun Mountain and shouted them-selves hoarse singing "John Brown's Body." But rebel sympa-thizers were waiting for an opportune time to take Washoe and its riches for the Confederacy.

A Yankee, inspired by patriotism and "tangle-leg," ran the Union flag up the pole that stood on the Tahoe House. Since this was Laura's property the little lady from Holly Springs, Mississippi, took violent exception when she heard that a "damned Yankee" flag was floating over the Tahoe House. Her jet eardrops quivered; her blue eyes flashed with Confederate rage. Laura picked up a revolver and headed for the roof quicker than she could whistle the first two bars of "Dixie." The exuber-ant Yankee was ordered to furl the offending stars and stripes. He refused. The irate Laura pulled the trigger, and the man fell down severely wounded and expertly ventilated by bullets.

Laura was arrested and tried for attempted murder. The *Territorial Enterprise* and northern sympathizers were against her. In Virginia City, interpretation of the law was not according to Hoyle or Blackstone. Judges could be bribed, juries fixed, and witnesses persuaded to give false testimony. Life was cheap, and the murder rate was high. It was the heyday of the individual, and Laura Fair was an extremely good-looking individual. By now, Crittenden was one of the leaders of the Washoe Bar. He impaneled a sympathetic jury, presumably twelve fire-eating secessionists, and made an eloquent plea for her defense, calling upon Shakespeare and Jeff Davis for support. Lovely ladies were a rarity in Virginia City, so Laura's gold curls and Crittenden's silver-tongued eloquence got her acquitted. For Laura, it was an instructive memory that lingered on.

One morning shortly after her acquittal, in the General Store, Laura, who had assumed that Crittenden was a widower, found out that there was a Mrs. Crittenden. Crittenden, with the role of widower cut from under him, clutched rather convincingly at the immortal part of the misunderstood husband. He told Laura he was married but that his marriage was a failure. He had been hoping to obtain a divorce and then confess everything on the way to the altar. He begged Laura to be patient and wait. Laura was very understanding, so much so that a few months later Crittenden pulled a real domestic idiot's delight. He walked into the dining room of San Francisco's Occidental Hotel with Mrs. Crittenden (Clara) on one arm and Laura on the other, while the carriage trade did a double take. If Crittenden had any remote hope of talking things over in a friendly manner, they were dashed. Mrs. Crittenden quietly left the dinner table a few minutes later on the polite plea of a headache, and Laura left for Virginia City tearfully and audibly pleading heartache.

Crittenden didn't give up easily. He followed Laura and was ordered out of the Tahoe House by Laura's mother, Mrs. Mary Lane. But Laura was a forgiving soul and wanted to believe Crittenden. She bought a house several blocks from the Tahoe House, on A Street, and moved in with her daughter and Crittenden. Crittenden was a fiend for punishment. He invited his wife to come to Virginia City, where she spent ten days in the house on A Street. Crittenden by some fast talking and some even faster nocturnal sprints from bedroom to bedroom, convinced each of the ladies that she alone was the queen of his heart, his affections, and his bed. Just what he hoped to accomplish by these abortive meetings is not clear. He was satisfied with things as they were and probably wanted both ladies to go along with the *status quo*. He loved them both. Crittenden's dilemma was obvious. That he loved Laura was certain. Their strenuous relationship over the long seven year haul was blood-sweat-and-tears proof. That he would not divorce his wife was certain. For a man of Crittenden's social and political background, such a step would be suicidal defiance, and Crittenden was no rebel, even with such a provocative cause as Laura.

By the end of 1866, Virginia City was slacking off. Crittenden no longer had business to bring him to the Washoe, and Laura followed him to San Francisco. The following years were a kaleidoscope of frustrations, quarrels, and reconciliations between Laura and Crittenden. Somehow, the divorce was a will-o'-the-wisp that gleamed and beckoned but remained an empty promise. There was a suicide attempt by Laura, presumably with a gun. Laura's mother was running a rooming house on San Francisco's Bush Street, and Laura had racked up a tidy fortune on the Comstock Lode. Laura would move in with her mother after a fight with Crittenden that would have made "Benecia Boy" Heenan flex his muscles in envy. Then with impassioned pleas, "I must love you with intensity until I die," Crittenden would brainwash Laura into taking unchaperoned rooms someplace else until the divorce came through. They had intimate suppers together; he called two and three times a day. Then, the divorce would hit another snag and Laura would go home to mother, while Crittenden would prowl through the lonely mansion on Taylor Street. Mrs. Crittenden had gone East for an extended visit, and Crittenden had vowed to Laura that he would keep her out of the state.

The passionate years were further enlivened by two occurrences. After a particularly bitter quarrel, Crittenden came back to make up, and Laura let it be understood that she was not in a forgiving mood this time. She blazed away at Crittenden with a five-shooter. She must have been upset to be so off her aim. "The shining light of the San Francisco Bar" took cover behind a thick door and escaped with everything unscathed except his dignity. Then, just to show Mr. Crittenden that her affections were to be trifled with no longer, she married Jesse W. Snyder, a lodger at her mother's rooming house. But Mr. Crittenden had an answer for that. Laura would simply have to get a divorce, and he would arrange it. Within a month, Jesse Snyder was a bachelor again, and Laura was back on Mr. Crittenden's knee. Evidently, Crittenden was better at getting divorces for other people than he was for himself.

It was like old times again until Laura heard that Mrs. Crittenden was returning from the East. Mr. Crittenden and his married daughter, Mrs. Sanchez, were furnishing a house on Ellis Street for a homecoming surprise. Their shopping spree was an orgy of velvet carpets, lace curtains, tapestries, inlaid tables, brocaded furniture, and Laura found out about it. "He promised to marry me. He promised to keep her out of the state. If she comes back one of the three of us must die." Sometimes to start knowing is to stop hoping. Laura had lived on hope for over seven years. The news of Mrs. Crittenden's return and the elaborate new home was for Laura the moment of truth.

She found Crittenden and did a little Western-type hell raising, but Crittenden, who admitted that Clara was returning to San Francisco—against his wishes, of course, said he would have everything ready for the divorce and their departure for the East. So what did it matter? The house was his farewell gift to Clara. Throughout the month of October, Laura nestled happily on Crittenden's knee and on the twenty-ninth of October, Crittenden casually broke the news to Laura that Mrs. Crittenden was returning on November 3. Laura traded in her gun on a new model—a Sharp four-shooter.

On November 3, he visited Laura on his way to Oakland to meet his family. She had been crying but allowed him to kiss her on the promise that "he would kiss no other." Laura seemed quite cheerful by the time Crittenden left. She bustled about with energy and businesslike precision. She put on a broad-rimmed hat, an all-enveloping veil, and a waterproof cloak, then walked with grim determination down the stairs, got into a hack she had ordered earlier in the afternoon, and boarded El Capitan, the next side-wheeler that was to ferry Mr. Crittenden across Oakland Bay to the collective bosom of his family. Crittenden, blissfully ignorant, sat on the deck while Laura lost herself in the crowded main cabin. When the ferry docked, she tried to see if Crittenden kissed his wife, but the crowd got in the way. She found them sitting on the upper deck. Mrs. Crittenden looked plumply complacent. A fourteen-year-old boy in the uniform of a military cadet tried to look very grown-up, and Mr. Crittenden appeared aggravatingly relaxed in his role of a fond husband and father. Laura watched from across the deck, saw them smiling affectionately, chattering happily, and loosened the strings of her reticule.

At ten minutes to six the El Capitan sounded the whistle and headed back to San Francisco. Laura saw Mrs. Crittenden take her husband's arms and that did it. She didn't know if he had kissed her or not, but this scene of wallowing domesticity was too much for Laura. She had waited seven years, but she was no Griselda. She walked across the deck, got the drop on Crittenden, and fired away. "I am shot," he groaned. Laura dropped her pistol and was waiting for the police in the gaslit saloon when the ferryboat chugged up to the San Francisco slip. Laura didn't give them any trouble. "Yes, I did it. and I meant to kill him. He ruined me and my child." All of which was a very admirable display of honesty on Laura's part, but it made things a little rough on her lawyer.

Laura was taken to the station house on Portsmouth Square, where she tore her hair and bit jagged pieces from tumblers. It took the combined force of a doctor, nurse, and policeman to get a sedative down the screamingly hysterical Laura. At the newly decorated house on Ellis Street, Mr. Crittenden was screaming, too. Laura's bullet had passed through his heart and both lungs, and the pain was searing and hot. In forty-eight hours he was dead. After four fate-haunted marriages, Laura could not afford to admit she had made a mistake with Crittenden. It would be emotional bankruptcy. So, she tried to blast away failure with a bullet.

Mr. Crittenden enjoyed the dubious honor of one of the largest funerals in San Francisco's history. The man who was constitutionally unable to live with just one woman was buried in Lone Mountain Cemetery, and the woman who shot him after seven years of existing on hope and broken promises stared through the bars of Portsmouth Jail. From now on, her memories would be a more effective prison than man-made bars.

The trial was held in the Fifteenth District Court of the Exchange Building, on the corner of Montgomery and Washington Streets, not too far from Mr. Crittenden's office. The defense was handled by Leander Quint and the courtroom tyro, Elisha Cook. Alexander Campbell, one of the Pacific Coast's outstanding criminal lawyers, and District Attorney Henry H. Byrne, with a reputation as an orator and prosecutor, represented the people of the State of California. The trial lasted twenty-six days, and crowds cross-sectioned the spectator seats with representatives from the Barbary Coast to Bay Society and the spectrum in between. Laura, for the first time in her life, was playing to a packed house. She was dressed in elegantly understated black silk, a wistful black tulle veil with just the right hint of widowhood, and she sat in a rocking chair with her small feet that Crittenden had so often admired on a foot warmer. Her ten-year-old daughter, a very beautiful child, and her mother, a grim guardian dragon, probably unable to suppress an I-told-you-so-look, sat beside her. There was a carafe of water for her sipping pleasure, and a comfortable couch for her to rest on leaned against one wall of the courtroom.

Laura's defense was simple. Everything went blank before she shot Crittenden. It was "emotional insanity" brought on by so many feminine ailments that one wonders if a lot of grief and pain couldn't have been avoided if Laura had reached for a bottle of Lydia Pinkham's Vegetable Compound instead of her four-shooter.

When Mr. Campbell referred to her as Crittenden's mistress, her right hand must have been itching for her four-shooter, but she had to content herself with verbal ammunition. "I am sure that Mr. Crittenden was the only friend I had in the world—and if he had been living now—he would have made Mr. Campbell on his bended knees apologize for it." All of which seemed to make Mr. Crittenden's death rather superfluous.

But the two sensations of the trial were the letters that turn up at Victorian murders almost as inevitably as rats and Laura's ideas on marriage. The letters were garden variety love letters of the time with references to dear faces, kissing, crossing the highest mountain, soul-mating, and heart music, nothing more graphic. But Laura's ideas on marriage were really original. According to her, she *was* Mr. Crittenden's wife. "God married me to him when we were both born. God made him for me and me for him. . . . That was adultery when I married Mr. Snyder." Coming from a more sophisticated woman, it would have sounded as if she were trying to fool the jury. Coming from Laura, it is more likely she was fooling herself. But either way, it left Mr. Stone, Mr. Grayson, and Colonel Fair out on a theosophical limb.

The prosecution tried to damage Laura's character and chastity and claimed her act was the poor sportsmanship of a woman who cannot have another woman's husband. She was a vile bad woman. The defense pictured Laura as a misunderstood woman who loved Crittenden to the end with a "fond, clinging affection"—well, almost to the end.

On April 26, 1871, the jury deliberated for forty minutes and found Laura Fair guilty of murder in the first degree. On June 3, 1871, Judge Dwinelle unhappily pronounced the first death sentence ever passed on a woman in the State of California. But Laura did not do the honors. On technical grounds, the Supreme Court reversed the decision and granted Laura a nerve-wracking stay of execution and a new trial.

There was a second trial and Laura was acquitted to a mixture of bravos for a brave little lady, and snorts about violating the sanctity of the home. Laura was a real pioneer. She was not the first or the last lady of the Old West to take a potshot at her man. Her aim was more accurate and her press notices were nation-wide. The plea that "everything went blank" and her defense of emotional insanity set a precedent that has had lawyers happily circumventing McNaughton's Rules defining legal insanity ever since, with varying degrees of skill and success.

Laura Fair is an example of Victoriphobia on the Last Frontier. By the time nineteenth-century morals had been stashed in a covered wagon or saddle bag, crossed the sun-baked plains and snow-tossed mountains, they had either sluiced down to a simpler form or been left along the way. The Oregon and Sante Fe Trails were littered with inhibitions as well as bones. The early West called for a physical and mental adjustment. A courage-shattering Indian war whoop, the moon-haunted howl of a coyote, the endless spread of land, the blue sky's suggestion of the infinite in its ever-vanishing horizon line made people either very big or very small. They either tried to imprint themselves on this yearning emptiness of space or they became part of the bigness. People were more direct in their actions, less evasive in their thinking. It was a land of raw-edged extremes.

The criminals were the worst. There were the dregs from the East, the Sydney Ducks from Australia, Billy the Kid, the Western juvenile delinquent, the Hell-bent-for-leather-and-loot Dalton Boys, dare-devil Jesse James, the bloody soaked Reno brothers, Henry Plummer, the Sheriff of Ruby Gulch who stained his shield, and David Terry, the shooting judge of the Washoe. The battles were the most heroic—the Alamo and Little Big Horn. The good men were the bravest, and Buffalo Bill, Kit Carson, Wild Bill Hickok, Davy Crockett, and Wyatt Earp have shot their way into the frontier mythology. Even the folklore was size conscious. Paul Bunyan, king of the lumberjacks, could fell two trees at once. Pecos Bill, the greatest cowboy of them all, rode a mountain lion and used a rattlesnake for a quirt. Tony Beaver, Jumping Mike Fink, and Johnny Appleseed are all large, economy-size legends. The echoing hang-over of this thundering tradition can be viewed weekly as "Paladin," "Gunsmoke," "Wagon Train," and the rest project their shadows and enjoy their Hooper ratings. Everything was extravagantly overstated in the West. Death was a pending presence, a sword of Damocles that looked like a Bowie knife. Life was an uncertain, bullet-happy fraction of time, and Boot Hill was the common denominator. In such a vast, up-tempo panorama, Victorian morality lost its spastic strangle hold, but it existed as a diluted caricature, still capable of insidious influence. Laura Fair translated Victorian concepts into Western action.

The rest is time-marking monotony. Laura made a not too successful lecture tour on the provocative topic, "Wolves in the Fold." Her mother died. Her daughter went East to try for a theatrical career and had no more success trodding the boards than her mother. She died in 1913 in New York. Laura tore off the pages of the calendar in an indistinguishable succession of San Francisco flats and furnished rooms. Her hair lost its gold.

Her figure lost its curves, and her life correspondingly was gray and shapeless. She never tried marriage again—at least not officially. She is always listed as "widow," and she was always alone. In October, 1919, at the age of eighty-two, Laura Fair cashed in her chips and started the long trek over the Big Frontier.

David Belasco was born in San Francisco and was a teenager at the time of the trial. Perhaps in later years, as a playwright in search of an idea, the memory of Laura Fair's golden curls and Virginia City background started him on the story trail of "The Girl of the Golden West." That's one nice thing about melodramas; they usually have a happy ending.

The Bloody End

Since the grim reaper worked overtime and harvested so lushly from 1820 to 1900, one book cannot pay full-length tribute to the profuse crop of nineteenth-century murderers. The following footnotes only attempt to give condensed credit where credit is due.

Forgotten Fiends

Two murderers who have been lost in the sanguine shuffle are an English housewife and a guide from the Old West. In 1873, Alfred Packer led a party of five hopeful prospectors into the gold-glutted San Juan mountains of Colorado. They were never seen again. Weeks later, Packer materialised, solo, at the Los Pinos Indian Agency and claimed his five companions had abandoned him while he was snow-blind. His friend, Chief Ouray of the Ute tribe, looked at him commenting, "Ugh, you too damn fat." Packer flourished a Wells Fargo draft, which had belonged to one of the men, and he spent a literally staggering sum in the local saloons. The authorities took a second look at the sleek, healthy guide and his pathetic story.

When questioned, Packer now told a story of starvation and decimation. The remaining men had lunched off their departed comrades until he was the only survivor. On the site of what is now called Cannibal Plateau, a search party found the skeletons of the five men with bashed-in skulls and stripped bare of flesh.

269

Packer was found guilty and got forty years at hard labor. The frontier judge was a white-heat democrat. After sentencing Packer, he leaned over the bench and hissed, "Packer, you depraved republican son of a bitch, there were only five democrats in Hinsdale County, and you ate them all."

Born in 1832, Mary Ann Cotton ran up an impressive box score. At sixteen, Mary Ann married William Mowbray, and produced six children with stair-step precision. But it was a lost effort. The children and Mr. Mowbray all died within a year or so of each other from "gastric fever." With forged references, the widow obtained employment as a nurse in an infirmary at Seaham Harbour and married one of her patients, George Ward. What was wrong with him at the infirmary is unknown, but after his marriage he died of gastric fever.

The repetitious widow found a job at Durham as housekeeper to a widower named Robinson with five children. The five children died. Mary Ann and the bereaved widower were married, and the two children of their marriage died.

Mary Ann was called home to Rainton, to nurse her sick mother who died from gastric fever, and Mr. Robinson found his life savings and his wife had disappeared. He got off cheap. Mary Ann then met Frederick Cotton. He invited her to his home where she helped out with the family, consisting of an ailing wife, a sister, and four children. Mrs. Cotton, anticipated things by dying of consumption. However, the sister and two children died from gastric trouble, and Mr. Cotton and Mary Ann were married. Three months later there was a child, and then Mr. Cotton joined the grim "gastric" procession. Three of the children and a lodger, who had been unwise enough to will his club money and his effects to his landlady, died, and with these last deaths the long arm of coincidence lost its elasticity. The four bodies were exhumed. Arsenic was abundantly present, and Mary Ann was attached to the noose end of a rope in 1873.

Juvenile Delinquent, Circa 1860

The twentieth-century can claim an exclusive credit line for astronauts, television, antibiotics, and Al Capone, but, Loeb and Leopold to the contrary, the first famous juvenile delinquent appeared in the nineteenth century. Constance Kent has often been cited as a perfect "for instance" of Victorian murder. She looked like Queen Victoria. There was even a rumor afoot that she was the illegitimate niece of Queen Victoria. She was the daughter of Samuel Saville Kent of Wiltshire gentry background. In 1829, Mr. Kent married and proceeded to father four children in rapid succession. After the fourth child, Mrs. Kent had to be put under restraint because of her active absorption in carving knives. In spite of this handicap, there were six more children, Constance being born in 1844. Mrs. Kent died raving in 1852.

Miss Mary Pratt, governess and housekeeper during Mrs. Kent's unfortunate spells, married Mr. Kent a year later. Mr. Kent with nonstop virility had four more children, and in 1860 the second Mrs. Kent was again "expecting." Constance had not been happy under the new regime. In 1885, she and her eleven-year-old brother, William, ran away from home. She cut off her hair and wore an old suit of her brother's. The two children were found in custody at Bath the next day. She brooded; she felt the second family was better treated than the first; she commented to a school friend that "mamma will not let me have anything I like." She treasured Mrs. Kent's remarks that slighted the first family, and Mrs. Kent, in a moment of exasperation with the sullen girl, told her she was getting as mad as her mother had been. Considering that today teenagers have been known to bash in either or both of their parents' heads for refusing them money for the movies or use of the family car, Constance exercised commendable restraint. However, on June 30, Francis, the favorite son of the second Mrs. Kent, was found in a disused outhouse on the family grounds, wrapped in a blood-soaked blanket, his head practically severed from his body. Constance was arrested and then released, protesting her innocence.

The family, driven by ugly rumors, moved to Wales, and Constance was shipped to a French convent for three years. She returned to England and entered St. Mary's Home at Brighton, an Anglo-Catholic Hostel for devout women. In April, 1863, pricked by conscience and driven by religion, Constance made a complete confession to the authorities. She had murdered her stepbrother to "get even with her stepmother." She was sentenced to penal servitude for life.

Murder Matriculates

Harvard, with its on-the-Cambridge imperturbability and well-bred understatement, is rich in classical tradition, and in 1850 the school suffered from an embarrassment of riches. It produced a murder that has become a classic.

Harvard Medical College was built on ground donated by Dr. George Parkman, and its three-storey building was presided over by Dean Oliver Wendell Holmes. Dr. Parkman had a reputation as a philanthropist, a scientist, and a tight-fisted business man. He was tall, thin, hatchet-faced and had an eye-catching set of false teeth. Prof. John Webster was Professor of Chemistry and Minerology at Harvard. He was short and plump, and his round face, rectangular spectacles, and bushy hair were campus landmarks. Webster was perpetually short on cash, and in November, 1850, Dr. Parkman was short on patience. He had obtained Professor Webster's job for him and held a $1200 mortgage on a mineral collection of Webster's. There was $483.64 dollars still due on this note when Dr. Parkman got wind that Professor Webster had sold the whole mineral collection to a third party. There was a rousing fight, and Webster wrote a note, asking Doctor Parkman to meet him at the Medical College on November 23. Parkman disappeared, and Professor Webster visited the doctor's worried family saying that he had seen Dr. Parkman on the day of his disappearance and had paid off the note for $483.64.

The next time Dr. Parkman was seen, he was scattered all over Harvard Medical College—in the furnace, under the lids of lecture tables, in the sink, in the cellar vaults where the anatomy class threw the remains from the dissecting room. Professor Webster was arrested, and Dr. Parkman's set of false teeth, unwinkingly survived the fiery blast of the furnace to provide enameled identification. Professor Webster was hanged on August 30, 1850, but the case survived and became legend. In 1869, Charles Dickens visited Boston and was courteously asked which of the great landmarks he would most like to see. "The room where Dr. Parkman was murdered," he answered with ghoulish enthusiasm. Then there's the story of the Boston lawyer who was chided by the judge because of his rough cross-examination tactics with a Harvard professor. "Yes, I know, Your Honor," replied the unimpressed attorney, "we hanged one the other day."

BEAUTIFUL DREAMER

Carlyle Harris of New York City had education, breeding, and blonde good looks. He also had a problem that is not uncommon with the male of the species: Harries wanted to get rid of his wife. As a twenty-two-year-old honor student of the College of Physicians and Surgeons, he had met Mary Helen Potts in the summer of 1889. He later confided to a friend that he "could not accomplish her ruin in any other way," so he married the pretty, intelligent schoolgirl secretly, under an assumed name. In the spring of 1890, Mary Helen gave premature birth to a child and told her mother everything. Harris explained to the irate Mrs. Potts that the marriage must be kept secret, because his uncle, who was putting him through medical school, would not approve. He had performed several illegal operations on the girl and was heard to remark that she was a "rope around his neck."

By the spring of 1891, Mrs. Potts delivered an ultimatum. Acknowledge her daughter as his wife, or she would not keep quiet. Harris went to an apothecary and ordered capsules containing $4\frac{1}{2}$ grains of quinine and $\frac{1}{6}$ grain of morphine. He gave them to Helen, who had been complaining of sick headaches. Several nights later, Helen, who was still a pupil at Miss Day's Ladies Boarding School on Fortieth Street in New York City, was found by her three roomates in a fuzzy state when they returned from a symphony concert. Helen told them she had been "dreaming of Carl . . . such beautiful dreams." Then she said she had taken some medicine Harris had given her and felt numb. She lapsed into a coma and was dead in eleven hours. Carlyle Harris was arrested and tried for her murder. Harris had kept two of the capsules. "No jury will convict me with these in my possession. They can be analyzed and proved to be harmless." But Harris must have taken stupid pills himself. The capsules in his possession only proved that the pharmacist did not make a mistake and that narrowed responsibility down to Harris. He died in the electric chair in 1892, still protesting his innocence, with a hollow ring that found echoes in Chester Gillette's spree on Big Moose Lake and Theodore Dreiser's "American Tragedy."

OGRES IN DAGUERREOTYPE

1888. Jack the Ripper is the *nom de guerre* of criminology's invisible man. The fog-and-gaslight atmosphere of London's Whitechapel was his happy hunting ground. He came, he saw, he conquered, and he disappeared. On August 31, 1888, Mary

Ann Nichols, a lady of price-tag virtue, was found dead and mutilated. In the cumulative order of their demise, three more ladies who bartered their charms were found in the Whitechapel area with slashed throats and mutilated torsos with minus a kidney or an ovary. Panic set in, and the newspapers coined the graphic name, Jack the Ripper.

On November 9, Mary Jeanette Kelly was heard by neighbors singing "Sweet Violets." The next morning she was found in her room in a far from lyrical condition. The girl was lying on the bed framed by her own internal organs. That was Jack the Ripper's farewell crime. There were stories that he had become a raving lunatic in an asylum, that he had committed suicide. Many police officials believed that George Chapman, the landlord of the "Crown," who was executed for poisoning three women in 1903, was Jack the Ripper. But everything is theory. The fact is that Jack the Ripper disappeared from life into legend as all enshrouding as his beloved Whitechapel fog.

1894. H. H. Holmes, a glib-talking, former medical student, made Bluebeard look like an ideal husband. His real name was Herman W. Mudgett, but he left that name and a wife in the green hills of Vermont and came to Englewood, still a suburb of Chicago. He started out modestly as a pharmacist in an Englewood drugstore, but he soon took over the drugstore and the beauteous wife of the drug clerk. By a series of frantic business deals, from a cure for alcoholism to fraudulent real-estate deals, he got together enough money to start building an enormous hotel in Englewood. It had three stories, one hundred rooms, and a series of lovely young ladies as tenants. The drug clerk's wife disappeared, so did a visiting heiress, Minnie Williams, and her sister, Anna.

Financially pressed, Holmes concocted a plan to defraud the insurance company with a small-time confidence man, B. F.

Pitzel. In reality, he murdered Pitzel, violating their gentleman's agreement to fake a murder so that the trusting Mr. Pitzel could enjoy his share of the take. When he was picked up for Pitzel's murder, police examined Holmes's "Castle" and found such sinister equipment as a slick chute to the cellar, airless gas chambers, a well-equipped crematory, acid vats, bones of women, and medieval torture racks. It was estimated that one hundred and fifty young women came to the castle either to work for Holmes as "typewriters" (nineteenth-century argot for secretary) or to marry him. Holmes admitted he either lived off their wages or conned them out of their inheritances. He took unblushing credit for the murder of twenty-seven of these women and was duly hanged.

THE INFERNAL TRIANGLE

The McFarland-Richardson case that rocked New York contains an imposing roster of names and proves the premise that the Victorians would swear black was white and vice versa to preserve the crenelated superstructure of their morality.

Abby Sage McFarland was married to Dan McFarland, a nonpracticing lawyer but an assiduously practicing alcoholic. In his cups, he was inclined to black his wife's eye, and sober he lived off his wife and friends. Out of grocery-driven necessity, Abby had started writing stories, including charming tales for children, that sold, and Edwin Booth gave her speaking parts in his theatrical company. In 1869, Abby had been separated from her husband for two years and was recently divorced. She was planning on marrying Albert Richardson, a popular nationally famous war correspondent and one of the owners of the New York *Tribune*. Mr. McFarland nailed Richardson with some accurate bullets when he came in to pick up his mail at the gaslit *Tribune* office. Mr. Richardson was taken to the Astor House, where on November 30 he and Abby went through a deathbed wedding ceremony performed by Rev. Henry Ward Beecher.

Mr. McFarland, in the belated role of protector of the sanctity of the home, had taken a potshot at Richardson earlier in the year. He had an intercepted letter from Richardson to Abby which he claimed proved that Richardson had debauched his wife. He read the letter in barrooms. He tried to sell it to rival newspapers for $100, and he brought suit for $45,000 damages against Richardson. His wife's shame was evidently subordinate to Mr. Richardson's checkbook.

The defense was based on "uncontrollable impulse," and Horace Greeley, editor of the *Tribune,* was accused of running a free-love establishment. McFarland was acquitted, and morality was vindicated. Abby McFarland Richardson lived under a cloud of social disapproval and continued to write charming stories. Mr. Richardson rested uneasily in a rake's grave, and it is reported that McFarland, that stirling champion of purity and home, drank himself to death.

Doctor's Dilemma

During the nineteenth century, an impressive number of doctors practiced murder instead of medicine and treated the Hippocratic oath with a deadly insouciance. That is not to say that murderers are prone to become doctors, or that doctors are prone to become murderers, but in those days medicine was a tempting combination of empirical diagnosis and trial-and-error dosage. A horse-and-buggy G. P. had a very good chance of "getting away with it" when he reached for his medicine bag to solve a problem or make a profit. Some of the more famous—and less fortunate—medical murderers are listed below:

1856. William Palmer of Rugeley, Staffordshire, came from a morally questionable but financially successful family. His student days were marked by misuse of funds and women, but he finally earned his degree and set up practice in Rugeley, where he was a regular churchgoer and was on a first name basis with the best families. However, the racetrack held more interest than his practice; he was soon in financial difficulties, and his career was marked by slow horses and quick death. One of his illegitimate children died after visiting him. His mother-in-law died while she was his house guest. A Mr. Bladon, who was pressing Palmer for a betting debt, died at Palmer's home. He insured his wife for £13,000 and she died in six months. His brother, Walter, also handsomely insured, went the same route. John Parsons Cook, a track associate, had a winning horse. Palmer collected £1,000 of Cook's money, but Cook sickened and died before he found out. He was cared for by Dr. Palmer. The perpetually smiling, chubby doctor, with hypertensive good looks, was hanged at the age of thirty-one in 1856 and is credited with being the first poisoner to use strychnine.

1859. Dr. Thomas Smethhurst, an English doctor with rather hazy qualifications, left his elderly wife to enter into a bigamous marriage with Isabella Bankes. The bride was an irresistible combination of youth and money. She possessed a lush figure and an equally lush nest egg of £1,800, which she obligingly but unwisely willed to the bridegroom. Within a few weeks, morning sickness turned into mortal sickness, and a post-mortem disclosed arsenic. Dr. Smethurst was arrested and tried, but missed the drop because of a forensic error.

The medical expert for the crown blushingly admitted that some of the arsenic discovered came from an impurity in the copper gauze used in the post-mortem tests. Smethurst was found guilty but received a pardon from the Home Secretary because of insufficient evidence. He did serve one year hard labor for bigamy, but Dr. Smethurst must have concluded that the game was well worth it, because he instituted and won a court action to prove the will of Isabella Bankes leaving him her property.

1865. Dr. Edward Pritchard was an ex-naval surgeon who set up practice in Glasgow. He liked to give lectures on his travels and offered such inaccurate puffery as "I have hunted the Nubian lion in the prairies of North America." The doctor was a regular churchgoer and an active Mason but was generally considered a glib humbug.

Pritchard was having an affair with the downstairs maid, Mary McCleod, and his visiting mother-in-law caught him and McCleod in the consulting room in a most unprofessional position. Mrs. Taylor died shortly after this scene. She was followed by her daughter, who had taken whining exception to the doctor's unsavory affair. The bodies of Mrs. Taylor and Mrs. Pritchard contained copious amounts of antimony. In spite of the fact that he had Mrs. Pritchard's coffin opened so he could kiss his "dearest Mary Jane," in spite of crocodile tears and plaintive questions of his motherless children, Dr. Pritchard was tried and convicted for the double murder. He finally admitted his guilt and blamed it on the use of ardent spirits. His was the last public execution in Glasgow. "Sir," he said to the attending minister at his execution, "I shall meet you in heaven." The man of the cloth answered with noncommital caution, "Sir, we shall meet at the Judgment Seat."

1882. Dr. George Lamson had a distinguished medical career in the Franco-Prussian War and served with the British Red Cross in Serbia, Roumania, and Russia. He married a girl with revisionary interest of £15,000 on the death of any of her brothers or sisters. One sister and a brother had already died, and Mrs.

Lamson turned the money over to her husband. A married sister and a crippled brother survived. Dr. Lamson bought a practice in Bournemouth, but, in spite of his excellent record, he was soon having financial difficulties and hitting the morphine bottle in his medicine bag. He visited Percy John, his eighteen-year-old crippled brother-in-law, who wheel-chaired his way around a school in Wimbledon. The headmaster produced sherry, and Dr. Lamson observed the amenities with plum cake and preserved fruit. Percy John died two hours later. Dr. Lamson was arrested, convicted, and hanged for administering aconite.

1885. Dr. J. Milton Bowers was a moderately successful San Francisco practitioner, but his wives died with suspicious regularity. In 1885, his third wife was plump, jealous, twice-married Cecelia Benhayon Levy. The current Mrs. Bowers died suddenly, and an autopsy gave phosphorous poisoning as the cause of death, rather than the abcessed liver diagnosis hopefully offered by her bereaved husband. Dr. Bowers was tried for murder and cried on the witness stand. In reply to the accusation that, after a buggy accident, he had said to his wife, "I wish you had broken your damn neck," he explained with injured patience to the judge and jury that what he had really said was "darn the buggy so long as your neck is not broken."

He was found guilty, but the dead woman's brother, Henry Benhayon, was found with a flask of whiskey, a bottle of liquid cyanide of potassium, and a note confessing he had killed his sister. There were many fishy angles about the suicide, and people suspected that it was really murder, masterminded by Dr. Bowers from the condemned cell. Bowers was released, married again, and opened offices, advertising himself with commendable modesty as a "specialist in the treatment of women." His fourth wife survived him.

1892. Dr. Neill Cream was born in Glasgow but moved with his family to Canada. He took his degree at McGill University and was described as rather good looking, except for an unpleasant and pronounced squint. He migrated to Chicago, where he scraped out a living as the "whore's doctor" and abortionist. When his mistress's husband, Daniel Stott, was found dead and full of strychnine, Dr. Cream was sent to Joliet for life. On his father's death, he inherited a large sum of money, and a kindhearted but weak-minded governor commuted his sentence to give him another chance. Dr. Cream arrived in England in October, 1891. In his role of whore's doctor, he started dispensing pills to the ladies of the evening around Lambeth for their complexions and other less socially acceptable eruptions. Ellen Donworth, Matilda Clover, Emma Shirvell, and Alice March died in screaming agony. Lou Harvey pretended to take the pill but threw it away. When she encountered Dr. Cream a month later, he gaped and beat a rabbitlike retreat. The squint-eyed doctor might have become the Lambeth equivalent of Jack the Ripper, but he wrote a lot of crank letters which were eventually traced to him. He was tried, convicted, and kept a long overdue appointment with the hangman.

1893. Dr. Robert W. Buchanan lived in the Greenwich Village section of New York City where he did a lot of drinking and loafing but not much practicing. He was small, wispy, and sported a limp mustache. His pretty, young wife, who had come with him from Nova Scotia, disappeared, and "Doc" told his cronies at his favorite restaurant, Macomber's, that she had left him for another man. Dr. Buchanan left his beloved haunts around Sixth Avenue and West Eleventh Street long enough to take a quick trip to Newark where he wooed and won Anna Sutherland. She was a ripe twenty years older than the young doctor, the proprietress of three high-class bordellos and the possessor of $50,000 from the wages of sin. She willed everything to the doctor at the time of their marriage.

But there were troubles in the May-December love nest. "Doc" was soon back on his accustomed stool in Macomber's, drinking his favorite whistle-wetter, rye highballs, and complaining that his wife had a sharp tongue. "I wish I could dump the old girl. Her face would drive a man to drink," he said and gave point to his statement by ordering another rye highball. "Carlyle Harris was a damn fool," he announced with rye-born superiority. If he had known enough to mix atropine with his morphine, the contraction of the pupils would have been counteracted, and nobody would have suspected the morphine." When Mrs. "Doc" died a short time later, Dr. Buchanan's statements, made in the warm, congenial atmosphere of the saloon, were repeated under oath in the cold, lucid precincts of the courtroom. Evidently the jury went along with the *in vino veritas* theory, and Dr. Buchanan gingerly seated himself in the electric chair vacated by Carlyle Harris two years previously, which goes to show a man can't be too closemouthed about his professional secrets.

And so they exit, trailing clouds of obituaries and memories of sudden death, headed for some dark-hued hall of fame where blood guilt and blood glory are indistinguishable and the escutcheon over the door blazes red with the mark of Cain. On the rim of the twentieth-century loom the Titans—Seddon, Armstrong, Crippen, G. J. Smith, and Landru, and then, in the era of booze and bullets, art descends literally to hack work. And so, crime marches on.